Principles of Liberty

FURTHER READING BY CHARLES G. FINNEY

Principles of Liberty

Compiled & Edited by
Louis Gifford Parkhurst, Jr.

BETHANY HOUSE PUBLISHERS
MINNEAPOLIS, MINNESOTA 55438
A Division of Bethany Fellowship, Inc.

Copyright © 1983
Louis G. Parkhurst, Jr.
All Rights Reserved

Published by Bethany House Publishers
A Division of Bethany Fellowship, Inc.
6820 Auto Club Road, Minneapolis, Minnesota 55438

Printed in the United States of America

Library of Congress Cataloging in Publication Data

Finney, Charles Grandison, 1792-1875.

    1. Bible. N.T. Romans—Sermons. 2. Sermons, American.
I. Parkhurst, Louis Gifford, 1946-   . II. Title.
BS2665.4.F55   1982   227'.106   82-20705
ISBN 0-87123-475-0

CHARLES GRANDISON FINNEY
AT THE AGE OF 40

A Portrait by Samuel Lovett Waldo and William Jewett completed in 1834: oil on hardwood panel. A gift of Lewis Tappan. Printed here through the courtesy of Allen Memorial Art Museum, Oberlin College, Oberlin, Ohio.

CHARLES G. FINNEY was America's foremost evangelist. Over half a million people were converted under his ministry in an age that offered neither amplifiers nor mass communication as tools. Harvard Professor Perry Miller affirmed that "Finney led America out of the eighteenth century." As a theologian, he is best known for his *Revival Lectures* and his *Systematic Theology*.

LOUIS GIFFORD PARKHURST, JR., is pastor of First Christian Church of Rochester, Minnesota, and Instructor in Ethics/Philosophy at Minnesota Bible College. He garnered a B.A. and an M.A. from the University of Oklahoma and an M.Div. degree from Princeton Theological Seminary. He is married and the father of two young children. This is his third Finney book.

CONTENTS

INTRODUCTION

The first two books in this series, *Principles of Prayer* and *Principles of Victory*, have been well received by the public, along with the other books of Charles G. Finney. Interest in Finney's life and work has been increasing, with churches of almost every denominational affiliation coming together in Rochester, New York, October 16-24, 1981, for a great *Charles G. Finney Sesquicentennial Festival* celebrating the "Great Awakening" there 150 years ago. With revival even now occurring in many churches throughout the world, these sermons of Charles Finney on a book of the Bible which has brought revival to many people through the ages is most appropriate.

One of the purposes of the series I have compiled and edited has been to make Charles Finney's works more accessible and more understandable to the general population, as well as to provide inspiration and helpful material to students of the Gospel, ministers, and missionaries throughout the world. I was greatly encouraged recently when I learned that a native missionary from India had read Finney's *Principles of Prayer* during an airplane flight here in the United States, and that he planned to take this book back to his fellow workers in India, because they had been employing many of Finney's principles (which they had learned from their independent study of the Scriptures), and they were having revival there.

This book, *Principles of Liberty*, is the companion volume of Finney's sermons on Romans, *Principles of Victory*. *Principles of Liberty* contains Finney's sermons and lectures on Romans from *The Oberlin Evangelist*, the newspaper published at Oberlin College from 1838, until the Civil War made its continuation impossible. The purpose of the newspaper's publication is stated on page 21. The sermons in this volume are an excellent complement to the sermons in the previous book, making a total of thirty-one sermons on Romans by Finney. Some of the sermons in each volume appear to have been preached consecutively; for example, the two sermons on Romans 8:28 were probably preached one after the other. One of them found its way into *The Oberlin Evangelist* and the other was published posthumously in *Sermons on the Way of Salvation*. Four of the sermons in this book, *Principles of Liberty*, are entirely different sermons on the same text found in *Principles of Victory*. These sermons are on Romans 1:18; 8:7; 8:28; 13:10. They show the

11

extent of Finney's indepth understanding of the Scriptures and human psychology, as he applies God's Word to his hearers extensively using only one verse to do so. The sermon on Romans 8:28, *All Events, Ruinous to the Sinner*, contains some of the most probing thoughts I have ever read on that verse.

These two books are essential to understanding the balance in Finney's work on faith, justification, and sanctification. Finney's views on sanctification are more thoroughly explored in *Principles of Victory*; hence the title given to that book of sermons. Yet, this book includes the important sermons on sanctification: *Sanctification Under Grace, Thanks for Gospel Victory*, and *The Way To Be Holy*. *Principles of Liberty* contains more material on justification and assurance of salvation than the previous book, hence its title. Especially to be read and considered are *The Foundation, Conditions, and Relations of Faith, Justification*, and *The Kingdom of God in Consciousness* (one of Finney's very best sermons!). The sermon which particularly gave this book its title is *License, Bondage, and Liberty.* Every person lives in a spirit of license, a spirit of bondage, or a spirit of liberty. These sermons on Romans contain the clear principles which lead to real Christian liberty. It is my prayer, as well, that when the last sermon in this book is read that the reader indeed can say, "I do have the kingdom of God in my consciousness!" This is real victory! This is the liberty which Christ came to bring upon the earth, until He comes again.

These two books of Finney's sermons also have been edited to contain extra materials on and by Charles G. Finney, materials particularly related to his preaching. It has been my desire to aid students of Finney and students of other great preachers and historians, by providing almost impossible to find resources regarding Finney as a preacher, professor of preaching, and theologian. It is also my desire to challenge preachers to be more diligent in preaching the *whole* Gospel in order to challenge their flock and to do the work of an evangelist, and to help laypeople to learn what effective preaching is about so they can evaluate better what they hear from the pulpit, and can challenge their pastors to preach "so as to convert somebody."* I pray that all readers would hear the truth of the Gospel clearly, perhaps for the first time, as they read these sermons on Romans, so that their minds might be enlightened, their hearts softened, and their spirits quickened, to the end that they may bow before Jesus Christ as Lord and Saviour in greater and renewed dedication to Him. Only Jesus Christ can give us the victory. Only Jesus Christ can set us at liberty.

As you read these sermons, you will notice something which made Finney's sermons so effective. He told his hearers everything he planned to discuss in his sermon within his first few words. His intentions have

---

*See *Principles of Victory*, p. 13 "How to Preach So As to Convert Nobody."

been placed in italics, and set apart with Roman numerals, as was the practice of his stenographers, in these books. You will be able to see at a glance what questions Finney intended to answer in that particular sermon. The sermons are well constructed, they show consecutive thought, they are easy to follow, and their style has been improved for the contemporary ear.

Finney also carefully defined his terms. You will notice this not only in these sermons, but also in his books on theology. If there was confusion about the meaning of a word, Finney was careful early in his sermon to tell exactly what the Bible did or did not mean by that particular word. This was vitally important, because some people would argue about things they had never taken the time to properly define. Finney carefully defined "debt"; for example, in his sermon, *Being in Debt,* on Romans 13:8. Unhappily, I had forgotten Finney's excellent definition of "debt" when I received a call one evening by a person deeply concerned because he had been told that it was unchristian to take out any loan or purchase anything on credit. Finney answered this question with thoroughness. I have been pleased with the contemporary relevance of the material in these books.

Other materials of interest included here are "Professor Finney's Charge" to the graduating class of Oberlin at an ordination service of those who had been called to the gospel ministry. The charge should be taken personally by any ordained or licensed minister. "The anxious seat" was one of the most confusing things regarding Finney's revivals, and its use has been maligned. The material on page 17 on "The Anxious Seat" from an unpublished portion of Finney's *Autobiography* was provided me by Gordon C. Olson of the Bible Research Fellowship, Inc.

I have included materials kindly provided me by W. E. Bigglestone, Archivist, Oberlin College Archives, Oberlin College, Oberlin, Ohio. The photograph shows Finney at the height of his youth and revival labors about the age of 40, almost 150 years ago. This is a photograph of a painting of Charles Finney, which is in the Art Museum of Oberlin College, and it is published by their kind permission.

I wish to thank Ardis Sawyer, Librarian of the Minnesota Bible College, Rochester, Minnesota, and Nowell Herzog, Puritan scholar, for their able assistance in research during this manuscript's preparation. I wish to thank my secretary, Judy Bonadore, for typing portions of the manuscript. I wish to thank Jack Key, Librarian of the Mayo Clinic, for encouragement and use of equipment to read and copy the sermons in this book from microfilm copies of *The Oberlin Evangelist.* I owe a debt of gratitude that I can never repay to Gordon C. Olson, Harry Conn, and David Birch, Jr., who have inspired me to continue my study and application of the principles of Christian living contained in the works of Charles G. Finney. Finally, I wish to thank Mrs. Carol A. Johnson and Bethany House Publishers for their continued interest in making the works of Charles Finney available to many interested readers.

May the principles found in this series be a trustworthy guide for you as you follow faithfully and put your whole trust in the only Way, Truth, and Life, even Jesus Christ our Lord and Saviour.

To the Praise of His Glory,

L. G. Parkhurst, Jr.
First Christian Church
Rochester, Minnesota
Epiphany, 1982.

PROFESSOR FINNEY'S CHARGE

*The following is a brief summary of a charge given by Professor Charles G. Finney at an ordination service in 1841. It was written from memory because the person who published it in **The Oberlin Evangelist** in Volume III; September 15, 1841, was not able to take notes at the time. If all ministers of the Gospel would take seriously what Finney charged these ministers to do and preach, then God might bless our churches with revival even as He blessed the efforts of Charles Finney and those he educated at Oberlin College, Oberlin, Ohio.*

1. We charge you to preach the whole Gospel, and in its proper proportions. Some neglect important parts of the Gospel altogether—others make a hobby of some particular truth—and if men become Christians at all under their preaching, they are monsters. Preach the *whole* Gospel, and in such proportions as is calculated to secure the most perfect symmetry of Christian character.

2. We charge you to live for but one object.

3. We charge you to aim at healing the divisions in the Church. Do nothing unnecessarily to increase the bitterness and heartburnings that now exist among Christians—but do all in your power to sweeten and heal them.

4. We charge you not to heal the hurt of the Church slightly. Do not, on the plea of peace, cover up sin, and thus leave the sores to fester instead of heal. Thoroughly probe them to the bottom, and then they can be soundly cured. Aim at the eradication of all sin; and rest not till the Church is "made whole of whatever disease she has."

5. We charge you to be men of prayer. Do not go to your work in your own strength. Do not depend upon your discipline, your talents, nor anything else, but upon Christ. Live in constant communion with Him, and derive your very life and all your strength from Him.

6. We charge you to be men of deep thought. In this age of the world you can never succeed, and do any good, unless you think deeply, think consecutively, and think rightly.

7. We charge you not to expect your *office* to give you permanent influence. The time was when a minister was greatly respected on account of his office, but that time has passed away. If you depend upon your office for influence, men will be quick to see it and despise you. Nothing

but a fearless, faithful, meek and humble discharge of the duties of your office ought, and nothing else will, give you influence. See to it that you deserve, and on that condition only have, influence.

8. We charge you not to grasp at ecclesiastical power. Your business is to preach the Gospel—to win souls to Christ—to present to the Church her great inheritance. You have nothing to do with ecclesiastical power. It is a dangerous weapon. Be careful how you seek for or try to use it.

9. We charge you to avoid censoriousness. The very fact that you go from this school, and this association, will make many look upon you with distrust, some perhaps will oppose you. You will be tempted to feel and speak censoriously to and of them, and thus grieve the Spirit of Christ and wound your own soul. Be on your guard here. Never suffer yourselves to *feel* censoriously, and then you will never *speak* censoriously.

10. We charge you not to be diverted from your work. You have been called and educated to preach the Gospel. Do not turn aside from this to some other work. Abide in the calling wherein ye are called. Continue to preach the Gospel.

11. We charge you to give a candid attention to the remarks of those who oppose you. They may teach you many things in regard to your real faults. These you should be anxious to know and correct. And your enemies may often speak of deficiencies or faults, which the partiality of your friends will overlook. Take advantage of all such circumstances, without regard to the motives of those who make the remarks.

12. We charge you in all things to show yourselves workmen needing not to be ashamed. Be sure that in everything—your studies, your devotions, your preaching, your conversation with your people, your business, the management of your families—you study to "commend yourselves to every man's conscience in the sight of God." (In this connection, Prof. Finney said that he had been greatly encouraged in his relationship with the members of the Senior Class, while under his instruction. They did not seem to him to suppose themselves to know half as much as when they began their studies. They seemed to feel their ignorance, and to be willing to acknowledge it. This had greatly interested and encouraged him. He hoped they would cherish the same willingness to be taught, and avoid all dogmatism, and exhibitions of self-sufficiency.) *Be examples* in everything—be "living epistles, known and read of all men." In a word, *in everything* study to show yourselves workmen needing not to be ashamed.

THE ANXIOUS SEAT

The anxious seat, or what we know now as the altar call and the counselor's meeting, which followed the preaching of the revivalists and evangelists of the nineteenth-century, was first used by Charles G. Finney during the Rochester, New York revivals in the 1830s. This feature of Finney's preaching and the reasons for it are recorded in his autobiography, but were more extensive in the unpublished and handwritten manuscript omitted from the autobiography, which was published after his death.

The unpublished material is included here in the context of what Finney wrote in the published version, and is enclosed in brackets.

I had never, I believe, except in rare instances, until I went to Rochester, used as a means of promoting revivals, what has since been called "the anxious seat." I had sometimes asked persons in the congregation to stand up, but this I had not frequently done. However, in studying upon the subject, I had often felt the necessity of some measure that would bring sinners to a stand. From my own experience and observation I had found, that with the higher classes especially, the greatest obstacle to be overcome was their fear of being known as anxious inquirers.

I had found also that something was needed to make the impression on them that they were expected at once to give up their hearts; something that would call them to act, and act as publicly before the world, as they had in their sins; something that would commit them publicly to the service of Christ. When I had called them simply to stand up in the public congregation, I found that this had a very good effect; and so far as it went, it answered the purpose for which it was intended. But, after all, I had felt for sometime that something more was necessary to bring them out from among the mass of the ungodly to a public committal of themselves to God.

At Rochester, if I recollect rightly, I first introduced this measure. This was years after the cry had been raised of "new measures." A few days after the conversion of Mrs. M——, I made a call, I think for the first time, upon all that class of persons whose convictions were so ripe that they were willing to renounce their sins and give themselves to God, to come forward to certain seats which I requested to be vacated, and offer themselves up to God, while we made them subjects of prayer. . . . I remember one evening after preaching, three lawyers followed me to my room, all of them deeply convicted; and all of them had been, I believe, on the anxious seat, but were not clear in their minds and felt that they could not go home until they were convinced their peace was made with God. I conversed with them and prayed with them, and I believe, before they left, they all found peace in believing in the Lord Jesus Christ.

[The means used for the promotion of this revival were precisely the same that had been used in all the revivals that I had witnessed before, with the exception, as I have said, of what has since been termed "the anxious seat." I found, as I expected, that this was a great power for good. If men who were under conviction refused to come forward publicly and renounce their sins and give themselves to God, this fact disclosed to them more clearly the pride of their hearts. If, on the other hand, they broke over all those considerations that stood in the way of their doing it, it was taking a great step, and as I found continually, was the very step which they needed to take. And when the truth was explained to them, and they were made intelligent, and the very duty to be performed was placed before them before they were pressed to come forward, in great numbers of instances, as was afterwards ascertained, they indeed did as they promised to do, and this was one of the means used by the Spirit of God to bring them to a present submission to and acceptance of Christ. I had long been of the opinion that a principal reason why so few were converted while under the voice of the living preacher was that they were not brought to the point of instant submission demanded of them. Ministers had been in the habit of preaching to sinners sermons pointing out to them their duty; but then in all probability admonishing them at the close that their nature must be changed by the Spirit of God or they could do nothing. Ministers had been so much afraid of dishonoring the Spirit of God as to think it their duty to call the sinner's attention to his dependence on the Spirit of God at the close of every sermon, and every exhortation to repentance.

The doctrine that sin was constitutional, and belonged to the very nature, that the very nature itself must be changed by direct physical influence exerted by the Holy Spirit, compelled ministers who believed it to remind sinners of their inability to do what God required and what in their sermons they urged them to do; and thus just at the point where the sinner needed to think of Christ, of his duty, of the important thing to be done, his attention was turned back to see whether any divine influence was going to change his nature, and let the Spirit of God act upon his nature like an electric shock, while he remained passive.

Thus the sinner's mind was mystified, and under such preaching it was no wonder that few souls were converted. The Lord convinced me that this was no way to deal with souls. He showed me clearly that moral depravity must be voluntary; that the divine agency in regeneration must consist in teaching the soul, in argument, in persuasion, and in entreaty. That therefore the thing to be done was to set the sinner's duty clearly before him, and depend on the Spirit's teaching to urge him to do it; to set Christ before him and expect the Holy Spirit to take of the things of Jesus and show them to the sinner; to set his sins before him and expect the Holy Spirit to show him his awful wickedness and lead him voluntarily to renounce his sins. I saw therefore clearly that to cooperate with the Spirit of God as an intelligent agent in this work, I must present the truths to be believed, the duties to be done, and the reasons for those duties. This is the very thing that the Spirit is doing to make the sinner see and understand the force of the reasons urged by the minister, the truth of the facts stated, and to give the sinner a realizing sense of those truths which the minister presents to him, to induce him to act.

Therefore, to me it was plain that to divert the sinner's attention, just at that point, to his dependence on the Spirit of God, was necessarily to hinder rather than to help forward the work of the Spirit. It is the minister's duty to urge him, and the offices of the Spirit to make his urgency effectual, to overcome his voluntary opposition to the Gospel. Therefore to me it was plain that it was totally unphilosophical and absurd when calling on the sinner to do his duty, to tell him that he could not do his duty, and to remind him that he was dependent on the Spirit of God, that his nature must be changed, and all those things which in their very nature were calculated to prevent his taking the very step which the Spirit of God was urging him to take. This kind of teaching leads the sinner to resist the Spirit of God, to wait for God to do something and to change his heart before he turns to God. The fact is, the fundamental error consists in supposing that a change of heart is a physical instead of a moral change; that is, a change in the nature instead of a change in the voluntary committal and preference of the mind.

By the kind of teaching of which I am speaking, sinners were constantly hindered and almost never converted under the voice of a living preacher. If they were convicted of sin and ever converted, it must of necessity have been when they forgot the theory in which they had been instructed, left entirely out of view their inability, their dependence on the Spirit of God, acted upon their convictions, and complied with the urgency of the Spirit's teaching. It is the Spirit's office first to convict the sinner of sin, or of righteousness, and of judgment to come; and when taught the need of the Saviour, to present the Saviour in His divine nature, His offices and relations, His atonement and mercy, His willingness, His readiness, His ability to save unto the uttermost. Thus Christ promised the Holy Spirit as a teacher, to lead men by a divine moral persuasion to renounce their sins and give themselves to God. That of which the sinner is conscious of under his agency is not the personal presence of any divine agency in his mind, but he sees the truth clearly, so sees it that it makes a deep impression. His difficulties are cleared up, his errors are corrected, his mind is enlightened, the truth presses his conscience, and he feels an urgency upon his spirit immediately to submit to God. It is the truth that engages his attention. If he is a reader of his Bible, he will infer of course that this urgency that is upon him is from the Spirit of God. It is often well that he should be told that this is the way in which the Spirit of God works with him; that in resisting the truths that are before his mind, he is resisting the Holy Spirit; and that in accepting these truths cordially, he yields to divine teaching. But he should understand distinctly that the Spirit's work is not to convert him while he is passive, waiting God's time; but that the Spirit of God converts or turns him by inducing him to turn himself; that the act of submission is his own act, and the Spirit is persuading him to do this; that faith is his own act, and the Spirit of God gives faith only by so presenting the truths to be believed with such a divine clearness and persuasiveness, as to lead the sinner to trust the Saviour; that He gives faith by inducing us to believe; and that He leads us to perform every duty, to repent, to believe, to submit, to love, by presenting the truths which are calculated to lead to these acts in so clear a light as to overcome our reluctance, and induce us voluntarily with all sincerity and with all our hearts, to turn to God, to trust him, to love Him, to obey Him. With these views of the subject, I saw clearly that just at the point where the sinner is thoroughly instructed, and while under the voice of the living preacher, with the strong pressure of truth sent home by the Holy Spirit, something was needed to induce him to act then and there upon his convictions. I concluded then, and have always thought since, that to call the sinner right out from the mixed multitude to take a stand for God, to be open and frank in his renunciation of sin before the world as he had been in committing it; to call him to change sides, to renounce the world and come over to Christ, to renounce his own righteousness and accept that of Christ—in short, to do just that which constitutes a change of heart, was just what was needed.

I was not disappointed in the use of this measure. I have always found it a thing greatly needed; and I might relate scores of instances in which proud men, after resisting it for a time, saw the propriety and necessity of it, and themselves came forward to the anxious seat and gave themselves to God. And I have often been told that they believed if they had not been called on to take that step, and if they had not taken it or something equivalent to it, they never would have been converted. If I labor for the conversion of a sinner, I must tell him the things that the Spirit of God wants him to believe and to understand. I need to present before him the considerations that ought to influence his present action. In this way I cooperate with the Spirit of God; for this is the very thing the Spirit of God is endeavoring to secure, his present action in accordance with the claims of God. And I never feel as if I have done my duty till I have pressed every consideration upon the sinner's mind that seems to me at the time to be essential to his rightly understanding his duty and doing it. . . .

In this revival at Rochester, I am not aware that there was ever any complaint of any fanaticism, or anything that was to be deplored in its results. The revival was so powerful, it gathered in such great numbers of the most influential class in society, it made so clean a sweep that it created a great excitement far and near.]

THE OBERLIN EVANGELIST

The Oberlin Evangelist began publication shortly after the founding of the Oberlin College, Oberlin, Ohio, by Asa Mahan, Charles G. Finney, and others. It ceased publication in 1862, when paper and other supplies became difficult to get after the Civil War began. Microfilm copies of The Oberlin Evangelist are available for purchase from The Oberlin College Archives, Oberlin College, Oberlin, Ohio. The purpose of The Oberlin Evangelist is reprinted here to demonstrate the breadth and depth of the commitment of these men, who dedicated themselves to changing the course of America and to bringing revival to her churches.

If it be inquired, what is the object of this paper, and what are the reasons for its publication; we answer,

1. It is no part of its object to wage a war of words or opinions with our neighbors.

2. Not to increase or perpetuate existing controversy in the Church.

3. Not to promote party or sectarian interests.

4. Not to promote *apparent* in the absence of *real* union in the Church.

5. Not to advance the interests of Oberlin, at the expense of sister institutions.

6. Not to promote any particular ecclesiastical organization.

7. Not to defend Oberlin against the injurious aspersions of those who misapprehend, or misrepresent it.

But,

1. We desire to promote purity, peace, and brotherly love among the saints of every denomination.

2. To satisfy the reasonable, and often expressed desire of multitudes, to know our views of the Gospel of Christ.

3. Because we are ignorantly, or purposely, misrepresented by many whereby evil results in two ways: (1.) Some who have confidence in us, are led, we fear, in some cases, to embrace and defend what we regard as error. (2.) Others, we fear, through misapprehension or misrepresentation of our real sentiments, imbibe prejudice, and speak unadvisedly of "things they understand not," thereby injuring their own souls.

4. To open a channel between us and our friends, that we may preach the blessed Gospel to them, though we may "never see their faces in the flesh."

5. To call the attention of Christians to the fact that the Millennium is to consist in the entire sanctification of the Church.

6. To exhibit the gospel view of sanctification in this life.

7. To promote the spirit of Christian union, and to investigate and diffuse its true principles.

8. It is intended to publish occasional sermons, on practical and important subjects. Most of the matter in this department may be expected from Professor Finney. He also intends, if health permit, to publish a series of sermons on Moral Government and the Atonement.

9. The paper will discuss freely the subjects of Christian Education, Slavery and Abolition, Moral Reform, Missions, the Christian Sabbath, Revivals of Religion, and any other subject that may seem to be of the highest importance.

10. It will contain such general religious intelligence as shall be deemed most authentic and important.

ASA MAHAN
HENRY COWLES
WM. DAWES
R. E. GILLETT
H. C. TAYLOR

Committee of Association

1

HOLDING THE TRUTH IN
UNRIGHTEOUSNESS*

Romans 1:18

"For the wrath of God is revealed from heaven against all ungodliness and unrighteousness of men, who hold the truth in unrighteousness."

In preaching from this text I intend to discuss,
   I. *What is "ungodliness"?*
  II. *What is "unrighteousness" in the sense used here?*
 III. *What is it to "hold truth in unrighteousness"?*
 IV. *What are we to understand by "the wrath of God"?*
  V. *Who is this wrath of God revealed against from heaven?*
 VI. *Why is the wrath of God thus revealed from heaven against all
      ungodliness and unrighteousness of men?*

Let us inquire,

I. *What is "ungodliness"?*
The original word means, primarily, to neglect God. It is the omission of duty to God; the withholding from Him of worship, love, confidence, and obedience. It is the withholding from God that which is His due.

II. *What is "unrighteousness" in the sense used here?*
The original word properly means neglect of duty to man, as ungodliness implies neglect of duty to God. It is an omission of duty, a withholding from man what is due him.

Unrighteousness, as the term is evidently used in our text, in distinction from ungodliness, means the withholding of that equal love to man which is his due—that regard to his interest, and feelings, and character, and whatever is to him a good.

The Oberlin Evangelist: Vol. XXIII; August 14, August 28, 1861. The companion sermon is in *Principles of Victory*. pp. 30-37: "The Wrath of God Against Those Who Withstand His Truth."

Withholding this from man is unrighteousness, as withholding it from God is ungodliness. Unrighteousness, in the broader sense, consists in withholding, either from God or man, whatever is their due from us.

But as the terms ungodliness and unrighteousness are here both used, we are undoubtedly to understand unrighteousness here as having reference particularly to the omission of duty to our fellowmen. Everything, then, is unrighteousness, which is short of doing our whole duty to our fellowmen; and everything is ungodliness which is short of doing our whole duty to God.

III. *I inquire in the third place; What is it to "hold truth in unrighteousness"?*

1. The word rendered *hold* in this case means to restrain, to hold down, to hold back. To "hold the truth in unrighteousness" is, for selfish reasons, to refuse to obey the truth.

2. When duty is once known or seen, indifference is impossible. Truth is the natural stimulus of the mind, and especially truth that reveals moral obligation.

When moral obligation is perceived, the mind cannot remain inactive. The perception of moral obligation *forces* the mind into a state of activity. The freedom of the will does not imply that in such circumstances the mind can remain inactive altogether.

But the freedom of the will implies that in every case of perceived moral obligation we have power to act one way or the other, to comply or refuse compliance with moral obligation.

When, therefore, moral obligation is perceived, passivity becomes impossible. The mind must act; it must either comply with the obligation; or it must refuse.

This should always be remembered—that indifference, or a state of non-activity, becomes impossible in the presence of perceived obligation. In such circumstances truth must be embraced or rejected; obligation must be accepted or rejected; duty must be performed or neglected.

To "hold the truth in unrighteousness," then, is to withhold the heart and life from obeying it; it is to persist in neglect of duty when convinced, and when obligation is seen.

3. To "hold the truth in unrighteousness" is to refuse to perform duty when it is known. *Neglect* in these circumstances is *real refusal.* There cannot be neglect in the sense of no action at all. The mind must act in opposition, must gird itself and *refuse*, in order to neglect when obligation is seen.

To "hold the truth in unrighteousness," then, is precisely this: when obligation to our fellowmen is perceived and admitted, we selfishly refuse to meet this obligation.

4. To "hold the truth in unrighteousness" is to unjustly neglect or refuse to perform our duty to God or man. Ungodliness, or withholding from God, is injustice or unrighteousness toward God.

All, then, who neglect to perform their duty either to God or man are guilty of holding the truth in unrighteousness in the sense of this text.

IV. *What are we to understand by "the wrath of God" in this text?*
The wrath of God is not a selfish anger such as selfish men exercise; but a benevolent, holy indignation, such in kind as a benevolent father or ruler might exercise toward injustice, selfishness, and madness in an undutiful child or subject. The term is a strong one. Wrath means something more than mere anger in a low degree; it implies an *intense indignation.*

V. *I inquire, against whom is this wrath of God revealed from heaven?*
1. The wrath of God is revealed against all persons who do not act upon, and up to, their convictions with respect to their duty either to God or to man. It is a very common thing to find persons admitting that such and such things they *ought* to do, and there they stop. They seem to make a virtue of admitting their obligation in *words*, while they deny it in *action.*

You press them with their obligation, and they will say, "Oh, yes, I know that I *ought*—but what then?" There they stop and do not lift a finger to perform their duty.

Now against all such persons, whether they be professors of religion or non-professors, the wrath of God is revealed from heaven.

2. The wrath of God is revealed from heaven against all who allow themselves shortcomings. I say *allow* themselves shortcomings respecting either God or man. It is not an uncommon thing for persons, in looking back, to accuse themselves of shortcomings, when after all they are not aware of having deliberately and knowingly, at the time, fallen short of their duty.

But observe, I say, that the wrath of God is revealed against all who *allow* themselves shortcomings—who are aware of their duty and really *indulge* themselves in neglect and shortcomings. As if a man owed a debt to a neighbor, and knowingly and deliberately neglected to pay him. Or when an individual admits his obligation to love, to confide in, to worship and obey God, and indulges himself in disobedience; or allows himself to neglect to perform his duty to God. Against all such, the wrath of God is revealed from heaven.

3. The wrath of God is revealed from heaven against all who stop short of living up to their *privileges* as well as their duty.

It is really a man's *duty* to live up to his privilege. A man cannot allow himself to live below his privilege, without at the same time allowing himself to live below his duty. It is certainly a man's duty to avail himself of all the means within his reach for promoting his own holiness and usefulness in the highest degree. To stop short of this, for selfish reasons, is a great crime against God; and therefore, the wrath of God is revealed against all who do this.

4. The wrath of God is revealed from heaven against all who rest, and

stop short of full sanctification—full obedience to God as they understand their duty. I say, *rest* short; by which I mean that they knowingly *quiet* themselves in this state of shortcoming.

There are a great many professors of religion who seem to have very little anxiety about being entirely sanctified and fully obeying God. If they can believe themselves *safe*, they seem very well satisfied; although they know they are indulging in more or less sin from day to day.

It is not with them a matter of intense struggle and effort to render to God full obedience. It is enough for them that they think themselves *justified*; the question of *sanctification* they are very willing to postpone.

They say they do not believe in sanctification in this life.

They seem to throw up the reins and live on loosely. They talk about continually sinning and repenting; while it is evident enough that they do not *care* to render to God a full and continued obedience. They care but little for sin, if they can be *forgiven*.

They care but little about *sanctification* if they can ensure *justification*. Now it is perfectly plain that the wrath of God is revealed from heaven against all such persons who are living on in known and allowed shortcomings with regard to sanctification—sinning and sinning and caring little about it—being anxious only to know that they are safe.

The fact is that such persons are *not* safe. You should understand at once that you are as far as possible from being safe.

You are under the wrath of God which is revealed from heaven against you. You are knowingly and carelessly withholding from God His due. You are allowing yourself in sin; caring more for your justification than for your sanctification.

Be not deceived, for God is not mocked. You cannot make Him believe that you are a sincere Christian, while you are so careless about sanctification.

What is sanctification but full obedience to God? And can you make God believe that you are a sincere Christian, while you are careless about rendering to Him, in all things, a *full* obedience?

5. The wrath of God is revealed from heaven against all whose religion is of the *negative* rather than of the *positive* kind.

The law of God is *positive*. It requires supreme love to God and equal love to man. It requires action toward God and man, *intense* action, energetic devotion to God and man. Now there are many who seem to suppose that this is *the doing nothing bad*, as they say.

They run hither and thither, and indulge themselves, and live in most things like the world around them. Their way of spending their time, of spending their money, of using their influence, is such that you inquire why they do this, and why they do that. "Why!" they reply, "what *harm* is there in it?"

With them the question is "What *harm* is there in this or that course of life?" And not "What *good* will this do? And how far will it glorify God?" If they live without committing flagrant sin they think they do well. It does not seem so much as to enter into their designs to do all they can for the promotion of God's glory, but only to avoid doing such things as will be an open disgrace to religion. Their religion is a mere negation (if it may be called religion), which, indeed, it cannot properly be religion, for all true religion is love, confidence, worship, and obedience. Let all who are satisfying themselves with this negative form of what they call religion remember that the wrath of God is revealed from heaven against them.

Indeed, there are some whose *history* seems to be one of *omission.* They are continually neglecting many forms of duty; and they *know* it. Perhaps some of you here are admitting from day to day that this, and that, and the other thing is your *duty*; and yet you never address yourselves seriously to the performance of it.

Some of you are perhaps neglecting secret prayer, neglecting your Bible, neglecting to pay your debt or neglecting in the outward life a great multitude of things, but in regard to God and man, and in your inward state you cannot but *know* that you are really neglecting to render to God all the love and confidence that are His due, and that you are neglecting to love your neighbor as yourself. Your history is one of *omission*. You seem to overlook the fact that omission is the very thing against which this text is arrayed; that this ungodliness and unrighteousness are omissions of duty to God and man.

Again, you seem also to forget that omission is a *real withholding*, a *real refusal*; that it is not a state of *inaction*, but of *contrary* action—a girding yourself to resist the claims of God and the claims of duty.

Your omission is not a mere *passive* state, but a state of *selfish activity*; the omitting to perform your duty to God and man for the sake of gratifying yourself.

Now can you not, some of you, right here, accuse yourself of living a life of omission? Is not this the *history* of your religion?

Are you not acknowledging from day to day in your conscience that you owe this, and that, and the other duty to God and man; while you are neglecting to perform these duties? Now remember, if this is so, the wrath of God is revealed from heaven against you. If you are neglecting any heart duty, or any outward duty, and if you allow yourselves in this neglect or continue to indulge in this omission, you are as far as possible from being safe. I pray you; lay it to heart.

6. The wrath of God is revealed from heaven against all sinners who neglect repentance and faith; in other words, who neglect to become Christians.

(1.) The wrath of God is revealed from heaven against all sinners who neglect God, who neglect prayer, and who neglect to perform all the duties enjoined upon every son and daughter of Adam.

(2.) The wrath of God is revealed from heaven against all *procrastinators*, whether in or out of the church. By procrastinators, I mean, those who have it in their mind at some *future* time to perform their duty; and who for some reason put it off for the present. This is the great sin of many persons. They know their duty—they know that now is the acceptable time and now is the day of salvation; but for unrighteous reasons they continue to procrastinate, to put God off.

(3.) The wrath of God is revealed from heaven against all sinners who neglect to do and be what God requires Christians to do and be. *All men to whom the Gospel is preached are bound to be Christians immediately.*

A great many sinners are constantly watching Christians and accusing them, but they seem not to understand that God requires of them what He requires of Christians, and that in condemning Christians they only condemn themselves; in pointing out the shortcomings of Christians they only point out their own. Now sinners, what you suppose God requires of Christians, you are bound to perform yourselves. For you seem to know what the Christian duty is; you continue to judge the Christian, and therefore you show that you know what he ought to do and what he ought to be. But if you neglect to do and to be what you require of him, then you fall short of your known duty, and the wrath of God is revealed from heaven against you for not doing what you exact of Christians.

(4.) The wrath of God is revealed from heaven against all who know better than they habitually do. Now all sinners are in this state; and this is what constitutes them sinners. They know better than they do; they know their duty but they do it not. And this is that for which the wrath of God is revealed against them.

Impenitent sinners are very apt to think of their sins only as *commissions* of something *outbreaking* in the outward life; but they seldom think much of their neglects of duty either to God or man. But it should be understood that all sin is either *neglect or refusal to render to God and man their due.* Indeed, there are many, both professors and non-professors, who allow themselves to live habitually in opposition to their convictions of duty. Now let it be understood that this is the very *essence* of sin; and against all such persons the wrath of God is revealed from heaven.

VI. *Why is the wrath of God thus revealed from heaven against all ungodliness and unrighteousness of men?*

1. *Neglect* of duty implies a *knowledge* of duty. A man cannot be said to neglect a duty of which he has no knowledge.

2. Neglect of duty implies *ability* to perform it.

3. Neglect of duty, as I have already said, implies a *refusal to do duty.* Indeed it *involves* it. A state of passivity in the presence of perceived obligation being impossible, neglect of duty must involve deliberate and persistent disobedience to God.

4. Neglect of known duty to God or man involves a rejection of God's authority as being not a sufficient reason for action.

It is virtually saying, "What if God *does* require of me such and such a thing? That is no good reason why I should do it. Who is God that I should obey Him, or what profit should I have if I should pray to Him?"

It involves a most insolent and contemptuous rejection of God's command as being a sufficient reason for action in that direction.

5. Holding the truth in unrighteousness involves a deliberate rejection of moral obligation as constituting an influential reason for action.

Observe, in this case the sinner *knows* his duty, he admits the obligation in *words* but rejects it in *practice*.

Now what is this but saying, "What do I care for moral obligation? To be sure, I admit that there *is* a moral obligation; but what do I care? Do you suppose I am going to be influenced by *moral* obligation? If you do, you do not know me; I hope you do not think that I am so weak as to yield to a mere moral obligation—to a mere command of God—to a mere sense of duty? Not I."

6. Holding the truth in unrighteousness involves a contempt for the idea of duty as being of no real *practical* account.

"Duty!" says the sinner, "Do you think I care for *duty*? What! My duty is to God, and my duty is to my neighbor! Talk not to me of *duty*. What do *I* care for *duty*?"

This holding the truth in unrighteousness is a real *contempt* for duty. It is virtually saying, "You never need expect me to be influenced by *that* consideration. You never need to tell me of my *duty*, for I care not for it. I will pursue my *inclination*—duty in any wise to the contrary notwithstanding. Why do you come to me whining about the idea of *duty*, and tell me it is my *duty* to do thus, and thus? Away with your cant! I will have nothing to do with duty."

7. This holding the truth in unrighteousness involves a real ruling down of all moral considerations. The consideration of duty to God—the consideration of God's authority—the consideration of God's rights, of man's rights, and of all rights—it is just ruling them down; putting the foot upon them; trampling them under the feet; and saying, "These considerations shall never influence me!"

8. This course of conduct in holding the truth in unrighteousness, in holding the mind back from obedience, is of course *decisive of the moral attitude*. It is taking a deliberate stand against God. It is taking a deliberate open stand before all His subjects, and pouring contempt upon His authority, upon His moral government, and upon all the moral considerations with which He attempts to enforce obedience. It is then taking the attitude of an open rebel, an open enemy, a persistent opponent of God.

9. Holding the truth in unrighteousness is decisive of *moral character*. It is a state of total depravity, of total dishonesty, in regard both to God and men. While the debt is admitted in *words*, and the obligation both to God and man in *words* is admitted; yet *practically* it is a denial of the obligation. The sinner virtually says, "I know I *ought* to obey God, but I will not. I know I am indebted to God, but I will not pay Him. I know I am indebted to man, but I care not for it—I will not pay him."

This, then, is making an open issue with God before the entire universe. It is a deliberate, known, practical, persistent rejection of His authority. Again, it is setting the worst possible example before God's subjects. Suppose a subject of any government stands forth in the presence of all the subjects, and deliberately refuses to obey the laws; not merely to obey some *one* law, but to obey the laws in general and universally. Suppose the subject to admit the obligation, to admit the wisdom and justice, and equity, and necessity of the laws, but for unrighteous reasons refuses to obey them; to take a course directly opposed to them; to persist in that course, and to hold fast his persistent resistance to the authority of the government—should not the wrath of the government be revealed against such a character as that?

But again—

10. Holding the truth in unrighteousness is the deliberate refusal to pay an acknowledged debt to God.

Suppose that someone is indebted to you. You greatly need your pay, and you go to him and demand it. He acknowledges the debt in terms, and you request him to pay it. He has the money; but he prefers to use it in some other way, to promote his own interest. You urge his obligation upon him; you tell him he *ought* to pay it; and he laughs you in the face, and says, "What do I care for that? Do you suppose I will be influenced by such a consideration as that? *Oughtness!* Shall that influence me? Never!" But you remind him of the authority of God, and of His command to pay his debts. He laughs again, and says, "And who is God? And what do I care for God's commandments? Do you suppose I am to be influenced by such a consideration as that? Never!"

Now you feel, in such a case as this, that such a deliberate refusal, and such a contempt of obligation, was a dreadful sin against you.

But just see that negligent professor of religion, see that impenitent sinner, deliberately refusing to pay an acknowledged debt to God; virtually saying to God, "What do I care for your authority? What do I care for my obligations to *Thee*? I will not be influenced by an obligation to pay my debts either to God or man."

But again, suppose a child should take such a stand, and deliberately and habitually and universally neglect obedience, refuse and omit all obedience—what would you say of such a child? Should not the parent be angry? Should not he reveal his indignation against that child?

And what would you say of your debtor, in case he should treat you in such a way? Would you not feel yourself called upon to put him in a way to pay you, if he deliberately contemned all obligation for selfish reasons, and deliberately refused to pay an acknowledged debt?

Suppose in this case you should go and sue him, and bring him before a court, and he should say, "Why, you appear to be *displeased*, you appear to feel *indignant* that I do not pay you." Would you not reply, "I have *reason* to be indignant. You are a scoundrel; you are a dishonest man; you contemn all *moral* obligation, and I will see what I can do by enforcing *legal* obligation. You treat all moral obligation with contempt; and what is left to me but to *compel* you to pay your debts?"

So in the case of holding the truth in unrighteousness: obligation to

God is treated with contempt; God himself is treated with contempt; His authority is treated as a mere trifle; His feelings are outraged and contemned, and is it not appropriate that God should be "angry with the wicked every day"? That He should have a benevolent indignation toward those who thus contemn their obligation? And is it not appropriate in Him to *express* or *reveal* this indignation, this wrath from heaven against such conduct as this? What would you think of a human ruler, who should let such conduct pass without manifesting the least displeasure at it; of a parent, who should let such conduct pass without manifesting any displeasure at it?

The fact is, God has infinitely good reasons for being highly displeased. His wrath must be enkindled against all ungodliness and unrighteousness of men, who hold the truth in unrighteousness.

Now, what will be said of Him if He does not manifest this wrath? What will His subjects think of Him? Can they maintain their confidence in Him? Will He not forfeit their confidence? Will He not inevitably lose the confidence of all His faithful subjects if He neglects to manifest or reveal His wrath against all ungodliness and unrighteousness of men, who hold the truth in unrighteousness?

Remarks

1. From this standpoint we can see the awful delusion of *mere moralists.*

There are many men who totally neglect God, and are, therefore, in the sense of this text, emphatically ungodly. They withhold from God the love, confidence, obedience, and worship which is His due, and still imagine that they are doing nothing very wrong. You speak of their danger of being lost and are ready to say, "Why, what have I done that is *bad*? Whom have I wronged?" Now the answer is plain, in the light of this text; you have wronged God out of His whole duty; you have never performed your duty to Him in any sense or degree. What if you should refuse to pay your debts to *men*?

Suppose you were indebted to many persons, and never paid them the first cent—habitually and universally neglected to meet their just demands. Then you should say you are a *moral* man and should ask, "What evil have I done?"

Suppose these creditors of yours should often demand their pay, and you should as often acknowledge in words that the debts were just, that you were just, that you *ought* to pay them, but still you should neglect and refuse to pay them, and never pay them at all; and then suppose they should complain of you, and you should say, "Why, what have I done?"—would not this be ridiculous?

But this is the manner in which you treat God; and you make little or no account of your neglect to pay what you owe to God. You would feel intensely if anybody owed you, and they should treat their obligation as you treat your obligation to God.

But just think! You are perfectly ungodly, and yet laying the flattering unction to your soul that you have done nothing very bad.

But again, you have neglected your whole duty to *man* as well as God. The law of God and the law of your own conscience requires you to love your neighbor as yourself; to regard and treat his interests as your own; to be careful of his reputation as of your own, of his feelings as of your own, of his interests as of your own. Now, have you done this? You satisfy yourself by saying you have not *wronged* him.

Wronged him! Have you not withheld from him that which is his due? Have you not refused to love him? Have you not refused to be interested in his welfare? Have you cared for his soul? Have you done anything to save him?

Suppose you had seen him asleep in his house, and the house was on fire, and you had let it burn down and consume him, and had given him no warning; and then you should say, "Wherein have I *wronged* him?"

The fact is you have wronged both God and man. You have withheld from both their due, and you have no more right to claim to be a *moral* man than Satan has to claim to be moral. For, a mere moralist, an unconverted man, a man that neglects his duty to God and his fellowmen (as all non-converted sinners do) is void of all moral honesty.

Why, how ridiculous it is for you to pretend to be morally honest, when you refuse, universally, to pay your debts. You do not hesitate to treat the claims of God, which you admit are just, with utter contempt in your practice. You withhold from Him all that is really valuable to Him. For if you do not love Him, if you do not regard His interests, your outward life (if it *appear* to be an honest and moral life) is a mere hypocrisy. Your kind treatment of your fellowmen is not, and cannot be, because you love them. For if you are a mere moralist, an unconverted man, you do not love your neighbor as yourself. You must, therefore, have some other reason than love to your neighbor for treating him kindly; it must be some other reason than real honesty of heart, and uprightness before God and man, that leads you to any *appearance* of honesty.

But suppose some individual owed you, and was under every possible obligation to you, and yet should contemn and depise the whole, and never perform his duty, or pay you a debt, or discharge any obligation, could you believe him an honest man? No, you could not believe that he had *one particle* of moral honesty in him.

But suppose you should see a son who treated his own parents as you treat God, would you believe that son an honest man, however much he might boast of honesty? Would you not be convinced irresistibly that any man who could treat honorable and upright parents with the contempt with which you treat God, could not be an honest man? Would you not regard him as void of all moral honesty? Would you not say irresistibly that a man beseech you to lay aside the claim of honesty and morality, and take home to yourself the charge that you are a totally dishonest and base man; you are one who has no real claim to be regarded as anything other than a wicked, unprincipled, and selfish being.

2. The same must be said of *many professors of religion*. What an awful delusion they are under! Supposing themselves to have been converted, they live in habitual and known transgression. Many things which they acknowledge to be their duty, they never pretend to perform.

They allow themselves all the time to live in the neglect of what everybody knows, and they themselves acknowledge to be their duty; and yet, they think they are justified—think they are penitent. But what idea can they have of repentance? Is not repentance the renunciation of sin?

But what is sin but withholding from God and man their due? Here then is a professor of religion that habitually withholds from God and man their due; living on in known omissions, confessing his omissions, continuing to confess them without end, and never addressing himself to the performance of these duties. Now what a delusion is this? Why, on the very face of it, it is hypocrisy and a fatal delusion.

3. This text does not agree with the doctrine of *inability* about which we hear so much.

There are many who are continually ready to acknowledge their shortcomings, and acknowledge in words their crime; but they plead their *inability* to obey. Inability! And does this text teach or imply any such doctrine as that? Why, this text assumes the very opposite of the doctrine of inability. It takes the ground that men, so far from being *unable* to obey the commands of God, are positively *resisting* them. And this is in fact true.

I have already said that truth, and especially the truth of moral obligation, is the natural stimulus of the mind. It wakes it up, and compels it to act in one way or the other. Moral obligation will at once enlist and engage the energies of the soul; and unless they be actively and positively withheld, unless the truth is held back, and restrained in unrighteousness, the mind will surely obey it. Here then, instead of being *unable* to obey, the individual *girds himself to resist*, in order to *prevent* obedience. Truth is a mighty impulse to draw him into conformity with itself; but, for selfish reasons, he girds himself and holds it back; restrains it in unrighteousness.

This, then, is your inability, sinner, and professor of religion.

Truth, if you did not restrain it, would at once quicken you into activity and into obedience. But you harden your heart; you stiffen your neck; you resist the claims of truth and of God.

This is plainly the doctrine of this text; as it is of the Bible universally when it is properly understood.

4. Men feel that neglect is sin, when *self* is the object of this neglect. Parents feel that the neglect of their children is sin; husbands and wives feel that the neglect of the other is sin; men in business feel that it is sin in their debtors to neglect to pay them, especially where this neglect is owing, not to inability, but to selfishness, or to carelessness of the rights of others. Selfish men are loud in their complaints of others who neglect to pay their debts to them; but it would surely be more consistent for them to cease complaining of anybody's neglecting them, while they are

neglecting to pay their debt to God. Thou that complainest that others neglect to pay their debts to you—dost thou neglect to pay thy debts to God?

5. How little stress is laid upon the neglect of duty as a *sin*. Now it should always be remembered that the law of God is *positive*. God is never satisfied with a man's doing *nothing*; He requires him to act, and that with all his heart, and soul, and mind, and strength. And now when God is totally neglected, when men are ungodly and unrighteous, neglecting their duty both to God and man, how strange it is that this neglect should be so little regarded as a great and abominable sin against God, and as indeed the essence of all sin.

6. *Church discipline* is often a great stumbling block on this account. Men are allowed to live in fellowship with the churches, and neglect their duty habitually and notoriously; men who neglect their duties to the church and their duty to God, and who live cold and formal lives, and who do not hesitate in words to confess it, while they do not reform.

How strange it is that persons are allowed to remain in the church as *accepted members*, who so neglect their duty both to God and man.

7. *Sinners are greatly misled* by the church in this respect. Children in Christian families see that their parents are living in constant neglect of duty; and if they attend meetings, they hear Christians confessing that they are constantly neglecting duty, and they know very well that they expect to continue to neglect their duty. Yet, very little stress is laid upon this by the church or by the ministry. Now this fatally misleads many sinners. They come to think but very little of omission of duty. The example of the church on this subject is the greatest stumbling block to them.They hear their parents say that they neglect God, and they neglect duty. Very well how little, then, do they think of neglecting their own duty!

It has come to this, that the example of the Church in this respect has completely hindered the world. Sinners are living for scores of years in the neglect of all their duty to God; and yet, do not consider themselves as very bad sinners. They say they have done nothing very bad. Now how have they acquired this idea? The fact is they have learned it from the Church. They have been in the habit of hearing the church members speak of the omission and neglect of duty as a thing *almost of course*.

8. *Orthodox* neglecters of duty are the *greatest sinners in the world*. I have said that neglect of duty implies a knowledge of duty. Now the more orthodox in sentiment men are, and the more enlightened men are, the greater, surely, is their obligation. Those, therefore, who are truly orthodox in sentiment, but heterodox in practice, living in the neglect of their known duty, are the greatest sinners in the world.

9. From this standpoint we can also see the actual difference between real saints and sinners.

I have just spoken of professors of religion who live in the habitual neglect of duty; and of the church, which is so largely composed of mere nominal professors, as being a stumbling block to the world. Remember, then, that I am now about to speak, not of *nominal* professors, of negligent souls, but of real saints and sinners. But I also wish to be understood as meaning by enemies all who live in the habitual neglect of known duty. Saints are converted persons; sinners are unconverted. Saints are penitent souls; sinners are impenitent. Saints are obedient; sinners are disobedient. Both *know* their duty; saints *do* their duty; but sinners omit theirs.

With the true saint, knowing God's will is *reason enough* to obey Him: he wants no further reason to influence his conduct. Such is God's will; and this with the true saint is enough. It is just this state of mind that constituted him a *saint*. He has given up his spirit of disobedience. He has ceased to hold truth in unrighteousness. He has yielded his mind to the influence of truth. God's will has been accepted by him. He has laid aside his rebellion, and become an obedient subject of Christ.

Now mark! He wants no better or higher reason for any course of conduct than to know that such is the will of Christ.

But with the sinner, the opposite is true. He knows his duty, but this is no influential reason with him at all. He has not accepted the will of God as his rule of life. He affirms it to be his duty to do so; but he does not do it. And it is this which constitutes him an impenitent sinner.

The revealed will of God is with him no sufficient reason at all to induce obedience. He knows his duty, perhaps as well as the saint does, but he does not do it. He holds the truth in unrighteousness. Again, with the true saint, the *omission* of any duty is a *dreadful thing.* What! To disobey a command of God!

To know that God requires of him a certain course of action, and for him to refuse! Why, it is a dreadful thing! A thing not to be thought of! But with the impenitent sinner, the omission of duty is a mere trifle, a thing scarcely worth considering. He goes forward omitting all his duty, and all with as little consideration or fear or regret as he would have in view of any trifle that you can name.

10. This text is more frequently suggested by facts around us than almost any other in the Bible. It is so very, very common to find persons neglecting what they know and even confess to be their duty, and it is utterly amazing when we consider that so many of these *con*fessors are really *pro*fessors. They confess themselves to be in the habitual neglect of some duties, and perhaps of many, and yet they profess to be the children of God; they profess to be converted, to be God's saints, His holy ones. Now, who can live with such surroundings without being constantly reminded of this text: "The wrath of God is revealed from heaven against all ungodliness and unrighteousness of men, who hold the truth in unrighteousness"?

11. The announcement of this text ought to shock such persons like a thunderbolt. See these dreamers! This multitude of souls that are crying peace, peace, when there is no peace! Neglecting their duty to God and to their fellowmen! Hark! Hear the thunder of this text, and let your nerves tremble!

12. Ministers have reason to tremble for their hearers. How perfectly

common it is for ministers to preach and hold out the claims of God, while their people will confess that it is truth, and that so they ought to do, but do they do so? Let such a minister watch his people. He holds out to them on the Sabbath the claims of God, and they go away, perhaps, eulogizing the preaching; at any rate, they confess that they have been instructed in regard to their duty—but does he find them the next day, and every subsequent day, addressing themselves to this duty? Does he *expect* them to do it? Does he even expect *his own church* to do it? I should like to ask ministers how many members of their church they have reason to believe, from acquaintance with them, will do their duty as soon as they are instructed in regard to it.

And I should like to ask them if it is not true that in a great multitude of instances, they have no expectation at all that the members of their church will wake up and be influenced by the truth, and will do what they know to be their duty. After preaching on the Sabbath and holding out to the church the claims of God, would they not be surprised on Monday to see the church all astir, and full of energy and vigor in carrying out the instructions of the Sabbath? How common it is for ministers to hold out the claims of God, to pour the truth upon their hearers; and then to see, right before their faces, that they hold the truth in unrighteousness. They know and acknowledge their duty, but they do not do it.

13. Let us reflect that it is the wrath of *God* that is revealed from heaven against all ungodliness and unrighteousness of men, who hold the truth in unrighteousness. It is the wrath of God; and therefore, it cannot be resisted. It is the wrath of God; and therefore, it cannot be endured. "Can thine heart endure, can thine hand be strong in the day that I shall deal with thee? saith the Lord. What then wilt thou do in the day when I shall punish thee?" Sinner and negligent professor, have you really considered what it is to have the wrath of an Omnipresent and Almighty Being revealed from heaven against you? Revealed from *heaven*! See, the holy mount is covered with dark clouds, the batteries are charged, the match is lighted—and *the Almighty is there!*

Are you not afraid to pursue your course of neglect of duty; holding truth in unrighteousness? In just such a time as you think not, and when you are crying peace and safety, these batteries of Omnipotence will open upon you—the discharge will wither you in a moment—and you will sink down, down, down in the blackness of darkness forever!

What then shall you do? I answer, immediately discard this spirit of delay—lay hold upon eternal life—let your heart go to Christ—no longer hold the truth in unrighteousness. Arise, and what you do, do quickly. Lay hold upon eternal life; for "now is the accepted time, and now is the day of salvation."

2

THE FOUNDATION, CONDITIONS,
AND RELATIONS OF FAITH*

Romans 4:1-5

"What shall we then say that Abraham our father, as pertaining to the flesh, hath found? For if Abraham were justified by works, he hath whereof to glory; but not before God. For what saith the scripture? Abraham believed God, and it was counted unto him for righteousness. Now to him that worketh is the reward not reckoned of grace, but of debt. But to him that worketh not, but believeth on him that justifieth the ungodly, his faith is counted for righteousness."

A passage in Genesis 15 refers to Abraham—to the promises God had made to him—to his faith in those promises, and to the Lord's acceptance of that faith. These topics are first brought to our view in Genesis 12, again in Genesis 17; and thenceforward, frequently in the course of Abraham's history. The case was highly instructive, and St. Paul could not fail to see its important bearings. Hence, he makes free use of it as an illustration; both of what faith is, and of its results.

In treating this subject, it is important,

    I. *To notice the foundation of Abraham's faith;*
    II. *Some of its conditions;*
    III. *Its governmental relations;*
    IV. *Its natural relations and results.*

I. *The foundation of Abraham's faith was not in any manner whatever in himself.* It was not the fact, either real or supposed, that he had been himself converted. There is no intimation that he ever so much as thought whether he had been converted or not. His faith seems to have been exercised irrespective of any opinions or thoughts on this question.

Nor did his faith rest on the assumption that he was himself in a right state of mind. He did not, so far as we can see, assume this; and thereupon, ground his confidence that God would do for him what He had promised.

Nor did his faith rest in the confidence he might have had in his own integrity of character. There is not the least intimation of this.

But positively, his faith rested on God's *veracity.* It does not appear

---

The Oberlin Evangelist: Vol. XII; February 13, 1850.

that Abraham took into view anything else whatever as a ground of his faith except the simple veracity of God. He simply relied on what God had said, because it was God who said it. God met him and told him certain things; he believed them, although they were apparently impossible. It was enough for him that God had said so. He rested in God as a Being of veracity of truth.

II. *Conditions of Abraham's faith.*

It is a very common thing for the conditions of faith to be confounded with faith itself. This is a fundamental mistake. For example, the rational recognition of God's natural and moral attributes is a condition of faith, but is not by any means faith itself. Unless a man sees and knows that God possesses the moral attributes ascribed to Him, he can see no ground for rational confidence in Him. How could Abraham have had confidence in God, if he had not believed in His natural and moral attributes? He must have believed this; else he could not rationally believe that God would and could fulfill His promises.

It is especially to be noted that Abraham must have had confidence in God's *moral attributes*, as a condition of faith. He must have believed that God is good; for of necessity this attribute of the divine character must be intellectually apprehended before the mind can rationally believe that God will certainly fulfill His promises. Hence the distinction between the conditions of faith and faith itself is really fundamental. One might intellectually apprehend these attributes as clearly as an angel in heaven does, and yet not have gospel faith.

Another condition of faith is the *promise of God.* It could have been no virtue in Abraham to believe that God would grant him a son, or give his posterity Canaan, if God had never promised to do so. God first revealed His covenant with Abraham, and connected with it precious promises; then a condition was fulfilled for faith on Abraham's part— *then*, but not before. In the same way the covenant of grace, clearly apprehended, as revealed of God, is a condition of saving faith now. When God in any way reveals the substance of this covenant—whether through dim types and prophecies as before Christ came, or in the broad blaze of gospel day as when He actually came, then the way is opened for the intelligent and acceptable exercise of gospel faith. No doubt Adam and Eve received sufficient revelation from God to lay a foundation for their faith. Eve obviously understood from the promise given in Genesis 3:15, that salvation from the power of Satan was to come through her posterity; for at the birth of Cain, her first born, she seems to have supposed that this was the promised seed. In this particular she was indeed mistaken, but not in her faith that God would bring salvation through her remote posterity. It is plain that both Adam and Eve received and believed at this time the revelation of divine mercy. The Lord was exceedingly kind towards them in His mode of convicting them of their first and great sin. How beautiful and how gracious that He should Himself clothe them to hide the shame of their nakedness! How significant too that this clothing should be of skins—of skins which almost beyond question were taken from animals now for the first time slain for sacrifice! It seems most fitting that here for the first time the idea of sacrifice should be developed, and the race be taught in the person of Adam and Eve that "without the shedding of blood, there could be no remission for sin." A most expressive and beautiful type! What could more forcibly express displeasure against sin—grace towards the real sinner—and the substitution of an innocent victim in place of the guilty, as a ground for the grace shown the latter!

The covenant of grace to Abraham God revealed yet more fully; thus expanding more distinctly His purposes of lovingkindness towards a sinning race, and making yet more distinct and definite this ground of saving faith.

III. *The governmental relations of saving faith.* What relations did Abraham's faith sustain to the government of God?

Scripture answers by saying, "He counted it to him for righteousness." It was set down—passed to his account as righteousness—as if it were perfect obedience. Businessmen will understand this phrase so current in their pecuniary transactions. A credit is passed to a man's account—a receipt in full—accounted as full payment of his debt. The obvious meaning seems to be that God accepted Abraham's faith instead of that perfect obedience which had been before required. All men have fallen into sin, and hence come under condemnation. Yet, God passes to their credit the righteousness of Christ, as if Christ had passed to their credit in the bank of heaven enough to cancel all their debt.

It should never be forgotten that the ultimate ground of the sinner's justification is God's great and pure love. In love alone, the whole scheme had its origin.

Another condition of this governmental justification is that the sinner believes. The simple belief of this record; the heart yielding itself up to the control of the truth believed—this is the condition on which the full blessings of Christ's work are conferred.

In the case of Abraham, faith gave him, as indeed it does all believers, the full benefit of all the work comprised in the death and resurrection of the Lord Jesus. All that Christ has done for the sinner becomes his on condition of his embracing it by faith. This is the *only* condition. Abraham was to believe the promise before Christ actually came; all believers since Christ's death are to believe on Christ as actually come. In each case the condition is substantially the same; it is believing what God has said, and taking hold of His promise to rely upon it as truth.

The term righteousness, as used in this connection, denotes *justification.* This is its proper meaning. Abraham's faith, therefore, is accepted of him in the place of perfect obedience as the ground of his pardon. Thus pardoned, he can be treated as if he had not sinned. He *had* sinned, indeed, but under the economy of grace, he is treated governmentally as if he had not sinned. Governmentally, he is regarded as perfect. By this I do not mean that the law did not regard him as a sinner, for it did so regard him, and could not do otherwise. It could not blot from its tablets the record of his past sins, but it could, so to speak, pass to his credit the faith he had exercised, which is accounted to him for righteousness. On this ground the Lawgiver can treat him not as sinful, but as righteous.

Yet, let it not be lost sight of that, *providentially*, he may be and is still treated as a sinner. Under the providential, disciplinary government of God, he is regarded as a sinner—as yet imperfect and needing discipline to improve his character and train him for heaven. Hence, while *governmentally* he is regarded as righteous and not doomed to hell, yet providentially, it is not forgotten that he has sinned, and that he still needs discipline to evolve and perfect the spirit and the habits of holiness.

IV. *Its natural relations and results.*

1. It is naturally connected with *obedience*. It stands related to obedience by its very *nature*. Faith is confidence in God's veracity. This naturally leads the soul to obey all God's requirements.

Cases sometimes occur in which we may get from our own observation very striking and just views of the nature of faith, psychologically considered. You may sometimes see persons give themselves up to another so completely as to believe everything they say, and be entirely controlled by their influence. I was much struck with this in the course of some Second Advent discussions. Some, then, seemed most manifestly to have unbounded confidence in all Mr. Miller said and believed.* Often they manifested a similar confidence in their subleaders. For example, I heard a man say, a man who I have reason to fear is a wicked man, "That woman will do just what I tell her to do, and I can make her believe anything I say." This was said in her presence, and I had but too much reason to think that it was literally true.

During the progress of these scenes, I felt constrained to say to one lady, "I am afraid you will go to destruction; you have given yourself up to be led anywhere, and I do greatly fear this will not end short of plunging you in absolute ruin. You believe the most utter nonsense as strongly and firmly as if God Himself had met you and told you to believe it."

This case may serve to illustrate the natural results of faith. Let one man commit himself to another as a leader and teacher, and the latter can lead him anywhere and any way he pleases. Let a soldier commit himself thus to his general; he can then be led right into the very jaws of death. So let confidence be cherished in another; its natural result will be to bring the confiding mind under the complete dominion of the mind confided in.

Such was the natural influence of Abraham's faith. We see him hang-

---

*William Miller (1782-1849) was founder of Adventism. He predicted Christ's Second Coming about the year 1843.

ing upon what God said just like a child upon its parent. If anything happened to try him, we see him coming forth from the trial in the utmost simplicity of character. How beautiful and how noble to see him stand firm as a rock while the storms of temptation dash around his feet! So it is with real faith always. Abraham's faith had in it nothing peculiar in character or in results. It was simple faith—nothing more.

2. *Faith naturally results in joy and peace.* The things believed are such that the mind cannot but feel the highest joy and the most quiet repose. If you really understand and believe what God says, why not feel at rest? What more need He say to inspire confidence in Himself? Who does not know that confidence in the One believed to be able to save to the uttermost must assuredly inspire the rest of sweet respose—the joy of unalloyed confidence and trust? Verily, God has said everything we need to have said to make us feel that His promised protection is round about us as the mountains are round about Jerusalem. Has He not told us that His everlasting arms are underneath us evermore? And can we ever sink, sustained by such supports? Who does not know that simply to believe in all this naturally results in peace, quietness, and assurance forever? Who does not see that these results flow as naturally as any other results flow from their appropriate cause? Who can believe this good news, and not be greatly glad? Is not that joy both intense and abiding which springs from peace, deep and broad as a river, and from a righteousness which flows and rolls its mountain waves as the sea?

3. *This faith overcomes the world.* By this I mean that it overcomes the influence of the world upon the mind.

Let a man believe what is said of the future state; he will then deem it a small thing to be judged of man's judgment. But, oh! To stand right in the eye of the Great and Final Judge—this will be his supreme concern. Let him only be assured of this, and all within is peace and joy. Let him only apprehend God's universal providence and put his trust in this all present and all controlling Deity, then all is peace and joy. Whether sick or well, it is all the same; nothing disturbs his peace; for he knows that under God's hand all things shall work together for his good. No matter whether he has much or little of earthly supply; he knows that he has just so much as is good for him, for the amount is wisely and kindly measured out to him by One who both knows and loves. He may enjoy honor, or dishonor; he may have much learning, or none. All is well, if he knows that God has appointed all just as it is, and if he can thoroughly trust it all to be perfectly right. Be the circumstances what they may, he knows that what is infinitely wise and good is taking place and always will be. Now he has only to believe this, and it is all the same to him whether he have little, or much, or none at all of this world's good things. If he will only believe with unfaltering faith that all is wise and well, he has a key in his own bosom with which he can unlock all treasures.

Here is a professor of religion, under God's glorious government, fretting about a *pin!* Alas! What is the matter? He has lost a single pin! This is not the worst thing—he has lost his *faith!* I saw him one day in great trouble and anxiety of mind. It was a few days after his conversion; then he seemed a bright and joyful convert, but he lost his way and fell into temptation. Alas! Go and ask him now what is the matter. He will reply, "I have lost my Jesus!" It is well that he knows it. Many do not seem to know it when the fact is most obvious to everybody else. Listen to the Psalmist and mark the beauty and pertinence of his words. He sinks into the deep mire of the Slough of Despond;* yet, opening his eyes somewhat to his condition, he cries out, "Why art thou cast down, O my soul? and why art thou disquieted in me? hope thou in God: for I shall yet praise him." He would excite his own soul to believe God, and hence he begins to arraign and catechize himself for his causeless unbelief. "Oh, my soul, Why art thou cast down? Believe thou in God!" Believe what? Believe *in God*. Believe that thou shalt still praise Him.

4. *Faith naturally overcomes the flesh.* If a man has faith, why shall he go about to gratify his appetites? Shall he make their gratification his chief good? Nay, verily. He will understand that the kingdom of heaven is not meat and drink. If you see a man given up to the indulgence of his appetites, you see an unbeliever. You see one who does not apprehend the great things of the eternal world as living and all controlling realities. He is under the dominion of his flesh. But faith breaks up this dominion, and asserts its own in its stead. What has faith to do with sensuality? What communion is there between light and darkness? What concord between Christ and Belial? Just the same as between faith and sensuality. Faith overcomes Satan. One who believes God knows that Satan is a liar and the father of lies. Without faith, you are Satan's dupe, Satan's slave, Satan's drudge; but faith in Jesus emancipates the soul from the dominion of his lies.

Remarks

1. The faith of Abraham was purely a mental act. The apostle speaks of it curiously. "If Abraham were justified by works, he would have whereof to glory"; but now he has nothing of which to glory; and therefore, he is not justified by works. Plainly he was not justified at all by works in the Jewish sense. It was not on the ground of certain external doings, but on the ground of his mental faith, that he was justified. The purely mental act of faith was the condition, itself antecedent to all external manifestations, and the condition of them. This faith is accounted to him for righteousness.

2. Some confound the condition of faith with faith itself. Some just knowledge of God is doubtless an indispensable condition to the exercise of faith, but this knowledge, this intellectual apprehension of God, is not to be confounded with faith itself.

---

*Shortly after Christian left the City of Destruction, he and Pliable fell into the Slough of Despond. See John Bunyan's, *The Pilgrim's Progress,* written from jail in 1675. (Editor's Note).

3. Some look to something within themselves as the ground of faith. Consequently, they attend continually to their own mental states instead of looking up to God. They are evermore looking within at their state of feeling for *evidence* upon which they are to believe. Believe what? Not believe in themselves, but believe in God. Under the pretense of self-examination, they are forever playing the fool with themselves, and looking down, as they suppose, into the depths of their hearts, to find evidence on which to believe. God announces to them a truth, and says, "Believe." They reply, "I can believe that, if I can only get the evidence on which to believe. God announces to them a truth, and says, "Believe." They reply, "I can believe that, if I can only get the evidence that I am in a right state of mind." But what is a right state of mind? A state of *faith*. Believing is the right exercise; nothing else is right. The great piety of Abraham, when brought out in the Bible, is simple belief—trust; this constitutes a right state of mind. He believed what God said, not on the ground of having certain right emotions and feelings, but because it was God who had said it. What if Abraham had said, "Oh, I could believe all God has said, if I only had the evidence." Of *what?* Do you want evidence that God is true? No, but I want evidence that I am in a right state of mind. Abraham was not such a fool as to back out of God's Light into the darkness of his own mind, and draw a vail of thick darkness over and all round about him. No, it was enough for him that God had spoken, and that God was true.

It would really seem as if God was unable to say anything to Abraham which he would not believe. God almost *seemed* to tell him lies to try his faith, but yet Abraham would believe. The Lord told him he should have a son, but still He went on in His providence as if He never meant to fulfill His promise. Continually He seemed to contradict Himself. After Isaac was born and grown, He told Abraham to take him far away to a specified mountain, and there kill him! Oh, what a scene was that! Yet Abraham believed God. He knew that God could even raise his Isaac from the dead; hence, why should he fear to obey God, even when He gave such a command? If this man of God were among us in our prayer meetings, would he do as some now do—be looking continually after his feelings? No! He would simply believe God.

Yet mark how sorely God tried him. "Take now," said He, "thy son, thine only son Isaac" (how every word sinks to the bottom of a parent's heart!), take him away from his loved home, and from his fond mother—forever! Set off on this dreadful expedition tomorrow. One night intervened. Did the tried father sleep quietly as ever that night? If he did, it must have been the rest of faith. In the morning he rose, said not a word to Sarah; he could not have her sympathy, for (probably) he could not trust her faith against her maternal feelings. His own faith stood, apparently, unfaltering. The simplicity of his faith was the glory of his piety.

Yet Abraham had but few things to believe. If those full revelations made to us had been made to him, what a mighty, triumphant life he must have lived! In what a sunset of glory he must have died! Only a single ray fell from heaven upon his eye, yet his eye caught this one ray, and his heart believed. On that ray he kept his eye fixed continually. Oh, if he were to live now and among us, what would he think of our faith? What could he think of us, always prating over our unbelief as if we had not faith enough to keep us above the fear of hell!

4. What many Christians say is greatly calculated to stumble young converts. They seem not to have gone a step beyond babyhood. They are no more able to stand alone than a mere child. Though counting the years of their Christian life, they ought for the time to be men of adult age and of adult strength.

When a young convert sets out in the Christian life with a flood of emotions and these soon subside, it happens not seldom that he falls into deep trouble. Like a raw hand aboard ship, he shows but too soon that he is no sailor. A storm comes on, the mountain waves dash high—such a wind he never knew before—his knees smite together, and he cries out, "Alas! I am lost, I am lost!" So the timid convert feels when he thinks he has lost his Jesus. The fact is he has only lost his faith. And perhaps this sad loss has befallen him because he was misguided by much older Christians, who should have strengthened his faith rather than weakened it.

How plain it is that God meant to confirm our faith and teach us to keep it always strong and earnest. Else why did He give us such a history as this of Abraham? Look at this man of living faith! See him pushing his way along with only one dim ray of light, yet firm as a rock amid the waves; steadfast, though all around be dark as death. But oh, what a zigzag course many now pursue! Faltering now, and now turning aside to shun the lions in the way; feeling their path along as if they could not trust the Mighty One who has said, "This is the way; go forward, and fear not, for I am with thee." How many such Christians would it take to promote a revival? Ten thousand of them would not promote one! In fact, the more such Christians there are, the worse for the cause of God; the greater the difficulties in promoting revivals where their influence is felt. Oh how weak and sickly they are! They need to be fed with a spoon like an infant. You might as soon march an army of invalids against Gibraltar, as lead such Christians out to conflict by prayer and faith in promoting revivals of religion. I can afford and endure to see infancy and weakness in young converts; but oh, when I see old Christians still shut up to the diet and leading-strings of infants, it is so afflictive, so disheartening! To see them go around and around forever in a circle after their feelings, *their feelings!* What an abomination that they don't learn to walk by faith! A perfect state of the physical system does not make a man think much about his health. It leaves him to mind his appropriate business and seek the proper enjoyments of life. If his digestion is good, he never thinks of his stomach. Why should he? Perhaps he never knows from any sensations felt that he has any stomach. But if his digestion is bad; then alas, the poor man has enough to do in thinking of his troubled stomach. So of the sickly Christian! You see him perpetually troubled about his feelings, *his feelings!* Oh, when will such Christians learn to have faith, and be strong in the Mighty God of Jacob.

5. It is a most unhealthy religion which is forever dwelling on views and frames and feelings. How is it in heaven? Are they thinking of their feelings and frames? No! They are so absorbed in the great objects before them that they are unconscious of the lapse of time. Perhaps a thousand of our years may pass over them and leave no consciousness of its having been a moment. Is this extravagant? No. Have you not been sometimes so engrossed that you could not mark the lapse of time at all? We mark time by noticing the succession of events. Have you not been so much engrossed as not at all to notice this succession? I recollect the case of a young convert in the northern part of New York State, who on one occasion prayed all night. When he came to consciousness of time and began to think what time it was, he was astonished to find it morning!

It is said of William Tennant that he rode all day in thought so profound that he never knew till he reached the end of his journey that he had been bleeding profusely from the nose.* Now in such cases, their own state is not the subject of thought at all. Of course, they are far indeed from studying and watching over their own feelings.

This latter is, as I have said, a most unhealthy state. He who is forever dwelling upon his own spiritual frames, instead of being absorbed in the objects of faith, is a poor, spiritual dyspeptic. This thinking of his own frames is the very thing which destroys his religion.

Suppose I go to England and leave my wife at home. Far away from her I set myself to examine my feelings to see if I love my wife. I turn my mind away from her, and fasten it upon my love. I make this love the only and the all absorbing subject of my thought. What will be the result? Who does not know that the affection of love is correlated to its object? In this case my affection is correlated to my wife, and cannot spring up and develop itself, except in view of its object. Hence, I must think of my wife, if I would make it possible for the affection of love to develop itself. Contemplation of the object is the condition of all manifestation of the affections. Consequently, by turning my mind wholly away from the object, and then demanding that love to the object should manifest itself, I demand a natural impossibility. Let me do this and I might pronounce myself a stark hypocrite, and be as well employed as many Christians are who withhold their contemplations from God, and all the proper objects of faith, and exercise themselves in scanning and trying to judge of their feelings. Oh, what misguided efforts are these!

---

*William Tennant (1673-1746) was a Presbyterian minister and educator who founded the "Log College" to train young men who were active revivalists, but who did not meet the educational requirements set by the Philadelphia Synod.

3

THE NATURE OF DEATH*

Romans 6:7

"For he that is dead is freed from sin."

In the discussion of this subject I shall notice,
  I. *The different kinds of death mentioned in the Bible;*
  II. *What kind of death is intended here in our text;*
  III. *What it consists in;*
  IV. *What is implied in it;*
  V. *How it is effected.*

I. *The different kinds of death mentioned in the Bible.*
1. *Natural death.* This is the death of the body.
2. *Spiritual death.* This is death *in sin.* It is total depravity or a state of entire alienation from God.
3. *Eternal death.* This consists in the endless curse of God.
4. *Death to sin.*

II. *The kind of death mentioned in the text is death to sin.*
The death here spoken of is manifestly a death to sin. This is very evident from the context. At the end of the preceding chapter, Paul had been speaking of the super-abounding grace of Christ, and commences the sixth chapter by saying, "What shall we say then? Shall we continue in sin, that grace may abound? God forbid. How shall we that are dead to sin live any longer therein?" Here Paul is speaking of those who were alive and yet dead to sin. He spoke of their having received a baptism into the death of Christ. By their spiritual baptism, they had been solemnly set apart or consecrated to the death of Christ. "Know ye not, that so many of us as were baptized into Jesus Christ were baptized into His death? Therefore we are buried with Him by baptism into death; that like as Christ was raised up from the dead by the glory of the Father, even so we also should walk in newness of life. For if we have

---

The Oberlin Evangelist: Vol. II; July 15, 1840. Original Title: "Death to Sin."

been planted together in the likeness of His death, we shall be also in the likeness of His resurrection; knowing this, that our old man is crucified with Him, that the body of sin might be destroyed, that henceforth we should not serve sin. For he that is dead is freed from sin. Now, if we be dead with Christ, we believe that we shall also live with Him." He speaks of them as not only dead, but by their spiritual baptism buried into the death of Christ. To carry the idea of their being still farther from the life of sin; he speaks of them as being planted into the likeness of His death, and crucified with Him that the body of sin might be destroyed. And then adds in the words of the text, "Now he that is dead is freed from sin." The term here rendered justification may be rendered "is made righteous."

It is plain from this connection, that Paul is speaking of those who had been so baptized by the Holy Spirit so as to be dead to sin, buried, planted, crucified, with respect to sin.

III. *What it consists in.*
Summarily, death *to* sin consists in the annihilation of selfishness, and the reign of perfect love to God and man in the heart and life.

IV. *What is implied in it.*
1. Death *to sin* is the opposite of death *in sin*. Death *in* sin implies living for self, or being dead to God's glory and interests and only alive to our own glory. Death *to* sin implies the reverse of this. It implies a death to our own interests and happiness as an end of pursuit, and a living wholly to the glory of God, and for the up-building of His kingdom.

2. Death *in* sin implies a will opposed to the will of God. *I speak here of a fixed and permanent state of the will in opposition to a single particular volition.* A will in this state is not at all influenced by the will of God. It has never submitted to His will, and consequently a knowledge of the will of God is no influential reason to determine its volitions. But death *to* sin implies a will wholly subservient to and under the control of the will of God. I speak now also of a *state* of will. *One who is dead to sin has no other will than that God's will should in all things be done.* Lay before him any question in which he is in doubt with respect to what the will of God is, and he will find himself unable to decide upon a course of action. All he can decide upon in such a case is to search and inquire what is the will of God. But until he is satisfied in some way with respect to the will of God, he is utterly in doubt and finds himself unable to make up his mind and come to any decision with respect to the question before him. This is a state of mind directly opposite to a death *in* sin. In a state of death *in* sin, the will of God is not inquired after as the great and only influential motive to decide the will. A man in this state has, as we say, a will of his own. He decides upon his own responsibility, in his own strength, and entirely in view of selfish reasons. While one who is dead *to* sin, has so submitted himself to the will of God—so bowed his will to God's will, that he decides nothing in view of selfish reasons, and

the will of God has come to be the controlling reason or motive of his conduct. Let him but know what is the will of God in the case, and his will is yielding as air. But shut him out from this knowledge, and he is in a state of the utmost perplexity and cannot decide upon any course of conduct. He can only say, "I have no will about it." However uncommon it has been for Christians to come into this state while in life and health, it has not been at all uncommon for them to be in this state while on a death bed. Every one conversant with death bed scenes has probably witnessed such cases of entire surrender of the whole being to the will of God, so that the individual was unable to choose whether to live or die and could only say, "I have no will about it." Not knowing what the will of God was there was no other choice than this, viz. that the will of God, whatever it was, should be done. Ask an individual whether sick or well, living or dying, who is in this state, whether he wills or chooses a certain thing; if it be a question with respect to which he is in doubt regarding what the will of God is, you will find him to be entirely at a loss. He is conscious of choosing that the will of God should be done. But until he knows whether this or that is the will of God he has no choice about that particular event.

3. Death *in* sin implies a self-indulgent state of mind. To consult ones own ease, happiness, reputation, and interests is natural to him who is dead *in* sin. If he is on board a steamboat, you will find him ready to contend for the best berth and hastening to obtain the best seat at the first table. If riding in a stagecoach, you will observe him seeking for the best seat. To consult his own comfort, his own indulgence and happiness, is the law of his mind. And in ten thousand ways will this state of mind develop itself.

But a death *to* sin implies a self-denying state of mind, a disposition to give others the preference, a choosing to accommodate others, to bless, and to benefit others, at the expense of self-interest or self-indulgence.

4. A death *in* sin implies the real and practical regarding of ourselves as our own. But death *to* sin is the real and practical regarding of our whole being as God's.

5. A death *in* sin implies the love of our own reputation. Death *to* sin implies the making of ourselves no reputation, as Christ did.

6. A death *in* sin implies the practical regarding of our possessions as our own. Death *to* sin implies the real and practical regarding of our possessions as God's.

7. Death *in* sin implies the dominion of the flesh and the will in subjection to the flesh. A death *to* sin implies a subjection of the body to the soul. It implies bringing the body into subjection, with all its appetites and propensities brought into subjection to the will of God.

8. A death *in* sin implies a state of mind that is influenced by sensible objects, by honors, riches, opinions, and things of this world as much as if its possessor expected to live here forever. Death *to* sin implies the giving up of the world substantially as a dying man gives it up. Its riches, honors, amusements, pursuits, ambition, strifes, and envyings; what are

all these to him? If he knows himself to be a dying man, he regards them not. He desires them not. He seeks them not. He does not, cannot, under these circumstances, will to have them. He chooses nothing of this world's goods, but those things that are really necessary for the few hours or moments which remain to him of this life. A little more breath—perhaps a few spoons full of water—a little of the kind attention of his friends are all that is left for him to desire of earthly good. Now death *to* sin implies this giving up all desire and expectation of the wealth, honors, and selfish pursuits of this world. The man who is dead *to* sin is as absolutely satisfied with a competency of earthly good as a man is who is on a bed of death. He would no sooner lay his schemes of earthly aggrandizement, or for enlarging and perpetuating his selfish gratification, than a man would upon a bed of death. In a word, he has given up the world as an object of pursuit as really and emphatically as if he knew himself to be doomed to live but one hour. He has entered upon a new and eternal life. All his plans, desires, and aims are heavenly, and not earthly, sensual or devilish.

IV. *How this death is effected, or how persons may enter into and exercise this state of mind.*

1. You cannot die *to* sin by the strength of your own resolutions. You will never die *to* sin by merely resolving to die to sin. It is one of the most common delusions among men to suppose that they can stand against temptation by the strength of their own resolutions. Peter thought himself able to follow Christ even unto death. But his resolution, like all mere human resolutions, failed him just when he most needed its support. A brother said to me the other day, "I have learned this about my resolutions; they are firm enough when there is nothing to overthrow them, and just when I do not need their support. But they always fail me when I do. Just when I have a trial that demands their sustaining power, I find they are like air and good for nothing."

2. This state of mind is never to be entered into by any unaided efforts of our own. Sin has too long had dominion over us. Our powers are too much enslaved by its protracted indulgence. Sin has too long been our master, to be at once put down by any unaided efforts of ours. But,

3. This state of mind is effected by the baptism of the Holy Spirit. The baptism of the Spirit does not imply the bestowment of miraculous gifts, as some seem to have supposed. The Apostles possessed miraculous gifts before they were baptized with the Holy Spirit. The power of miracles may or may not be incidental to spiritual baptism. But, by no means, constitutes any part of it. Nor does spiritual baptism imply great excitement.

But it does imply such a degree of divine influence as will purify the heart. The New Testament writers manifestly use the term baptism as synonymous with purifying. Water baptism is typical of spiritual baptism. Spiritual baptism is the purifying of the heart by the Holy Spirit. Miraculous gifts, great excitement of mind, great rejoicings, or great sorrows over sin may be incidental to spiritual baptism, but they are not essential to it. You that have read the memoir of J. B. Taylor will recollect that on the 23rd of April 1822, while he was engaged in prayer, he felt his whole soul sweetly yielding itself up to God. Such a sweet thorough yielding himself and all his interests for time and eternity into the hands of God, he had never before experienced.* Now I suppose that this was the effect of the baptism of the Holy Spirit. He ever after remained in a state of mind entirely different from anything he had before experienced.

In receiving the baptism of the Holy Spirit, we are by no means passive but eminently active.

This influence is secured by faith. Faith in Christ throws the mind open to the influence of His truth and gives the Spirit the opportunity of so presenting truth as sweetly to bring the entire person under its whole power. Christ administers spiritual blessings, and this is received by taking hold of His promise to baptize with the Holy Spirit, and throwing the mind open to His influences. The baptism of the Apostles, by the Holy Spirit on the day of Pentecost, will illustrate what I mean. Christ had promised them that they should be baptized with the Holy Spirit not many days hence. They fastened upon this promise, and waited in a constant attitude of prayer and expectation; throwing the door of the mind open to His influence. Now Christ has given to all believers a great many promises of the freeness of the Holy Spirit. He has said that the "Father is more willing to give the Holy Spirit to them that ask Him than earthly parents are to give good gifts to their children." The "water of life" which is so abundantly promised in both the New and Old Testaments is the Holy Spirit. This everyone knows who has attentively considered the real meaning of those promises.

And now if you would enter into this death to sin, you must be baptized with the Holy Spirit. If you would be baptized with the Holy Spirit, you must fasten upon the promises of Christ and take hold of them in faith—laying your whole soul open to receive His influences. Rest with the utmost confidence in His promise to give you of the "fountain of water of life freely." And when you have taken hold of His promise, be sure not to let go or let your confidence to be shaken until you feel a consciousness that "you are baptized into His death."

Remarks

1. In the connection of this text, Paul speaks of himself and others as dead *to* and freed *from* sin.

2. If death *to* sin does not imply entire sanctification, death *in* sin does not imply total depravity, for they are manifestly opposite states of mind.

3. As death *in* sin is consistent with persons doing many things

---

*James Brainerd Taylor (1801-1829) died at the age of 28, but left an autobiography of over 400 pages: see *Memoirs of James Brainerd Taylor*, New York: American Tract Society, 1833.

which the world regards as righteous, so death *to* sin may be consistent with many things which the world would regard as sinful.

4. Paul's history confirms the profession which he makes of being dead *to* sin.

5. The circumstances of the primitive Church rendered a death *to* sin almost inevitable, at least in many instances. The profession of attachment to Christ must inevitably have cost many of them all that the world holds or calls dear. They had to enter upon the Christian life by a renunciation of the world, by giving up worldly expectations and pursuits, as much as men do on a deathbed. The state of public sentiment was eminently calculated to faciliate their entrance into a state of physical death, and was no doubt a prime reason for their rapid advancement in the divine life.

6. We see why state and other violent persecutions have already greatly contributed to the spirituality of the Church.

7. We see also why state and worldly favor has crippled the energies and overthrown the purity of the Church.

8. We see how the idea comes to be so prevalent that Christians are not wholly sanctified until death. As a matter of fact, this no doubt generally is true, that Christians are not wholly and permanently sanctified until about the close of life, until they come into that state in which they expect very soon to die. I once knew a good man who was told by his physicians that, in consequence of the enlargement of the large blood vessel near the heart, he was exposed to instant death, and that at all events he must expect to die very soon. This intelligence, after the first shock was over, was instrumental in baptizing him into the death of Christ. He very soon entered into a most blessed and heavenly state of mind, let go of the world, and seemed to stand looking and waiting with most heavenly serenity for the coming of the Son of Man. In this state of mind, he was informed after a while that he might probably live for a long time, notwithstanding his disease. This so staggered him as to well nigh bring him again into bondage. Not seeming to understand the philosophy of the state of mind in which he was, and how to remain in it by simple faith, he staggered and groaned under this intelligence till Christ, true to His promise, interposed and set his feet upon eternal rock. After this he lived and died to the wonder of all those around him; few, if any, so much as dreamed that his state of mind was what is intended by a death *to* sin.

9. Payson and multitudes of good men have found it easy to enter into this state of mind when all expectation was relinquished of remaining longer in this world.* But it seems impossible or difficult for most persons to conceive that this state of mind may be really entered into with a prospect of any amount of life still before us.

---

*Edward Payson (1783-1827) was an American clergyman whose memoirs and sermons were quite popular: see *Payson's Complete Works*, Boston: Hyde, Lord, and Duren, 1846.

10. But there is no need of waiting until the close of life before we die *to* sin. We have only to thoroughly let go of all selfish schemes and projects whatever, and give ourselves as absolutely up to the service of God, as much as we expect to when we come to die, and we enter at once into this infinitely desirable state of mind.

11. If persons have entered into this state of mind, new trials may call for fresh baptisms of the Spirit. While we are in this world of temptation, we are never beyond the reach of sin and never out of danger. If selfishness could be called into exercise in holy Adam, how much more so in those who have lived so long under the dominion of selfishness? If a man has been intemperate or licentious, although these appetites and propensities may be subdued, yet it behoves him to keep out of temptation's way; and renewed temptation calls for fresh and more powerful baptisms of the Holy Spirit. *Be not satisfied then with one anointing. But look day by day for deeper draughts of the water of life.*

12. If we allow any form of sin to live, it will have dominion. It must be wholly exterminated or it will be our ruler. The principle of total abstinence in regard to sin is wholly indispensable to the reign of spiritual life.

Let us then, beloved, not rest satisfied until we are conscious that we are dead and buried by spiritual baptism into Christ's death; until we are planted in the likeness of His death; and so crucified with Him that the body of death is fully destroyed.

4

SANCTIFICATION UNDER GRACE*

Romans 6:14

"For sin shall not have dominion over you; for ye are not under the law: but under grace."

I shall attempt to show:
  I. *What sin is.*
  II. *When it may be said that sin has dominion in the soul.*
  III. *What it is to be under the law.*
  IV. *What it is to be under grace.*
  V. *That under the law sin will have dominion over an unsanctified mind, of course.*
  VI. *That sin cannot have dominion over those who are under grace.*

I. *I am to show what sin is.*

Sin is a state of mind which is the opposite of the law of God. As I have shown in a former lecture, the whole of true religion consists in obedience to this law, which requires supreme, disinterested love to God and disinterested and equal love to our neighbor. This is the opposite of selfishness or a supreme regard to our own interest. Selfishness, therefore, under all its forms, is sin; and there is no form of sin that is not some modification of selfishness.

Sin then is not any part of our physical or mental constitution. It is no part or principle of nature itself but a voluntary state of mind, that is, an action or choice of the mind, a preferring our own interest, because it is our own, to other and higher interests. It does not consist in any defect of our nature, but in a perversion or prohibited use of our nature.

II. *I am to show when sin has dominion in the soul.*

It cannot be properly said that sin has *dominion* because the soul has fallen under the power of an occasional temptation. Some have supposed this passage to teach that a person under grace could not sin un-

---

*The Oberlin Evangelist: Vol. I; April 24, 1839. Untitled: this title supplied by Timothy L. Smith, editor of Charles G. Finney, *The Promise of the Spirit*, (Minneapolis: Bethany Fellowship, 1980), pp. 117-124.

der any circumstances. They have maintained that to sin once is to be brought under the dominion of sin.

Now, although I am for making the promises mean all they say, yet I do not believe that such language as this can be justly interpreted to mean all that such persons contend for. For example, if a man should be once intoxicated, under circumstances of peculiar temptation, it would be neither fair nor true, in speaking of his general character, to say that he was under the dominion of ardent spirits and a slave to his appetite.

As an illustration of my meaning take a parallel promise, John 4:14. Christ says, "But whosoever drinketh of the water that I shall give him shall never thirst; but the water that I shall give him shall be in him a well of water springing up into everlasting life." Now some have understood this promise to mean that if a person became a partaker of the Holy Ghost, he could never again know what it was to thirst for the divine influence in any sense—that he would have such a fullness of the Spirit of God as to have at no time any thirsting for more. But this is certainly a forced construction of this passage. It is not in accordance with what we should mean in the use of similar language. Should you promise your neighbor that if he came and boarded with you then he should never hunger nor thirst, would he understand you to mean that he should never have a good appetite for his food, or merely that he should not be hungry or thirsty without being supplied? He would doubtless understand you, and you would expect him to understand you, to promise that he should have enough to eat and to drink—that he should not suffer the gnawings of hunger or the pains of thirst without the supply that nature demands.

Just so I understand this promise of Christ: that if any man have partaken of these waters of life, he has the pledge of Christ that he shall have as great a measure of His Spirit as his necessities demand—that whenever his soul thirsts for more of the waters of life, he has a right to plead this promise with an assurance that Christ will satisfy his thirsty soul with living waters.

I suppose this text to have a similar meaning. *It does not mean that no person, under temptation, can fall under the power of an occasional sin, but that no form of sin shall be habitual, that no form of selfishness or lust shall in any such case be habitual in the soul that is under grace; that no appetite or passion or temptation of any kind should in this sense be able to bring the soul into bondage to sin.*

III. *I am to show what it is to be under the law.*

1. *To be under the law is to be subject to the law, as a covenant of works*—in other words, to be under the necessity of perfectly fulfilling the law in order to obtain salvation thereby.

2. To be under the law is to be influenced by *legal motives or considerations*—to be constrained by the fear of punishment, or influenced by the hope of reward.

3. To be under the law is to be *constrained by conscience* and a sense

of duty, and *not by love*. Individuals seem to go painfully about their duty, under the biddings of conscience, and submit with about as much pain and reluctance as a slave to his master.

4. To be under the *condemning sentence of the law*, like a state criminal, and of course shut out from communion with God. A state criminal, under sentence, is of course shut out from all friendly intercourse with the government—is considered and treated as an outlaw. Just so with a sinner under the sentence of God's law. While he remains in a state of spiritual death and alienation from God, the sentence of eternal death is out against him; he is shut out from communion with God, and consequently sin will have dominion over him.

IV. *I am to show what it is to be under grace.*

1. *To be under a covenant of grace* is in opposition to a *covenant of law*. By a covenant of grace, I mean the covenant which confers all the blessings of salvation as a mere gratuity, and more than a gratuity, as being the direct opposite of our deserts.

2. To be influenced by *love*, excited by *grace* and not by legal motives.

3. To be put in *possession of the blessings* of the new or gracious covenant.

Jer. 31:31-34: Behold, the days come, saith the Lord, that I will make a new covenant with the house of Israel, and with the house of Judah: not according to the covenant that I made with their fathers in the day that I took them by the hand to bring them out of the land of Egypt; which my covenant they brake, although I was an husband unto them, saith the Lord: but this shall be the covenant that I will make with the house of Israel: After those days, saith the Lord, I will put my law in their inward parts, and write it in their hearts, and will be their God, and they shall be my people. And they shall teach no more every man his neighbour, and every man his brother, saying, Know the Lord: for they shall all know me, from the least of them unto the greatest of them, saith the Lord: for I will forgive their iniquity, and I will remember their sin no more.

Heb. 8:8-13: Behold, the days come, saith the Lord, when I will make a new covenant with the house of Israel and with the house of Judah: not according to the covenant that I made with their fathers in the day when I took them by the hand to lead them out of the land of Egypt; because they continued not in my covenant, and I regarded them not, saith the Lord. For this is the covenant that I will make with the house of Israel after those days, saith the Lord; I will put my laws into their mind, and write them in their hearts: and I will be to them a God, and they shall be to me a people: and they shall not teach every man his neighbour, and every man his brother, saying, Know the Lord: for all shall know me, from the least to the greatest. For I will be merciful to their unrighteousness, and their sins and their iniquities will I remember no more.

4. To be under grace is to be so united to Christ, by faith, as to receive a continual life and influence from Him. He represents himself as a vine, and His children as the branches. And to be under grace is to be united to Him as a branch is united to the vine, so as to receive our continual support and strength and nourishment and life from Him.

To be under grace is to pass from death unto life, to be translated from the kingdom of darkness into the kingdom of God's dear Son, to pass from the state of a condemned criminal into a state of redemption, justification and adoption.

V. *I am to show that under the law sin will have dominion over an unsanctified mind.*

1. Because this is the certain effect of law *upon a selfish mind.* A selfish mind is seeking its own interests, of course. And if it attempts to obey the law it will be through selfish considerations, either through hope or fear.* But in every such attempt the mind must fail, of course, for selfishness is the very thing which the law prohibits. And every attempt to obey from selfish motives is only a grievous breach of the law. Therefore, if all former sins were cancelled and salvation depended upon future obedience to the law, salvation would in this way be forever impossible. Hence, if the mind attempted to obey for the sake of obtaining salvation, this would be selfishness and disobedience; and in every such attempt the mind must fail, of course.

2. Sin must have dominion over a selfish mind that is under law, or it would amount to this absurdity: that the disinterested love demanded by the law would flow from selfish motives—a thing naturally impossible.

3. To produce disinterested love, salvation must be *gratuitous,* that is, the soul must understand that obedience to law is not the condition of salvation, it is impossible that this consideration should not influence a selfish mind in its efforts to obey. So that this consideration would render all attempts at obedience ineffectual, and sin would continue to have dominion.

4. Selfishness will of course seek *present* and *selfish* gratification until compelled by deep conviction to desist, in which case the will certainly takes refuge in a self-righteous attempt to obey the law, unless it understands that salvation is gratuitous, or a matter of grace. *There seems to be, as a matter of fact, no other way in which the power of selfishness can be broken, except to annihilate the reasons for selfish efforts by bringing home to the soul the truth that salvation is by grace, through faith.*

The effect of law upon a selfish mind is beautifully illustrated by the Apostle in the seventh chapter of Romans. The case here supposed is what the Apostle, as is common with him, represents as if it were his

---

*See especially Finney's sermon, "Religion of the Law and the Gospel," in *Principles of Victory,* pp. 137-145, for a fuller explanation of this theme.

own experience. It appears, from its connection, to illustrate the influence of law over an unsanctified mind. It is plainly a case where sin was habitual, where it had *dominion*, where the law of sin and death in the members so warred against the law of the mind as to bring the soul into captivity. Now some have contended and continue to contend that the Apostle in this chapter describes the experience of a saint under grace. But this cannot be, because in this case it would flatly contradict the text upon which I am preaching. As I have said, the case described in the seventh of Romans is a case in which sin undeniably has dominion—the very thing of which the Apostle complains. But the text affirms that sin shall not have dominion over the soul that is under grace. Besides, it is very plain that in the seventh of Romans it was the influence of *law*, and not of *grace*, which the Apostle was discussing.*

5. Another reason why sin will have dominion under the law is that under law men are left to the unaided exercise of their own powers of moral agency, without those gracious helps which alone can induce true holiness. The law throws out its claims upon them and requires the perfect use and entire consecration of all their powers to the service of God, and then leaves them to obey or disobey at their peril. It neither secures nor promises to them any aid, but requires them to go forth to the service of God—to love Him with all their heart and their neighbor as themselves—in pain of eternal death. Now in such circumstances, it is very plain that a mind already selfish will only be confirmed in selfishness under such a dispensation.

VI. *I am to show that sin cannot have dominion over those who are under grace.*

1. Because the law is *written in the heart*, that is, the spirit of the law has taken possession of the soul and made us forever "free from the law of sin and death" which was in our members.

2. Because the soul has become *acquainted with God and with Christ* and has fallen deeply in love with their character. It delights in God and exercises the very temper required by the law, uninfluenced by the hope of its rewards or by the fear of its penalty. It is overcome and swallowed up with that love that naturally results from a right acquaintance with God. Nor in this state of mind, sin can no more have dominion over the soul; no form of selfishness can be habitual, any more than a wife who loves her husband supremely can become a habitual adulteress. A woman who loves her husband might, by force of circumstances and by some unexpected and powerful temptation, be led to sin against her husband; but for this to become *habitual* while the supreme love of her husband continues is a contradiction.

3. Sin cannot have dominion over the soul because *Christ has become its life*. He is represented not only as the life of the soul but as the

---

Principles of Victory and *Principles of Liberty* contain four helpful sermons on this much disputed chapter 7 of Romans.

Head of the church, and Christians as members of His body and flesh and bones. Now as the vine supplies the branch and as the head controls the members, so Christ has become the mainspring, the well spring, of life in the soul; and sin cannot have dominion over such a soul unless it can have dominion over Christ. *Christ may find it necessary to permit the soul to fall into an occasional sin, to teach it by experience what perhaps it will not learn in any other way.* But that sin, under any form, should become habitual cannot be necessary to give the soul a sense of its dependence; and Christ, by express promise, has secured the soul against it.

4. Because the soul so *reposes in the blood of Christ* for justification and salvation as to have no motive to selfish efforts, being released from the responsibility of working out a legal righteousness. It is constrained by such a sense of abundant and overflowing grace that it loves and serves God, having no reason to serve itself.

5. Because it is so constrained by a sense of the *love of Christ* as to be as unable to indulge in sin, and vastly more so, than the most dutiful and affectionate child is to indulge in habitual and willful disobedience to its parents.

6. It is impossible for sin to have dominion over a Christian because it implies a *contradiction.* To be a Christian is habitually to love and serve and honor God. *Obedience is the rule and sin is the exception.* It is therefore impossible that sin should have dominion over a Christian, for this would be the same as to say that a person might be a Christian while sin was his rule and obedience the exception or, in other words, that sin his habitual and obedience only occasional. If this is the definition of a Christian, then I know not what a Christian is.

7. Sin cannot have dominion because the veracity of the God of truth is pledged that it shall not.

8. Because the very terms of the covenant of grace show that to be under grace is to have the law written in the heart—to be made or rendered obedient to God by the residence of the Spirit of Christ within us.

9. Because every form of sin is hateful to the soul, and can have no influence—[save] only during a moment of strong temptation, when the involuntary powers or emotions are so strongly excited by temptation as to gain a momentary ascendancy over the will, while the deep preference of the mind, although for the time being comparatively inefficient, yet remains unchanged.

10. Because the soul, under grace, is led by the Spirit to such an understanding and use of its powers as to make the soul a partaker of the divine nature. John says a man "born of God, doth not commit sin, for his seed remaineth in him," that is, the Spirit of Christ dwelling in him renders it unnatural for him to sin.

11. Because *old things are passed away and all things are become new.* The grand leading design of the mind has undergone a radical change. And as the leading design of the mind must of course control the habitual conduct of the soul, and as deviations from its influence will

only be occasional and not habitual, so the soul under grace will not, cannot be under the dominion of sin.

Remarks

1. There is no sound religion where there is not universal reformation. It should be constantly and strictly observed, in all cases of professed conversion, whether the reformation in habits and life is *universal*—whether it extends to selfishness and sinful lusts and habits of every kind and under every form. If any lust is spared, if selfishness under any form is indulged and habitual, if any sinful habit still remains unbroken and unsubdued, that is not a sound conversion. *No form of sin will have dominion where conversion is real. Occasional sin may occur through the force of powerful temptation, but no form of sin will be indulged.*

2. Want of attention to this truth has suffered a great many unconverted persons to enter the Church. In some respects a reformation has been apparent. In such cases, without sufficient discrimination, hope has been indulged by the individual himself and encouraged by members of the church, and he has been admitted to the communion to the great disgrace of religion. It does not appear to me to have been sufficiently understood that grace not only ought but actually does, in every case where piety is real, so overcome sin as to leave no form of it habitual. It has indeed been a common maxim that where sin is habitual there is no real religion. But this has manifestly not been adopted in practice: for great multitudes have been admitted and are still permitted to continue as members in good standing in Christian churches, who habitually indulge in many forms of sin. I think the Gospel demands that no professed convert should be thus encouraged to hope or suffered to become a member of the church, whose reformation of life and habits is not *universal.*

3. You see that all those persons who have frequent convictions and conflicts with sin, and yet are habitually overcome by it, are still under the law and not under grace, that is, *they are convicted but not converted.* The difficulty is *their hearts are not changed so as to hate sin under every form.* Temptation is too strong, therefore, for their conscience and for all their resolutions. Their hearts pleading for indulgence will of course render them an easy prey to temptation. This seems to have been exactly the case described in the seventh chapter of Romans, to which I have referred. Where regeneration has taken place and the *heart* as well as the *conscience* has become opposed to sin—in every such case the power of temptation is, of course, so broken as that sin will at most be only occasional, and never habitual. In all cases, therefore, where individuals find themselves to be or are seen by others to be under the dominion of sin or lust of any kind, they should know or be told at once that they have not been regenerated, that they are under the law and not under grace.

4. What can those persons think of themselves, who know that they are under the dominion of selfishness in some of its forms? Do they believe this text to be a direct and palpable falsehood? If not, how can they indulge the hope that they are Christians? This text asserts, as plainly as it can, that they are under the law and not under grace.

5. You see the state of those who are encouraged by the seventh chapter of Romans, supposing that to be a Christian's experience. If they have gone no further than *that*, they are still under the law. I have been amazed to see how pertinaciously professors of religion will cling to a legal experience, and justify themselves in it by a reference to this chapter. I am fully convinced that the modern construction of the chapter from the 14th to the 24th verses, interpreting it as a Christian experience, has done incalculable evil and has led thousands of souls there to rest and go no further, imagining that they are already as deeply versed in Christian experience as Paul was when he wrote that epistle. And there they have stayed, and hugged their delusion till they have found themselves in the depths of hell.

6. There may be much legal reformation without any true religion.

7. A legal reformation, however, may generally be distinguished by some of the following marks:

(1) It may be only partial, that is, extend to certain forms of sin, while others are indulged.

(2) It may and almost certainly will be temporary.

(3) In a legal experience, it will also generally be manifest that some forms of sinful indulgence are practiced and defended as not being sin. And where there has not been a powerful conviction that has deterred the soul from indulgence, selfishness and lust are still tolerated.

A *gospel* or *gracious* experience will manifest itself in a *universal* hatred of sin and lust, *in every form*. And, as I have said, sin will have no place, except in cases of such powerful temptation as to carry the will for the time by the force of excited feelings, when a reaction will immediately take place and the soul be prostrate in the depths of repentance.

8. By reference to this test and the principles here inculcated, not only may the genuineness of each pretended conversion be decided, but also the genuineness or spuriousness of religious excitements. *That is not a revival of true religion, but falls entirely short of it, that does not produce universal reformation of habits in the subjects of it.* There is many a revival of conviction, and convictions are often deep and very general in a community where, for want of sufficient discriminating instruction, there are very few conversions.

9. You see the mistake of those sinners who fear to embrace religion lest they should disgrace it by living in sin, as they see many professing Christians now do.

Sinner, you need not stand back on this account. Only come out from under the law and be truly converted, submit yourself to the power and influence of sovereign grace, and no form of sin shall have dominion over you, as God is true.

10. This text is a great encouragement to real Christians. They often tremble when they have once fallen under the power of temptation. They greatly fear that sin will gain an entire ascendancy over them. Christian, lift up your head and proclaim yourself free. *The God of truth has declared that you are not and shall not be a slave to sin.*

11. This is a proper promise, and an important one, for Christians to plead in prayer. It is like a sheet anchor in a storm. If temptations beat like a tempest upon the soul, let the Christian hold onto this promise with all his heart. Let him cry out, Oh Lord, perform the good word of Thy grace unto Thy servant, wherein Thou hast caused me to hope that sin shall not have dominion over me, because I am not under law but under grace.

12. Let those who are under the law—over whom sin, in any form, has dominion—remember that under the law there is no salvation; that "whatever things the law saith, it saith to them that are under the law"; and that "cursed is every one that continueth not in all things written in the book of the law to do them."

5

THE REVIVAL OF SIN AND THE LAW*

Romans 7:9

"I was alive without the law once; but when the commandment came, sin revived, and I died."

In my remarks upon this passage, I shall pursue the following outline,

I. *Show in what sense Paul was without the Law;*
II. *What were the consequences of this state;*
III. *In what sense the "Commandment came";*
IV. *The consequences of this "coming of the commandment."*

I. Show in what sense Paul was without the Law.

1. Paul was thoroughly a Pharisee. He had been brought up and instructed in the Oracles of God according to the best teachings of his time, and therefore could not have been "without the law" in the sense of not having the letter of it in his hands and before his mind. He had the law as given to Moses, the whole of it, both moral and ceremonial. Indeed, he had given much of his life to the study of it. Having been brought up at the feet of Gamaliel, he enjoyed the best advantages his country could afford for knowledge in the Jewish law.

2. Yet Paul was really ignorant of the true meaning and spirit of the law. His grand mistake was that he regarded it only in its relations to his outward life. He assumed that it had no other relation, made no other demands. His moral and spiritual eyes were not open. I mean by this language that he did not see his moral and spiritual relations to God and to his fellowmen, and did not even seem to recognize the fact of the existence of any such relations.

3. As to his outward relations, his course of life was objectively just, while subjectively it was altogether unjust. By subjectively just, I mean just and right *at heart*, being and doing in reference to the law what it requires. In the state of his heart he was all wrong, for he was supremely selfish. Here lay the great error of his school of moralists. Their whole attention was directed to the *objective* and withdrawn from the subjective.

The Oberlin Evangelist: Vol. XV; July 6, 1853. Untitled: this title supplied by the editor.

In other words, they thought everything of the outside, nothing of the heart. Exclusively regarding the letter and the ceremony, they seemed never to ask, "Is the *heart* honest and pure before God?" Thus the moral and spiritual eye was not trained to discern or even to notice the real meaning of the law. Consequently, it is not strange that Pharisees, so trained, should suppose themselves to be obeying the law, while in truth they entirely overlooked all that is really valuable. So with Paul, his spiritual consciousness was not awake.

4. Here let us make a distinction which is somewhat important in reference to this subject. There is a natural consciousness, a moral consciousness, and also a spiritual consciousness. The natural is exercised upon things merely natural and worldly—external and not in regard to their moral relations. The moral relates to things of a moral nature, and when distinguished from spiritual, should refer to our relations to fellow beings, while the term spiritual may be applied to our relations to God. An active spiritual consciousness keeps the mind awake to the presence of God, as naturally as we are conscious of the presence of each other. It keeps us alive to all that is embraced in our relations to God. Moral consciousness respects moral questions; yet, in the strict sense, only as they lie between ourselves and our fellow-beings. The difficulty with Paul was that, his moral and spiritual eyes being closed, he entirely overlooked his own subjective state of mind, the very thing which God's law primarily regards.

II. *I am now to speak of the consequences of being in this sense "alive-without the law."*

1. Paul was in a state of both *moral and spiritual delusion.* He supposed himself to be performing his duty to his fellowmen when really he was doing no such thing. He had only the idea of objective justice, justice viewed in its outward relations. If he did not cheat a man, it mattered in his view little or nothing how much he coveted his goods, or how utterly void his heart might be of true love to his neighbor. Consequently, he never performed the duty which the law required of him towards his fellowmen.

The same was true of his spiritual relations to God. He regarded simply what the law required *externally*; went around and around with the routine of his outside duties, while his heart all this time was dead and cold, and as it showed itself subsequently bitter as hell itself towards the lovely and innocent Son of God.

2. Another consequence was a *false hope.* Supposing himself to be complying with the law of God, he expected to be saved as much as he expected anything whatever. Yet this expectation was altogether unfounded. Although he was very zealous, he was also very bitter in his spirit, showing that his zeal sprang from any other source rather than real benevolence. Indeed, he showed that his spirit was as bitter as the bitterness of the pit. How then can it be supposed that his hope of heaven was anything better than a delusion?

3. Another result was a *self-righteous performance* of all he called his religion. But here I must explain: I am afraid many are not well aware of what the Bible means by self-righteousness; certainly it is the case that many professed Christians do not well understand this matter. For explanation of the point that is most important for discrimination, take the case of Paul. When he performed what he called his *duties*, and thanked God, Pharisee-like, that he prayed and fasted, and paid tithes, *did he feel himself so utterly lost that he ascribed all his acceptable work to Christ, working in him?* Far from it. He had done all these things *himself.*

When he came ultimately to know himself and then to know Christ, he could speak on this subject with intelligent discrimination and ever wakeful interest. Then he dwelt much upon the fact that the Jews depended on their own works and upon themselves alone to do their own works; while on the other hand, he insisted that while left to themselves they never did anything but sin. He always maintained that the energetic power of the Divine Spirit wrought in them all that was ever acceptable to God. Often does he illustrate this by his own experience. Before he was a Christian, he performed religious duties as regularly as now; he says "I profited in the Jews' religion above many mine equals," but all along, he regarded his obedience as in such a sense rendered in his own strength so that he made no hearty acknowledgments of dependence on sovereign grace. Of that grace which comes through divine mercy, and first moves the heart to good, he seemed to know nothing. His own righteousness was self-originating and self-performed. There was nothing else of it but what came of himself. It had no spiritual life or power in it, for the reason that there was no power of God in its origin, no influence from God moulding its character. Paul did not truly recognize God's grace in this obedience, and God did not impart His grace to subdue selfishness and beget true love in his soul.

Now here is a curious distinction which spiritually-minded persons make, but which others, if they use it, never understand. The spiritually-minded say with Paul, "By the grace of God I am what I am." With many, this language degenerates into mere cant; but really there is a world of meaning in it, and a meaning which is inexpressibly dear to the real Christian's heart. The man who truly enters into the spirit of religion never regards *himself* as having done it; he knows it is all of grace; nothing can offend him more than to have it assumed that it is himself and not God's grace that has wrought in him all good. He knows deep in his consciousness, that if left to himself, there never was and never will be any good thing in him. Hence, he honors and praises divine grace with a fullness of meaning and an outgushing of heart which self-righteousness never knew. This deep recognition of God's grace comes to be wrought into the very life, intertwined through all the fibers and incorporated into the substance of the soul. Through all his being he feels that all is of rich grace and nothing of praise is due to himself.

Not that his exercises are not *right*, for to deny this were to impugn the efficiency of God's grace; and not that they are not his own acts, for to deny this were to set aside man's agency and responsibility, and involve the Bible doctrine of God "working to will and to do" in us, in entire confusion. The simple idea is that the Spirit of God, acting upon our minds in harmony with the laws of mind, instructs, stimulates, draws, and thus substantially *causes* right voluntary action on our part.

III. *We are next to consider in what sense "the commandment came" to Paul.*

The law was sent home to both his moral and spiritual consciousness and perception. He was led to see what the law meant in its moral relations to himself and to his neighbor—that without *love* all was nothing. He saw the same also in regard to prayer, to alms, to worship, that all is nothing, only a grievous abomination in the sight of God when the subjective state of the heart is wrong. He became fully aware of this, all suddenly, as if a flash of lightning had broken upon him. He saw the reality of this spiritual meaning, and with it a purity and blessedness in the law itself which commanded his most intense regard.

IV. *And what was the result of this new view of God's law?* This is the point we are next to consider.

1. It quickened his selfishness. This was the *first* result of bringing the spirituality of the law home to his selfish heart. This new light as it flashed upon his mind found him in a most self-complacent state, altogether satisfied with himself. No sooner did he see the spirituality of the law than one of two results must inevitably have taken place—either he must break down at once, acknowledge his guilt and empty himself of all his self-righteousness; or if he resist this, his selfishness must be quickened into fresh activity. In Paul's case the latter result ensued; his selfishness was aroused and stirred up as if Ithuriel's spear had touched him.* The long unnoticed enmity of his heart was developed. We are not to suppose that during all the time he was persecuting the Church, he enjoyed an easy, self-complacent state of mind, and that all was quiet until the moment when the great light from heaven broke upon him. By no means. It must not be assumed that he had no serious thought about his moral relations to God prior to the scenes at Damascus. Doubtless his mind had been stirred up long before. He had heard of the sermon on the mount; had heard about Christ's pungent and terrible denunciations against the Pharisees; he had known that Christ had publicly rebuked and exposed their favorite interpretations of the law, and had torn up their system from its very foundations, and that the masses of the common people heard Him gladly. This had greatly quickened the selfishness and stirred up the enmity of his heart against that Man, so that his very soul was maddened. You recollect he says of himself, "I verily thought with myself that I ought to do many things contrary to the

---

*From John Milton, *Paradise Lost,* Book IV. (Editor's Note.)

name of Jesus of Nazareth." It was obviously under color of being very zealous for the *truth*; but really his selfishness was all on fire and all the malign passions of his soul were astir. It is exceedingly plain from the history that Paul was all this time warring against his own consciousness. This great fact was perfectly known to Jesus, and hence, when He came down in that flood of overwhelming light and arrested the burning persecutor, what did He say? "Saul, Saul, why persecutest thou Me? It is hard for thee to kick against the pricks."

Here we have the secret of Saul's state of mind. He is kicking against the pricks. The sharp points of his moral sense are against him, and he is resisting and is wounding himself upon those piercing points continually. He is like a hampered animal trying to run away, while every step drives the goads into his quivering flesh. He tries to kick, he winces and shrieks, yet has too much obstinacy to yield. Sometimes, perhaps, he half persuaded himself that he ought not to oppose Jesus of Nazareth; but the whole case shows that he was ill at ease in that impression, and that on the whole he knew better and was truly fighting against his prevailing convictions of duty.

2. When the law came home to his soul, it compelled reflection. This almost always supervenes when the law comes home more and more to the soul. There will be hours of deep and earnest reflection, producing first consternation, then a deep sense of shame; the mind waking up to see things in their true light. This leads to great consternation, remorse, self-condemnation; and then, often to despair. The man is stripped of all his excuses; and then, not having yet seen the great love of God, and having therefore no faith and trust, he settles down in the conviction—"*I ought to be damned and I certainly must be!* There can be no help for me!" More than one such case have I seen where men, a long time settled down in infidelity, are awakened to see themselves as they are before God and His holy law, and they cry out, "I deserve eternal damnation!" One such I have in my mind's eye. I shall never forget how he looked. Every feature of his countenance depicted horror. Every muscle was in a tremor. A little reflection had brought him into an attitude in which he could not stand before God. There was also the case of Deacon H., whom I well knew in his years of infidelity. He is now in heaven, but when an infidel, he professed to be entirely satisfied that the Bible was all priest-craft. He verily thought that soon this delusion (Christianity) would be swept from the earth. Returning at one time from the sale of infidel books, full of self-complacency, all elated with his success, he conversed frely with his wife upon his labors for the day—when all suddenly, a new view of the truth and meaning of God's Word broke in upon his mind. Intuitively he saw himself a sinner and undone; he could no longer shut his eyes to the fact that Jesus, whom he had been opposing, was truly the Saviour of the world. He knew that the Bible he had been gainsaying was really God's own revelation to lost men. Seeing all this he was in agony. His wife, alarmed, cried out, "Deacon H., what is the matter with you?" Still he groaned as a man in agony of body, and still she

pressed her question; *"What's the matter?"* At last he broke out saying, "The stubborn oak must bow! Jesus Christ *is* the Saviour of the world!" She was thunderstruck! It could not have surprised her more if a bolt from heaven had broken through the roof and smote him to the floor. There he was—but how changed! Go and ask him now what Paul meant by saying, "When the commandment came, sin revived, and I died." He can doubtless tell you.

Paul had long thought on this subject and was troubled. But at last the matter came to a head. Jesus met him in the way and broke him down. He let in light upon his already troubled conscience. He made him see the purity and the spiritual meaning of His law; and now mark what follows—self-condemnation, shame, and dreadful remorse! See him writing his own death warrant in spite of himself! Nothing is more common than for despair to supervene for a season in such cases as this. In the case of Paul, this was momentary. Yet we must suppose that he utterly gave up his old hope, and this to him was like the giving up of the ghost. It was as *death*. No wonder, therefore, that he should say; "Sin revived, and I died." When he saw how strangely the rebellion of his heart burst forth, and sin in this sense "revived," his hope perished, his heart sank within him—such revelations were made of himself as suddenly blighted all his hopes of being in the divine favor, and he died in the darkness of despair. This seems to be the obvious explanation of his language, and corresponds entirely with what we must infer from the laws of mind and the uniform course of similar experiences.

Remarks

1. The Pharisees generally in those days, and all Pharisees in heart in every age, are under the same delusion. Yet they were then and are often supposed to be the most pious people. It was a common saying then that if only two men were to be saved out of all mankind, one of them must be a Pharisee. But they were entirely deceived—their moral perceptions were blunted; the subjective state which alone constitutes true religion was not even apprehended in their minds. When you hear them speak, you hear nothing of religious experience, like that of David for examle; they do not cry out—"Oh how love I thy law!" "Cleanse me from secret faults;" "My soul thirsteth for God, yea, for the living God." Indeed, you seldom hear any of them go farther than to pray for those states of mind which they know God requires. They do not profess to *have* them already, nor do they use language in the honest simplicity of their hearts which *implies* that they have a right subjective state of heart now. Many do nothing more than hold on to a hope. With no small difficulty they manage to do so much, and often they call into exercise the utmost pertinacity of purpose to effect even this.

2. Manifestly the teachings of Christ roused up the whole tribe of Pharisees. It deeply disturbed their peace. They were like a hive of bees as you have seen them when somebody breaks up their house, or as when

they are forced to swarm, or are led out to battle. So thoroughly had He torn up their entire system, root and branch, and so fully had its great defects been laid open to the eye of the world, that they could rest no longer. This general result was produced by the lingering yet almost departing rays of the Spirit's light upon the nation. God was giving a corrupt people their last call. Here was a deep and damning delusion fastened strongly on the hearts of thousands, and if any were to be saved, this terrible delusion must be broken up by outspoken and crushing truth. It was but natural and necessary that in such an effort many hearts should become excited, maddened, and thrown into a state of most bitter opposition.

So in our own day many professed Christians, who are living along in a legal and pharisaic state, get now and then some scattering rays of new light—glimpses of truth break in upon their minds as they hear the true Gospel faithfully preached, or as the Spirit sets home upon their souls some portions of God's word. Something within says, "That is true Religion, but I have not got it. I have no such experience as that." Sometimes in seasons of searching prayer, the Spirit of God hurls His arrows broadcast, and many are pricked in their heart and constrained to say, "My hope is vain and I am yet in my selfishness, and know nothing yet of true religion as I must know it. *I must give up this old rotten hope, or be lost!*" But they resist at the moment. They cannot quite bring their minds to give it all up now and throw their naked souls on divine mercy as lost sinners; and, thus resisting, they relapse into tenfold greater hardness and delusion. If under such appeals from God, they would not resist, then light would increase, and they would doubtless be soon brought forth into day. I knew the case of an elder who took an honest course, unlike most persons in similar circumstances. I was preaching in the place of his residence. The Spirit was pressing truth on some minds, as I endeavored to aid His searching scrutiny into the heart by preaching on the case of Achan and the accursed thing. I was progressing in my sermon, in search after that accursed thing, when suddenly he rose in the midst of the congregation and cried out; "Mr. Finney, Mr. Finney, you need not say another word, it's found; I am the man, I am the very man!" There he stood pale as ashes. "If there were no other Achan here," said he, "I am enough to curse the whole church. I did not want to disturb the congregation," he added, "but I saw that I *must* speak. I have been brought almost to this point before, but I drew back and my soul relapsed into darkness. I knew that I must meet the demands of my conscience now, or my soul would be lost."

So with many, there are times when God lifts the vail and lets them see their naked hearts. Constrained by truth they cry out; "I am deceived, I know I am," but instead of making thorough work and acting with decision, they hesitate, lose the light God gave them, grieve the Spirit away, fall back to their old position, go on as before, and perish utterly in their own corruptions. I should not be surprised if in fact there had been hundreds in this place who have passed through this very course, doomed, unless they earnestly repent, to reach the same awful end. Influenced by your pride of character, and by the force of an old hope, you delay, and put over the thorough examination you ought to make, and thus slide on to ruin. Oh, that everlasting spirit of *delay*! How many souls it has lured along to ruin!

3. There are many non-professing sinners, who are laboring under this same difficulty. They have the objective, but not the subjective, of religion. Externally they are upright; but alas, internally there is no *true love* to God or man. Some of you here in this congregation are in just this position. I know you well; I have had business dealings with you and know you to be honest and upright in all those things; but what shall I say of your treatment of your God and Saviour! Nobody denies you the credit of being prompt in your business with men and of doing your work as you ought to do it; you would scorn to do objective wrong—but you seem not to realize that this, in itself, is nothing towards real obedience. Suppose any of you, students, were as upright in externals as Saul of Tarsus himself; you might nevertheless be as guilty a sinner as lives out of hell! What did Paul say of himself when his eyes came to be opened? Speaking of sinners he says, "Of whom I am chief." He looked upon himself as a heart hypocrite! He did not attempt to say one good thing of his former Pharisee life, but condemned it all. You mean to do right, you say, but you think only of *objective* right—right as to the *external* only. You know that all your *rightness* is only this, no more. You know that all you think of when you speak of doing right is of the external and objective; you do not even inquire whether the heart, the motive, is pure before God. You know that real *love* to God and man is not the life and spring of your activities. Precisely here is your deep and ruinous delusion!

Suppose my wife should claim to do right in her relations as a wife, and think, like you, only of the objective, the outside appearance. She says she means to do all right, but what does she mean by that? Suppose she trims her ways to answer the demands of external propriety; but suppose also that everybody has reason enough to know that she loves somebody else with all her heart! What would you say to that? Suppose you know that any wife is absolutely devoted to some other man than her husband. Would you not abominate all her professions of doing *right* towards her husband? Suppose it to be your own wife. Would you not spew her out—nauseated and sick of such *right doing?*

Let every mere moralist know that you have never done one thing in all your life of which God did not say—"Who hath required this at your hand?" You need not come and tell Him it is all right, that you mean to do right; all is utterly wrong since your heart is after your idols and is not yielded up trustfully to God. How can all your right-doing be anything but an abomination so long as you do not give God your heart!

4. This text does not profess to give the whole of Paul's conversion. It only gives us his *conviction*. "I was alive without the law once—(in my self-righteous hopes) but when the commandment came—(revealing God's holy law) then sin revived, and I *died*—my hopes perished then.

There he was until he gave himself up to the Lord Jesus Christ. Substantially this experience of being slain by the law must always precede the acceptance of Jesus Christ as our own Saviour. The reason for this is that men will not accept Christ's robe while their own apparel suits them better. They will not rely on another for salvation while they are strong in their self-dependence.

5. We can see in the light of our subject what the work of the Spirit is in both conversion and sanctification.

Some are forever enquiring, "What *is* the work of the Spirit?" Others think there is no need of any divine Spirit in order to produce conviction of wrong, for they assume that natural conscience is all-sufficient for this result.

But who does not know that the light of nature and all the force of mere conscience will never slay the enmity of the sinner's heart and break him down in real penitence and humiliation? The Spirit of God must wake and rouse the moral and spiritual consciousness. The Spirit must take God's holy law and hold it up as a molten looking-glass. *There* the sinner must see the meaning of that law and his own awful sin in having so long trampled it beneath his feet.

The Spirit also reveals the spiritual nature of the *Gospel*. Having with one hand held up the spiritual nature of the law, with the other He reveals in like manner the love of the Gospel, unfolding the heart of Jesus, until the sinner says, "How can I abuse such love! How can I refuse to trust such a Saviour!"

6. Those of you who are not conscious of such things as these in your experience are not converted. You who have not had before your mind's eye this looking-glass of law and Gospel—what do you know about the Gospel? If Christ has not been revealed to your soul, what do you know about faith in Christ?

Do not some of you see that you are certainly deluded? You who are merely moralists. Impenitent sinners still, have you utterly failed to see today the utter abomination of all your offerings and sacrifices?

What awful danger there is lest some of you should put out the light of the Holy Ghost as it shines in upon your souls! What result can be more fatal and more awful than this? How can we account for the moral state of many men except on the supposition that they have grieved away the Spirit of God? They go and come, go and come with God's people; but they seem never to see the very thing that stands right out before their eyes—their own self-deception and impending damnation!

I have seen some of you writhe under the truth as if an arrow had struck you. And did you then at once give up all and say, "I am a deceived wretch! I must repent!" Did you not rather say, "I will look this subject over after I get home"? Several times during the last season, I thought I saw most clearly that some of you were on the very pivot of life; and I said, "Come now—come right forward and settle this matter at once for all. But you did not come, and what was the result? Go and see—*all gone back*. You did not come up to the light and therefore of course fell back into deeper darkness than ever.* And are you still waiting for more light? I beseech you, be not so absurd as to *wait*; such resistance to God surely grieves away the Spirit and sinks the soul into yet more fatal darkness. Have not some of you young men waited for more light until you have lost all you had? The Bible doctrine is: "Use and you gain more; neglect and you lose." "From him that hath not shall be taken away even that which he hath." Why? Because the fact that he hath not proves that he has not improved.

To professors of religion let me next say, "It is becoming most alarmingly true that there is a great want of discrimination in distinguishing what is essential from what is merely incidental to a good Christian life." Often in attending examinations of candidates for admission to the church I have been pained to hear questions put which did not at all touch the real merits of the case. They might have been answered in the most favorable way and yet the answers should have afforded no decisive testimony of real conversion. The questions altogether failed to show whether the candidates had ever really felt themselves to be lost sinners, and as such had thrown themselves upon God's mercy. Did this conviction of being lost and self-ruined fasten on them, and then under its impression, did they search for the remedy and find it in casting themselves wholly on infinite grace? Where this is wanting, there can be no Christian experience.

Often, and perhaps I may say always, *where under Gospel light true conversion does not take place, something binds the mind.* Truth adapted to wake up the consciousness, first to fear and then to love, fails to produce its effect. Do you ask the reason? *Selfishness has bound up the mind* all round about and it has no enlargement, no freedom, to go forth in confidence or in penitence. When some attempt to pray, it is as if something bound up the mind. There is no earnest going out of soul after God. When they say, "I will go and seek God," they go not. It is not with them, as with those whom the Spirit of God is drawing, who feel as if their very soul would go out after Christ—even almost out of the body. This going out of the soul I often compare to what you may have noticed often when you put a burning candle in a strong draft of air: the wind bears the blaze away and almost forces it entirely from the wick, yet it flickers and hangs—yet you can see it borne quite a perceptible distance from the wick—but the connection is still maintained and when you arrest the draft, the candle burns again as before. So the Christian almost goes off from the body—his soul being drawn away by the power of his ravishing views of Jesus.

Right over against this is the state which I have been noticing; no spontaneous going out of the heart after God either in prayer or in attempted consecration. Ask such a person, "Do you feel your whole soul *going, going,* as if nothing were held back?" "No; I know nothing about that," he would reply. Yet when one really yields himself to the drawing

*See "The Anxious Seat," page 17, of this book.

of the Spirit, he is as conscious of giving himself up as he ever is of giving anything to another. A lady, whom I saw last winter, said, "I went to my room to give myself to God there and as soon as I knelt down there was a spontaneous going forth of my heart to God and it seemed hardly necessary for me to say a word for my heart had already gone out to Christ. Words seemed too poor to express my mind to God, for it seemed as if my very soul had gone itself, and no words were needed." She came down from her room so wonderfully filled with the Holy Ghost that her soul was all on fire and some suggested that such a woman must be crazy. But many are utterly hard and unmoved—no going out of heart towards God and no melting of soul before Him.

Christian, do you know what it is to be slain by the law and truly made alive by the Holy Ghost? Or is it the case that you are living along with a hope that does not assimilate you to Jesus Christ? Are not some of you aware that you have so long resisted God and His truth, that it will not do for you to try it again? Now is your time—you need not pause to make terms with God; for all the terms are fixed already. Let your inward heart go! Say, "Lord, I come to thee! It is long enough that I have lived on in my sins. I am ashamed to ask another hour's life in which to fight and war against God! Let it be enough that I have lived in sin so long: now and forevermore I will be the Lord's!"

6

THANKS FOR THE GOSPEL VICTORY*

Romans 7:25

"I thank God through Jesus Christ our Lord."
"Thanks be to God who giveth us the victory through Jesus Christ our Lord."
1 Corinthians 15:57

In both these passages, Paul gives thanks for deliverance from a sinning and sinful state. To bring the subject fully before us, I remark,
I. *The Bible everywhere teaches and facts prove that unconverted men are morally and spiritually dead.*
II. *Christians, on the other hand, are represented as being alive, but not in good and perfect health, and not mature in their growth.*
III. *If there be not some efficacious remedy for sin in the soul, sinners must be either annihilated at death or damned.*
IV. *God in Christ is the only efficient and all-sufficient power to reach and remedy this direst of all things, sin.*

I. *The Bible everywhere teaches and facts prove that unconverted men are morally and spiritually dead.*
They live as if there were no God. They appreciate neither His rights nor His feelings. To all intents and purposes, they are, towards God, as dead men. Considerations concerning God have no influence on them. This is one of the most obvious facts in human life. So true is it, that in fact we often find men pleading as their excuse that they have no inclinations towards God. Thus they reveal their moral death, not in their *lives* only, but in their very excuses; showing that they are conscious of their moral apostasy and death, and but too well aware that they have no tendencies in themselves towards God.

II. *Christians, on the other hand, are represented as being alive, but not in good and perfect health, and not mature in their growth.* At first they are newborn babes, needing the pure milk of the word. Then they are youth, needing counsel. Then they are fathers and mothers in Israel, of "full age," and "having their senses exercised to discern both good

---

The Oberlin Evangelist: Vol. XVIII; January 30, 1856.

and evil." Often the Scriptures represent Christians as being very weak, so that they have great liability to stumbling and falling. This stumbling and falling becomes a sad stumbling block in the way of wicked men—those men who are prone to look for and seek stumbling blocks for their excuses. They do not realize the condition of Christians, who are only in part reclaimed from their death in sin. They do not consider that though born, they are yet babes, or at best, but children. But they are not disposed to make allowance for these circumstances—a fact which only serves to show how unreasonable sin is.

Returning to the fact that Christians are usually weak, I remark, this weakness is moral, not natural. *Natural weakness pertains to one's created faculties; moral, to one's voluntary purposes. Weakness of nature is a misfortune; weakness of moral purpose is a fault.* Death in sin is simply a fault—always and altogether, a *fault*. This weakness in Christians is also a fault, because it results from a want of faith in Christ, and love to His Name.

This weakness and moral death of sinners is a fact of experience. I have myself had but too much reason to know what it is. I found a total discrepancy between my convictions and my actions. I could say, "So I *ought* to do, but so I do not." When I questioned myself, asking, "Why is this so?" I could only say, "It is wholly unaccountable." Wide awake on all other subjects, and to all other interests, yet perfectly dead to this; I found myself in a strange state, and if not a "wonder to many," I was at least to myself. In a wretched state, I knew I had no disposition to get out of it. And every sinner who reflects knows that this is just his state.

The spiritual weakness of Christians manifests itself in a conscious want of promptness to act upon, and fully up to, their convictions of duty and sense of obligation. They are more deeply conscious of these defects than sinners are, or can be, of theirs. Sinners have little anxiety or trouble about their own moral death; but not so with Christians. They recognize their obligations, and are usually conscious of being ready, prompt, and anxious to meet them, yet painfully aware that while "the spirit is willing the flesh is weak." Sometimes they are strong in the Lord, and their sense of weakness has passed away; anon, perhaps, they trust to their own strength, and find out their weakness to their cost; they fall sadly short, and come into darkness and trouble.

This state in both saints and sinners is among the most patent and obvious facts in the world. Who can doubt that there is moral life in real Christians, and moral death in sinners? This the Bible everywhere teaches or implies. It is a fact that no man can doubt who has eyes to see, and a mind candid enough to apprehend and admit a plain fact.

I often think it strange that unconverted men allow themselves to be so stumbled by the weakness of professed Christians. I have met some impenitent men who had thought candidly on this subject, and who seemed to appreciate fully the state and difficulties of Christians, and consequently were not stumbled at all by any mistakes or errors into which they might fall. They did not at all wonder that Christians are no better. If I had not considered this matter, and had not ceased to stumble myself on the imperfections of professed Christians, I never could have become a Christian. If I had not seen that all this is according to the Bible and reason, I could not have come into a state of mind towards God and Christianity in which my conversion from sin would be possible. Usually, in places where there are many Christians, there will be some who stumble constantly upon them, as if utterly unable or unwilling to apologize for their failures on the score of infant piety, superinduced upon long-standing habits of sin.

III. *If there be not some efficacious remedy for sin, in the soul, sinners must be either annihilated at death or damned.* So of Christians, if there be not some efficacious remedy, giving them victory over sin, they too must be lost. In my early life, I was much more ready to doubt whether any could be saved, than to believe that *all* would be. There seemed to me more reason to suppose all would be damned, than all saved. The great enquiry was, "How can any be saved?" It was never this, "How can God damn any?" Let any sensible man get a clear and full idea of what salvation is, and he will see it can be no easy thing. He will assume that the law must go into full execution against all, and that being so, none can be saved. My mind before my conversion ran on this text, "If the righteous scarcely be saved, where shall the ungodly and the sinner appear?" I could see that even Christians must have mighty help from some quarter, being only babes in Christ, and their salvation a work of many difficulties.

It has always seemed strange to me that any man could be a universalist. Even before my conversion it was a profound mystery. "Why," said I then, "does not everybody see that men must become holy or be lost?" If the Holy Ghost does not go down into hell to convert sinners, surely they cannot be saved *there.* Unless there be some efficacious remedy for sin, taking effect to the full extent of actually giving the victory over it, salvation in heaven is impossible."

In Romans 7, Paul describes a state in which there is the greatest effort to get rid of this state of sinfulness. There he cries out, "O wretched man that I am! Who shall deliver me from this body of sin and death?" Then, the Gospel opening on his anxious eye, he thanks God for deliverance through Jesus Christ. He saw the remedy.

This remedy is never in ourselves. Nowhere, in the wide range of the material system all round us, can it be found—nowhere outside of God. It might be demonstrated that in our own nature there is no efficacious remedy. Yet by this I do not mean to say that *if* any man would use his powers right, he could gain no relief; but I do mean to say that, *apart from God, he never will use his own powers right for this end. His own will is committed in an opposite direction. He has fallen into the slough of his corrupt propensities.* These propensities are fearful adversaries to his being holy, and must be, until they are subdued. Hence we are constantly pressed with the question, *"Where is the power that can subdue them and give us the victory?"*

Paul answers by thanking God who giveth us the victory through our

Lord Jesus Christ. In Him we have it! Yet until men come to know the Gospel by an inward apprehension, it is to them dark, and almost without meaning. They feel but little if any interest in it. But when the Divine Spirit reveals Jesus to the mind, these dark things become precious realities. Light breaks in and illumines the chambers of the mind so recently in thick darkness. Under this influence, Gospel truth becomes intensely interesting, and even exciting. Men who have been swept away by the influence of worldly objects, who would not look at spiritual things, and were almost mad in their pursuit of objects which appeal only to the senses, are now wonderfully changed. Christ reveals himself so clearly that He overbalances and overcomes these earthly excitements. Especially is this the case when the Spirit reveals God as being truly *love*. This revelation at once takes prodigious hold on us. Said one, who had long professed Christ and had known something of the Gospel in her own experience, "All at once, after so long walking in comparative darkness, the Lord showed me that I had hitherto known Him but very imperfectly. I did not *know* God was *love*, before. I did not see this in its own true sunlight. I had opinions; I had notions; but it could not be said I had knowledge. I had heard of Him by the hearing of the ear; but now mine eye has seen Him, and my heart has been ravished with His love."

From this time onward her whole soul seemed all glowing with love to God, and radiant with the love of God revealed to her. So it will always be when the Spirit reveals Jesus to the soul, and we see why He died for us, and why He has in so many ways done so much for us. When these things come up from the realms of theory and into the position of *fact* and of *experience*, then apathy ceases; the sensibilities are no longer stagnant; all is wakeful; slavish fear is gone; the soul approaches God freely, and in the spirit of a child. He is no longer religious because he *must* be, nor reads the Bible because he *must*; nor does he pray, or give in benevolence for such reasons. All these forms of dead experience have passed away, and the mind looks back on it as a loathesome abomination. While these views of Christ are before his mind, he will make no more legal efforts—will no more strive to gain the favor of God by mere works of law. Christ, thus revealed, breaks the power of sin.

Turning now to my impenitent hearers, I ask you if you do not know and admit that I have given a fair account of your case. You know that you have no proper regard, practically, for God, no more than if your heart and intellect were separated, and all mutual influence of one over the other were broken off. Your convictions of truth are often clear and strong; but the response of your heart to this truth is utterly withheld. The state of your affections and will seems to have no correspondence to your own convictions of what they should be. Yet this strange discrepancy is altogether within your power, and you *ought* to put an end to it at once. You have no right to live on so; God asserting His claims, but your soul utterly disowning them. This is precisely the state of the sinner; his conscience dissevered from his heart. When his attention is turned to this, he is conscious of this utter disagreement and discordance. In my days of sin, I was just as sensible of this as of my own existence.

Do you ask, "What is the reason for this? Am I ever to become self-consistent?" Said one of the first lawyers in New York: "There is no use in trying to vindicate myself. I can make no defense; I can offer no explanation. It avails nothing for me to argue my case, for I have nothing to plead." So you know you have no reason to offer for your course of sin. If I were to put it to you all, to say by a public expression, if this be not your case, you would at once, if honest, rise to give assent. You are in a lost state. You feel, sometimes, a deep sense of this *lostness. Is there a remedy for you?*

Some of you who profess religion are in great doubt whether you have any spiritual life. Let me ask you if you have not been greatly tried with the fact of your own spiritual impotence, and of your having so little rallying power in yourself? Are you not surprised and troubled at your want of energy, your inefficiency in duty? Have these things pressed you, and have you been led to enquire, anxiously, whether there is a remedy? Do you want to get hold of one, if it be yet possible?

IV. *Our text gives us the true and only remedy. God in Christ is the only efficient and all-sufficient power to reach and remedy this direst of all things, sin.* Everywhere in the Bible, the condition of this victory over sin is declared to be faith in Jesus Christ. "This is the victory that overcometh the world, even your *faith.*" Without faith the gospel never takes effect in us.

What the Bible thus declares is true also in philosophy and in fact. Goodness revealed has attractions even over sinners. It is its very nature to attract all human hearts.

Some of you felt this attraction even when you were in your sins. Perhaps you feel it somewhat even now. In my own case, I recollect the circumstance of weeping profusely at an instance of goodness. I thought then it came near to winning me over to sympathy with goodness. I could not help crying out, "This is not in me; I know my heart is not in sympathy with God": so strangely did this manifestation of goodness affect me.

You who have read *Uncle Tom's Cabin* will remember the story of Topsy and little Eva. Topsy seems never to have seen any manifestations of kindness and goodness towards herself. Always beaten about, every influence only driving her the farther from goodness, no wonder she became surly and morose. Little Eva approached her on one occasion as she sat, and looking her mildly and sweetly in the eye, asked her if she could not be good. Now, for the first time, she saw an interest manifested in her happiness, and saw also, in contrast with Eva's spirit, what her own was. This is represented as the first step before the great moral change.

No doubt this is true in philosophy. There is something in goodness which strongly tends to draw a moral being into sympathy with itself.

Christians are made strong by the revelations which Christ makes of himself to their minds. "Beholding as in a glass the glory of the Lord (Jesus), they are changed from glory to glory." The view of His own glory, which the Lord gave to Moses when he prayed, "I beseech Thee show me Thy glory," and the Lord answered, "I will make all My goodness pass before thee," strengthened Moses greatly. It seemed to cast the mantle of Jehovah upon him, and make him a new and wonderful man.

When the Lord gains the confidence of a sinner so that He can reveal himself, the first step is to reveal His goodness. So we should expect, and so it is.

But this goodness must be *believed*. Confidence must be reposed in Christ, else He cannot reveal His goodness in any saving manner.

A conscious victory over ourselves and sin is the only evidence of a saving change. An *apparent* victory is the only evidence to *others* of our being savingly changed. This victory consists in being saved from sin, and in becoming like God. Nothing less than this is real salvation.

Love revealed to faith is the power of God unto salvation. Suppose one of you comes into a state in which you have not a particle of confidence in any one who tries to do you good—all that any friend should attempt to do for you, you ascribe to some sinister motive. As long as you withhold confidence in him, his love is not revealed to your faith; for you have no faith to which it can be revealed. In this case, by a natural law of mind, all the goodness he reveals to you only makes you more wicked and only works out a deeper ruin.

The love of God revealed to faith is the power of God to bring the soul out of its bondage. But love manifested, yet through unbelief rejected, works ruin to the soul by a natural law; and by the same law, the clearer the revelations of that love, the more rapid and fearful the ruin wrought. The case of the Jews, taught by Christ in person, is in point a most striking and affecting example. The way they rejected their Messiah served fearfully to deprave their hearts and to hasten the ruin of the nation. Christ himself said, "If I had not come and spoken unto them, they had not had sin, (that is, comparatively none) but now they have no cloak for their sin." When Christ went through all Judea and Galilee, manifesting everywhere the evidences of His being the Messiah, and bearing himself with so much kindness, dignity, and humility, it seems amazing that the people in mass and their priests and scribes especially, did not open their hearts to bid Him welcome. But when instead of this, they withheld their confidence, and rejected Him in stern and wicked unbelief, then they became fearfully hardened. Every step in the process of this rejection worked only mischief and ruin. Suppose you have in your family a son whom you are trying to save; but the more you labor for this result, so much the more does he withhold his confidence, traduce your motives, and pervert to evil all your intended good. Such a course as this on his part throws him fearfully into the power of Satan, and he is led captive by that arch-deceiver at his will.

None can appreciate our texts, and other passages of this class, except those who have had experience. "Thanks be to God," cries Paul, "who giveth us the victory:" a song in which none can truly join but those who have gained this victory, and know its power and blessedness. What can an impenitent man know of such emotions? What can he say? Can he thank God for victory of which he knows and experiences nothing? No; he has been only vanquished, and Satan sings the peans of victory over the ruin of his soul.

To the Christian, really victorious, there is the utmost occasion for gratitude and thanksgiving. He esteems this far above all his other mercies; he finds himself lifted above the power of temptation, his old chains broken, his religious exercises and purposes become spontaneous, and religion the life and joy of his soul. How earnestly does he bless the Lord who hath given him the victory!

It is sad to see how little there is, in our day, of this thanksgiving for victory over sin. How rarely do you hear such thanks for grace received and victory obtained! We have been in the habit here of having a thanksgiving meeting, for the purpose of expressing our individual grounds of thanksgiving. When the next thanksgiving day occurs, shall we hear any offerings of praise to God for giving the victory over sin? We used to hear thanks for grace received; shall we have such thanks again? Once, giving thanks for victory over sin was more common with us than thanks for temporal mercies; shall it be so again?

If the numbers who return to give thanks for this blessing are small, what shall we infer? Is it not fearfully sad and perilous that the gospel should lose its power in any community?

Many seem not to be aware of their real state. It is hard to convince them that they are not altogether right; yet they have no thanks for this victory. Yet, if they had gained this victory, then they surely would acknowledge it and express their gratitude to God for it. No other victors are more grateful than *Christian* victors. If they find themselves victors, they will not conceal the blessed truth, but will naturally wish to shout the praises of victorious grace!

Many professed Christians spend their time and breath in brooding over their great weakness, talking it over, praying about it, and discouraging themselves and others as if the Lord were a hard master, who imposed heavy tasks and allowed only the least possible amount of grace to help His children perform them. Yet, they do not usually quite despair of help in themselves; do not cease from legal efforts; are not dead to this class of efforts, as those who have utterly renounced them, and who trust in Christ alone. They still think they shall gain the victory by some work which they shall do in themselves. By efforts made without faith, they hope to get faith, and so work out their own righteousness. *But it is only when self is really despaired of that deliverance comes. When you see a sinner on the verge of despair in himself, then you may know he is near the kingdom of grace and mercy. When he has done everything he can do in himself to save himself, and is compelled to despair of doing anything more, then he is ready to trust in Jesus.* Who of us has not seen this experience in others, and felt it in ourselves? At first we thought we could get religion with little effort; we started off self-righteously, made some ineffectual struggles to pray, and soon learned that our case was far worse than we had supposed. Before my conversion, I had never prayed much. For a short time previous, I used to lock my office door, stop the keyhole, and whisper out a short prayer in the greatest perturbation lest somebody should hear my voice, or in some way learn that I was praying. But this answered no purpose; I knew I must pray better than this. I seemed to be bound up and hemmed in on every side and could not pray. But it occurred to me that if I could get entirely away from everybody, and could meet God alone, that then I could pray. So I went off into the woods, far beyond any danger of being overheard or seen. But even then I could not pray. My heart refused to pray; there seemed to be no prayer in it. I felt fearfully faint and said, "All is over with me; I never can pray." Despair came down on my heart for a moment; the last prop was knocked out from under me, and there was nothing more I could do but to fall helpless at Jesus' feet and find mercy there!

Often persons talk and complain much of their weakness, but do not despair of yet further efforts in their own strength. They are not so shut up to God that they know they cannot take another step to purpose in any other direction. They seem little aware of the fact that Jesus Christ is knocking at the door of their heart every moment, as He said, "Behold I stand at the door and knock"—yet they do not bid Him enter with welcome. In fact, they even bolt the door against Him.

A lady of my acquaintance, hopefully a Christian, felt her need of sanctifying grace, and really exhausted her strength in efforts after her own ideas of the matter, to get the command of her temper. At length she fell into despair; she said she was not a Christian and could do no more, and would profess piety no longer. At this crisis, Jesus revealed himself to her, and in a moment she found deliverance. She was completely saved from the power of her giant temptation. Years after this, she said to me, "I have no more expectation of committing those sins of temper than I have of committing murder."

Real despair of help in one's self does not make men careless and lead them to drop all efforts; on the contrary, the more they despair, the more their soul reaches out on every side for help and hope.

Until the church is sanctified, the world cannot be converted. Until Christians can testify with their lips and lives, it cannot be expected that the truth will take effect.

A man of much prominence in New York had a pious wife. When the subject of sanctification came to be agitated there, some eighteen years ago, she was enough of a Christian to understand it and to feel her need. She studied it and embraced it. When her unconverted husband saw the astonishing change it wrought in her, he said, "The Church must have this. When they do, the world will understand the Gospel. They will have something intelligible to aim at." How true! Until the Church gets the victory, and, rejoicing in this victory, can show it to the world, she need not think she is greatly recommending religion, or is likely to secure many converts.

Converts are likely to be converted only to the current standard of piety in the church where they are. Often you see this illustrated in a very striking manner. Although they have the Bible in their hand, and although they have excellent preaching, yet their practical ideas of religion are usually drawn from the observed life and spirit of their Christian friends. The living patterns have the practical power. Hence, if young converts have before them high examples, it puts them upon high aims and efforts. They aspire to the standard of those whom they most esteem. Oh, how precious to them to have high and holy examples for their imitation!

Church members are in their own light when they reproach converts, for they only reproach themselves. They often do not consider that these converts are only *themselves reproduced*; a mirror in which they can see the reflection of their own faces. So, also, for the church to complain of each other is only to complain of themselves. We are every one of us responsible in our measure for the state of the Church, and we are to blame for its state being no better than it is. It is therefore of no use for us to recriminate.

Some professors of religion say, "All this does not apply to me, for I don't profess sanctification." A great mistake; for you *have* professed sanctification. Scarcely could you make a more solemn profession than you made when you joined the church. Then you publicly avouched the Lord Jehovah to be your God, Jesus to be your Saviour, and the Holy Ghost to be your Sanctifier. You solemnly promised to abstain from all ungodliness and every worldly lust, and if this is not a profession of entire sanctification, what is? Certainly, your promise and profession went the whole length of pledging yourself to full and wholehearted obedience—an obedience not so complete as you may, perhaps, render in after years with a more and better knowledge; for holy obedience may progress with knowledge through all time and all eternity. But after such a covenant, it avails nothing to say that you have not committed yourself to a life and a state of entire consecration to God.

Is it not a fact that some of you, instead of coming up to the gospel standard, keep shy of it. You are more than willing to waive the question about entire consecration, and are really anxious to build up a new highway to heaven; which shall not be the "highway of holiness?" Brethren, such building of other highways for the Christian life must be a fearful failure. There is perdition at the end of such a pathway, and there *ought* to be. If God's redeemed people rebel against being constrained by redeeming love, and insist that some little sin must be indulged and admitted into the standard Christian life, ought not God to give them up to their own lusts? Nay more, *will* He not do this as sure as He is holy, and as surely as He hates sin with utter hatred?

7

JUSTIFICATION*

Romans 8:1

"There is therefore now no condemnation to them which are in Christ Jesus, who walk not after the flesh but after the Spirit."

In this discussion, I shall notice,
   I. *What it is to be in Christ Jesus;*
  II. *What is intended by no condemnation;*
 III. *Why there is no condemnation to them who are in Christ Jesus;*
  IV. *What is intended by not walking after the flesh, but after the Spirit.*
   V. *None, except those who walk after the Spirit, are in a justified state.*

I. What it is to be in Christ Jesus.

Four answers have been given to this question, three of which I will briefly consider, and then I will give what I suppose to be the true one.

1. The first answer is the doctrine of eternal justification by imputed righteousness. The doctrine states that a certain number were unconditionally chosen from all eternity, to whom Christ sustained the relation of Covenant Head, in such a sense that they are eternally justified. This gross and absurd notion is now exploded and generally rejected.

2. The second answer is that of perpetual justification by one act of faith. The doctrine states that the first act of faith brings the soul into such a relation to God that never afterwards will it be condemned or exposed to the penalty of the law, whatever sins it may commit. The simple idea is that respecting Christians the penalty of the law is wholly set aside.

(1.) Now respecting this, the first remark I make is; justification is of two kinds, legal and gospel. Legal justification consists in pronouncing a moral agent innocent of all violation of the claims of the law so that it has no charge against him. Gospel justification consists in pardoning a sinner for whatever transgressions he may have committed; that is, in

---

The Oberlin Evangelist: Vol. V; July 19, 1843.

arresting or setting aside the execution of the penalty which he has incurred.

(2.) Legal justification is out of the question, since all the world has become guilty before God. And to maintain that a soul is perpetually justified by once believing is antinomianism, and one of the worst forms of error. It is to maintain that with respect to Christians the law of God is abrogated. The law is made up of precept and penalty; and if either is detached, it ceases to be law. It matters not whether it be maintained that the precept be set aside, or the penalty; it is to maintain an abrogation of the law, and is a ruinous error. It is the nature of a pardon to set aside the execution of the penalty due to past violations of the law, and to restore the person to governmental favor during good behavior. More than this it cannot do without giving an indulgence to sin. If no future sins can merit their penalty, it follows that the Christian would not be in danger of hell no matter how many or how gross the sins he might commit; or even if he should die in a state of the foulest apostasy. What an abomination is such a doctrine!

(3.) This doctrine cannot be true, for no being can prevent condemnation where there is sin. I said in a former lecture that the law is not founded in the arbitrary will of God, but in the nature and relations of moral beings. Whatever penalty is due to any act of sin, is due, therefore, from the nature of the case, so that every act of sin subjects the sinner to the penalty. Pardon cannot then be prospective—sin cannot be forgiven in advance, and to maintain that it is, is to make Christ the minister of sin.

(4.) Again, if Christians are not condemned when they sin, they cannot be forgiven, for forgiveness is nothing else than setting aside the penalty. And therefore, if they are not condemned, they cannot properly pray for forgiveness. In fact, it is unbelief in them to do so. What else can it be, when the sin, whatever it may be in enormity, has not exposed its perpetrator at all to the penalty of God's law?

(5.) This notion cannot be true, because the Bible uniformly makes perseverance in holiness, that is in *obedience,* just as much a condition of final acceptance with God as repentance or one act of faith. For my part, I must say, I don't know where the Bible makes salvation depend on one act of faith. Those who hold this dogma ought to tell us where it is taught.

(6.) The Bible, to the contrary, expressly declares that "when a righteous man turneth away from his righteousness, and committeth iniquities, and dieth in them, for his iniquity that he hath done, shall he die." What can be more distinct or explicit than this declaration? I know not how it has been overlooked or can be evaded.

(7.) If this doctrine were true, it would follow that if Christians are not condemned for one sin, they would not be for ten thousand, and that the greatest apostates could be saved without repentance. But what kind of a gospel is that? It would overthrow the entire government of God. A pretty gospel! Strange kind of good news!

(8.) Moreover, as I have said before, if the penalty is abolished with respect to believers, then the law must be. To them, its precept ceases to be anything else than simple advice which they may do as they please about adopting or obeying.

(9.) Finally, every Christian's experience condemns this doctrine. Who of them does not feel condemned when he sins? Now, he either is condemned when his conscience affirms that he is, or his conscience is at opposition to the government of God—affirming what is not true. And when under its rebukes, persons go and ask pardon, in yielding to it, they are guilty of disbelief in their doctrine, and thus add one sin to another. The truth is every Christian's conscience condemns the doctrine, and it obviously is evil, and only evil, and that continually in its whole tendency.

3. The third answer is that there will be no final condemnation. Without saying anything about the truth or falsity of that doctrine here, I remark that the text says no such thing. It says, "there is *now* no condemnation." With this agrees Romans 5:1. "Therefore, being justified by faith, we have peace with God, through our Lord Jesus Christ." Indeed, this is the general representation of the Bible.

4. The fourth answer which has been given is this: "To be in Christ is to have a personal, living faith in Him—it is to abide in Him by a living faith." John 15:4-7, "Abide in Me, and I in you. As the branch cannot bear fruit of itself, except it abide in the vine, no more can ye, except ye abide in Me. I am the vine, ye are the branches: he that abideth in Me, and I in him, the same bringeth forth much fruit; for without Me, ye can do nothing. If a man abide not in Me, he is cast forth as a branch that is withered; and men gather them and cast them into the fire, and they are burned. If ye abide in Me, and my words abide in you, ye shall ask what ye will, and it shall be done unto you." 1 John 3:5, 6, "And ye know that He was manifested to take away our sins: and in Him is no sin. Whosoever abideth in Him, sinneth not: whosoever sinneth, hath not seen Him, neither known Him." 2 Cor. 5:17, "Therefore, if any man be in Christ, he is a new creature: old things are passed away; behold, all things are become new." I might quote many other passages all setting forth that there is no condemnation to those whose faith secures in them an actual conformity to the divine will. To all others, there is.

To be in Christ is to be under His influence so as not to walk after the flesh but after the Spirit; that is, to receive constant divine influence from Him, as the branches derive nourishment from the vine. This intimate connection with Christ, and spiritual subjection to His control, are fully taught in many passages in the Bible. Gal. 2:20, "I am crucified with Christ: nevertheless I live: yet not I, but Christ liveth in me: and the life which I now live in the flesh, I live by the faith of the Son of God, who loved me, and gave Himself for me." And Gal. 5:16-25, "This I say then, walk in the Spirit, and ye shall not fulfill the lusts of the flesh. For the flesh lusteth against the Spirit, and the Spirit against the flesh, and these are contrary, the one to the other; so that ye cannot do the things that ye would. But if ye be led by the Spirit, ye are not under the law. Now the works of the flesh are manifest, which are these; adultery, fornication, uncleanness, lasciviousness, idolatry, witchcraft, hatred, variance, emulations, wrath, strife, seditions, heresies, envyings, murders, drunkenness, revellings, and such like; of the which, I tell you before as I have also told you in times past, that they which do such things, shall not inherit the kingdom of God. But the fruit of the Spirit, is love, joy, peace, long-suffering, gentleness, goodness, faith, meekness, temperance: against such there is no law. And they that are Christ's, have crucified the flesh with the affections and lusts. If we live in the Spirit, let us also walk in the Spirit."

II. *What is intended by no condemnation.*

1. *To be condemned* is to be under sentence of law. Those who are condemned *are not only not pardoned for the past*, but *also their present state of mind is blameworthy and condemned.* They are not justified on the ground of either law or Gospel, but the whole penalty due to all their iniquity is out against them.

2. When it is said that there is no condemnation, it is not intended that they never were condemned, but that *their past sin is all pardoned.* They are wholly delivered from exposure to the penalty due to their sins. In addition to this, it is intended, that *in their present state of mind they obey the law so that the law does not condemn their present state.* It does not mean that they will not be again condemned if they sin, but that *while they are in Christ Jesus they are free from all present condemnation.*

III. *Why there is no condemnation to them who are in Christ Jesus.*

1. Not because they are of the elect and eternally justified.

2. Not because Christ's righteousness is so imputed that we can sin without incurring exposure to the penalty of the law.

3. Not because we are perpetually justified by one act of faith. This, as we have attempted to show, is an antinomian and pernicious error.

4. Not because God accepts an imperfect obedience. There is a general opinion abroad, that somehow or other, God accepts an imperfect obedience as genuine. Now it seems to me that this is a very erroneous view of the subject. The truth is that God has no option about this matter any more than any other being; for the law exists and makes its demands wholly independent of His will and whatever it demands; that is, whatever the nature and relations of moral beings demand, that, as moral governor, He is bound to enforce and nothing else. Now what is there in reason or the Bible to sanction the idea that God will, or can, accept an imperfect obedience? The Bible insists on our serving Him with the whole heart—on our being perfectly benevolent—and proposes no lower standard. Nor could we believe it, if it did. What kind of obedience is half or imperfect obedience? No one can tell; and consequently, no one can intentionally render it. The very idea of it is absurd.

5. But to him that is in Christ Jesus, there is *now* no condemnation because he *is* in Christ Jesus in the sense above explained. Not that Christ shields him from the penalty while he continues to violate the precept, but that He saves him from sin; and thus, from desert of the penalty. Says the text, "to those who walk not after the flesh, but after the Spirit." Now mark the result; let us read right along. In the seventh chapter, he spoke of a law in his members which brought him into captivity to sin and death; that is, under condemnation. Now he says, (8:2-4) "For the law of the Spirit of life in Christ Jesus, hath made me free from the law of sin and death. For what the law could not do, in that it was weak through the flesh, God sending His own Son in the likeness of sinful flesh, and for sin, condemned sin in the flesh, that the righteousness of the law might be fulfilled in us, who walk not after the flesh but after the Spirit." Here he asserts that the reason why God sent His own Son in the likeness of sinful flesh and for sin and condemned sin in the flesh was "that the righteousness of the law might be fulfilled in us, who walk not after the flesh, but after the Spirit." Now, public justice having been satisfied by the Atonement, when the heart is thus brought into conformity to the law, is a good reason why they should be pardoned. The same thing is meant by "writing the law in the heart."

6. Again, there is no condemnation to him who is in Christ Jesus, because he "walks not after the Spirit." This same thought is contained in Gal. 5:16-24, "This I say then, walk in the Spirit and ye shall not fulfill the lust of the flesh. For the flesh lusteth against he Spirit, and the Spirit against the flesh: and these are contrary the one to the other; so that ye cannot do the things that ye would. But if ye be led by the Spirit ye are not under the law. Now the works of the flesh are manifest, which are these; adultery, fornication, uncleanness, lasciviousness, idolatry, witchcraft, hatred, variance, emulations, wrath, strife, seditions, heresies, envyings, murders, drunkenness, revellings, and such like, of the which I tell you before, as I have also told you in time past, that they which do such things shall not inherit the kingdom of God. But the fruit of the Spirit is love, joy, peace, long-suffering, gentleness, goodness, faith, meekness, temperance; against such there is no law. And they that are Christ's have crucified the flesh, with the affections and lusts." Here the fruit of the Spirit is just what the law requires; and therefore, there can be no condemnation.

7. This assertion must either mean that when we are in Christ we do not sin, or that in Him we can sin without condemnation. Now, what does it mean? It cannot mean the last for that would make Christ the minister of sin. No individual can sin without breaking the law, for sin is the transgression of the law. The first, then, must be the meaning and this agrees with what the Scriptures teach: "Without holiness no man shall see the Lord." The reason then why there is no condemnation to them who *are in* Christ Jesus, is,

(1.) That in Christ their former sins are pardoned on the ground of His Atonement; and,

(2.) That while in Him they do not sin. He saves them from their sins; and therefore, from condemnation.

IV. *What is intended by not walking after the flesh, but after the Spirit.*

1. By the flesh is meant the appetites, desires, and propensities of the sensibility. To walk after the flesh is to indulge these—to give up the will to self-gratification. It is to be in bondage to the propensities so that they are our masters and govern us. It is to be selfish.

2. But to walk after the Spirit is to obey the Spirit of Christ—it is to obey the law of God.

V. *None except those who walk after the Spirit are in a justified stage.*

1. By this I do not intend to say that they never were justified. For it is true that individuals who once obeyed, and were of course justified, have fallen. This is the case with the angels, who kept not their first estate, and Adam and Eve. These were justified in the legal sense before they sinned. But many have also fallen into grievous iniquity, who have once been justified in the gospel sense.

2. I do not mean that they are in no sense Christians. In the common acceptation of the term, it is not limited to those who are in a state of actual conformity to the will of God, but applies to all who give credible evidence of having been converted. Moreover, it is true of Christians that they sustain a peculiar relation to God, and the term does not indicate that they never sin or fall into condemnation, but that they sustain a certain relation to God which others do not.

3. But I do mean that no one can commit sin without condemnation. When a Christian sins, he is as really condemned as anyone else, and he is no longer justified any more than he is obedient.

4. I mean that no one is justified or pardoned until he obeys the law or repents, which is the same thing. By the way, it is important that all should understand that repentance is not *sorrow* for sin, but a real turning away from all sin to God. Now when any individual sins, he must be condemned till he repents or forsakes his sin. A great many people talk about *always repenting*—that the best acts we ever perform need to be repented of, etc. Now, this is all nonsense and nothing but nonsense. I say again that religion is no such thing as this, and to represent it so is to talk loosely. "The soul that sinneth it shall die." Repentance is a hearty and entire forsaking of sin and entrance upon obedience to God.

5. I mean that when one has truly repented, he is justified, and remains so just as long as he remains obedient, and no longer. When he falls into sin, he is as much condemned as any other sinner, because he is a sinner.

6. I also mean that justification follows and does not precede sanctification as some have vainly imagined. I here use the term sanctification, not in the high sense of permanent sanctification, but of entire

consecration to God. It is not true that persons are justified before they forsake sin. They certainly could not be thus *legally* justified, and the *Gospel* proffers no pardon until after repentance or hearty submission of the will to God. I add, that *Christians are justified no longer than they are sanctified, or obedient, and that complete permanent justification depends upon complete and permanent sanctification.*

Remarks

1. I have often thought and could not help drawing the conclusion that the great mass of professors of religion are mere antinomians living in the habitual commission of known sin and yet expecting to be saved. And when they are pressed up to holiness of heart, they say, "I am not expected to be perfect in this life. I expect Christ to make up for my deficiencies." Now such religion is no better than universalism or infidelity. See that professor of religion. What is he doing? Why indulging his appetites and propensities in various ways which he knows to be contrary to the divine will! Ask him about it and he will confess it—he will confess that this is his daily practice; and yet, he thinks he is justified. But if the Bible be true, he is not. "Know ye not that to whom ye yield yourselves servants to obey, his servants ye are to whom ye obey; whether of sin unto death, or of obedience unto righteousness?" But he can tell of an "experience." Perhaps he wrote it all down lest he should forget it, and he tells it over to the hundredth time, how he felt when God pardoned his sins—while he is now living in sin every day. Perhaps he never tells of an "experience" at all, but yet rests back upon "something which he felt" when he imagined he was converted. Now this is nothing but antinomianism, and how astonishing it is that so many should cry out so vehemently about antinomianism when they are nothing but antinomians themselves. What a terrible delusion this is!

2. Men are justified by faith in Christ, because they are sanctified by faith in Him. They do not have righteousness imputed to them, and thus stand justified by an arbitrary fiction, while they are personally unholy. But they are made righteous by faith, and that is the reason why they are justified.

3. To talk about depending on Christ to be justified by Him, while indulging in any form of known sin, is to insult Him. It is to charge Him with being the minister of sin. A lady, not long ago, was talking with her minister about certain women who were given over to dress in the utmost style of extravagant fashion. He said he thought the most dressy people in his church were the best Christians. They were the most humble and dependent on Christ. That was his idea about religion. *What did he mean?* Why, that such persons did not pretend to be holy, but professed to depend wholly on Christ. They acknowledged themselves sinners. And well they might! But what kind of religion is that? And how did he get such a notion? How else but by supposing that persons are not expected to be holy in this life, and that they can be justified while living

in sin? Now I would as soon expect a pirate, whose hands are red with blood, to be saved, as professors of religion who indulge in any form of sin, lust, pride, worldliness, or any other iniquity:"Do we make void the law through faith? God forbid; yea we establish the law." But what a state of things must it be when a minister can utter such a sentiment as that?

4. Such an idea of justification is open to the infidel objection that the Gospel is a system of impunity in sin. The Unitarians have stereotyped this objection against faith. Ask them why they say so. They answer, "because the doctrine of justification by faith is injurious to good morals." A circuit Judge, some years ago said, "I cannot admit the Bible to be true. It teaches that men are saved by faith, and I therefore regard the Gospel as injurious to good morals, and as involving a principle that would ruin any government on earth." Now, did he get this idea from the Bible? No, but from the false representations made of the teachings of the Bible. It teaches no such thing, but plainly asserts that a faith that does not sanctify is a dead faith.

5. There are many *hoping* that they are Christians who yet live so that their conscience condemns them. "For if our heart condemns us, God is greater than our heart, and knoweth all things." Now to teach that persons may be justified while their conscience condemns them contradicts this passage. If our own conscience condemns us, God does. Shall He be less just than our own nature?

6. A great multitude of professors are merely careless sinners. Now do let me ask, "If from the way many persons live in the Church, compared with the way many careless sinners live, is it not perfectly manifest that they are in no wise different? And is it censorious to say that they are mere hardened sinners? What will become of them?"

7. Many who are accounted the most pious are only convicted sinners. It is a most remarkable thing, and one which I have taken great pains to observe, that many, thought to be converted in the late revivals, are only convicted sinners; that is, mere legalists. The preaching makes them so. The claims of the law are held up and obligation enforced to comply with it. They are told to trust Christ for pardon and they attempt it. Many really do, while others stop short with mere resolutions. All this class will go back, or stay in the Church, almost constantly distressed by the lashings of conscience. If you hold up the law they are distressed, and if you hold up Christ they are distressed by the consciousness that they do not exercise faith in Him. Hold up either and they have no rest. They are really convicted sinners, and yet they think this is religion. In time of coldness they always sink back, but in times of revival they are aroused and driven to the performance of a heartless service which continually fails to appease the demands of conscience. They know of no other experience than this. They refer you to the 7th chapter of Romans to prove that this is Christian experience and thus bolster up their hope. I recollect some time ago, when I had preached against this as Christian experience, a minister said to me, "Well, Brother Finney, I

can't believe that." Why? "Because that's my experience, and I believe I am a Christian." A strange reason! I suppose it was his experience! Great multitudes have it and suppose it genuine. I fear, in some instances, whole Churches are made up of such, and their ministers teach them that this is genuine religion. What would the minister just referred to say? "That is Paul's experience, and mine too." And the people often derive much comfort from what the minister says is his experience. Oh, what teaching is this? It is high time there was a change of mind in the Church on this subject. Whoever has no experience but that of the 7th chapter of Romans is not justified at all, and were it not that great multitudes are deluded, it could not be that so many could sit down contented under this view of the subject.

8. One who walks after the Spirit has this inward testimony that he pleases God. An individual may think he does, when he does not, just as persons in a dream may think themselves awake, but when they really awake, find it all a dream. So individuals may think they please God when they do not, but it is nevertheless true that those who please God know it. He that believeth on the Son of God hath the witness in himself.

9. This view of the subject does not touch that of the final perseverance of the saints. What I am attempting to show is,

(1.) That true believers are justified or pardoned, and treated as righteous, on account of the Atonement of Christ.

(2.) That those who truly believe are justified because they are actually righteous. The question is not whether a Christian who has fallen into sin will die in that state, but whether if he does he will be damned. Whether, while in sin he is justified.

10. Those who sin do not abide in Christ. "And ye know that He was manifested to take away our sins; and in Him is no sin. Whosoever abideth in Him sinneth not: whosoever sinneth hath not seen Him neither known Him. Little children, let no man deceive you: he that doeth righteousness is righteous even as He is righteous. He that committeth sin is of the devil; for the devil sinneth from the beginning. For this purpose the Son of God was manifested, that He might destroy the works of the devil. Whosoever is born of God doth not commit sin; for His seed remaineth in him: and he cannot sin because he is born of God." While they abide in Christ, they are not condemned, but if they overlook what abiding in Christ is, they are sure to fall into sin; and then, they are condemned as a matter of course. The secret of holy living, and freedom from contamination, is to abide in Christ. Says Paul, "I am crucified with Christ, nevertheless I live; yet not I, but Christ liveth in me; and the life that I now live in the flesh, I live by the faith of the Son of God." We must have such confidence in Him as to let Him have the entire control in all things.

11. Sinners can see how to be saved. They must believe in the Lord Jesus Christ with all their heart. They must become holy and walk after the Spirit.

12. Convicted professors can also see what to do. Have you felt

misgivings and a load on your conscience? Are you never able to say, "I am justified—I am accepted in the beloved.'"? You must come to Christ *now*, if you now experience condemnation.

13. There is neither peace nor safety except in Christ, but in Him is all fullness and all we need. In Him you may come to God, as children, with the utmost confidence.

14. If you are in Christ, you have peace of mind. How sweetly the experience of a Christian answers to this. Many of you perhaps can testify to this. You had been borne down with a burden too heavy, crying out, "Oh wretched man that I am; who shall deliver me from the body of this death." But your faith took hold on Christ, and suddenly all your burden was gone. You could no longer feel condemned. The stains of sin all wiped out by the hand of grace. You can now look calmly at your sins, and not feel them grind like an iron yoke. Are you in this state? Can you testify from your own experience that there is *now* no condemnation to them that are in Christ Jesus? If so, you can reflect upon your past sins without being ground down into the dust under the guilty burden which rolls upon you. The instant you experience a freedom from condemnation, your whole soul yearns with benevolence for others. You know what their state is. Ah, yes, you know what it is to drink the wormwood and the gall—to have the arrows of the Almighty drink up your spirit, and when you find deliverance you must of course want to teach others what is the great salvation—to strengthen those that are weak. And an individual who can sit down at ease and not find His benevolence like fire shut up in his bones—who does not even feel agonized, not for himself, but for others, cannot have yet found that there is *now* no condemnation. He may dream that he has, but if he ever awaken, he will find it but a dream. Oh, how many need to be aroused from this sleep of death!

8

MORAL DEPRAVITY*

Romans 8:7

"Because the carnal mind is enmity against God: for it is not subject to the law of God, neither indeed can be."

In this subject, I proceed,
  I. *What is moral depravity?*
  II. *It behooves us to enquire into the attributes or qualities of moral depravity.*
  III. *What is the "carnal mind"?*
  IV. *The "carnal mind" is a state of enmity against God.*
  V. *The "carnal mind" is a state of* mortal *enmity against God.*
  VI. *The "carnal mind" is a state of* supreme *opposition to God.*

I. *What is moral depravity?*
The words "moral depravity" mean, literally, *crooked manners*, from *mos*, manners, and *pravus*, crooked. The *de* is intensive. Hence, moral depravity means manners wholly crooked.

By manners is intended not merely the outward life, because the outward life has not in itself any morality or immorality. All that is strictly or properly *moral*, all that has moral character, belongs to the mind. Moral manners, therefore, are the manners of the inner will, the moral agent, the mind itself. The outward or bodily manners are only expressions of the inward or real manners of the subject.

When we speak of manners as crooked, we of necessity refer to something straight with which the manners are compared. A thing may have a natural crookedness, or a physical crookedness, or a moral crookedness. Moral crookedness is a deviation from the straight rule of action prescribed by the moral law. It is crooked when compared with the moral straightness of the law of God.

Again, moral depravity lies entirely back of individual actions and volitions, and is the source from which these actions and volitions spring.

The Oberlin Evangelist: Vol. XXIV; March 12, March 26, 1862. The companion sermon is in *Principles of Victory*, pp. 109-127: "Total Depravity."

II. *It behooves us to enquire into the attributes or qualities of moral depravity.*

1. As already intimated, *unlawfulness* is a quality or attribute of moral depravity. This depravity must be a thing prohibited by the moral law. If it were not, it would not be morally crooked. Whatever has moral character must be either in accordance with moral law or in violation of it.

2. Another attribute of moral depravity is *sinfulness.* Dr. Woods defines moral depravity as being "sinfulness."* By this is meant that this state of mind called moral depravity, which is contrary to God's law, is sinful. This is the term by which we express its moral turpitude.

3. Another attribute of moral depravity, is *blameworthiness.* It is not only contrary to God's law and sinful; but it is worthy of blame and of punishment, and justly brings the subject of it under the penalty of moral law.

4. Moral depravity is a violation of moral obligation. It is a state of mind the opposite of that which we are bound to be in. We ought not to be morally depraved. If it were not a violation of moral obligation, it would be neither unlawful nor blameworthy.

5. It is a state of mind that ought to be instantly abandoned. Of course, if it is sinful, if it is blameworthy, if it is a violation of moral obligation, it ought to be instantly renounced.

6. Moral depravity is a state that *can* be instantly abandoned. It *ought* to be, and therefore it *can* be. To say that it ought to be abandoned, that we are under moral obligation to abandon it instantly, and yet to deny the possibility of abandoning it instantly, involves a gross contradiction.

7. I have said that moral depravity must be a state of mind. It cannot be a state of body. Depravity of body is physical depravity, not moral. It is simply disease.

8. You will observe that moral depravity consists in moral manners; that is, in mental action, and is no part of quality of soul or body. Whatever belongs to the essence or substance of either soul or body, must of necessity be in its nature physical; and if depraved, therefore, its depravity must be physical and not moral. It is plain that whatever is strictly constitutional in the sense of being an attribute, quality or part of soul or body, cannot have the distinctive characteristics of moral depravity. For example, it cannot be unlawful or contrary to the law of God, for the law legislates over man's mental activities, and not over the essential qualities of either body or mind.

Again, that which is a part or attribute of either soul or body cannot be a violation of moral obligation. Nor can any attribute of body or mind be a violation of conscience. It cannot be a violation of duty; it cannot be instantly abandoned; it cannot be blameworthy.

9. Again, moral depravity cannot consist in things created or trans-

---

*Leonard Woods (1774-1854) was a member of the Andover faculty, and he wrote *Letters to Unitarians* in 1820 to challenge their view of human nature.

mitted; such as, the appetites, passions, or propensities. These have none of the attributes of moral depravity. They are not contrary to moral law. It is only their unreasonable indulgence that is contrary to moral law, and not the appetites or propensities themselves. They are not blameworthy. They cannot be immediately abandoned so as to exist no longer. Their existence is no violation of moral obligation. Consequently, the existence in the constitution of these appetites and propensities is not moral depravity or bad manners.

10. Moral depravity should not be confounded with temptation, or excited feelings, or propensities. I have just said that the existence of these sensibilities in the soul is not in itself sinful. Nor is an excited state of the propensities necessarily in itself sinful. If they are indulged unreasonably, this is sin; but no merely excited state of feeling, that does not secure the consent of the will, can be a violation of moral obligation.

11. From its very attributes, moral depravity must certainly be a voluntary state of mind. For whatever is involuntary has none of the attributes of moral depravity.

12. *Moral depravity is the state of mind called in the Scriptures— the wicked heart.* It is that in us to which moral character belongs. I speak of it as a state of mind, to distinguish it from mere volitions, or mere executive acts of mind. It is that state of mind from which wicked words and acts naturally proceed. Words and acts are means to an end. They proceed from a choice of an end, and have moral character only as they partake of the moral qualities of the choice that gives them existence.

Moral depravity must consist in a settled ultimate choice, the choice of an end. It must consist in the voluntary devotion of the mind to self— self-interest and self-gratification. Human activity is rational and responsible. Men are moral agents; that is, they act under the responsibilities of moral obligation; they are subjects of moral law and of moral government. Moral law requires of all moral agents sincere, perfect, universal devotion to God and to the interests of His kingdom. In other words, it requires perfect, universal, perpetual, *unselfish* benevolence.

Moral depravity is the opposite of what this law requires; or, more strictly, it is want of conformity to this law. It is primarily a withholding—a refusal to be devoted to God and to the interests of His kingdom. It sets up self above God. It deliberately prefers self-interest and self-will to God's interest and God's will. It practically makes self of supreme importance. In one word, it is selfishness. *Moral depravity is the mind's commitment to self as the great supreme good of life.*

Moral depravity is a standing choice as distinct from a volition. It is a choice of the supreme end to which the mind shall devote itself. It is the choice of an ultimate end; that is, *self-gratification is chosen for its own sake.* We know from consciousness that when the mind is made up and has decided upon the end to be secured, its whole activities will be directed to the accomplishment of that end. Volition, as distinguished from the choice of an end, is the mind's effort to secure the end. *When we speak of individual sins, we speak of volition and consequent action. When we speak of moral depravity, as distinct from individual sinful acts, we mean that abiding and wrong, selfish, choice from which these volitions proceed.* Please observe the distinction I make between sinful acts and moral depravity. Moral depravity is originally a choice, and therefore a mental act. It is the choice of an end, and therefore an abiding, standing choice. Volitions are individual efforts to secure the end chosen. Sinful acts are found in the outward life. Moral depravity lies back of the outward life, and back of volition, in a standing preference of self-interest over God's interests and all other interests.

III. *What is the "carnal mind"?*

1. It is not the substance of either soul or body. it has been common to speak of the "carnal mind" as being identical with the mind itself. I recollect that Dr. Griffin, in his Park Street Lectures, confounds the "carnal mind" with the substance of the soul.* Since the Bible affirms the carnal mind to be enmity against God, he insists that the more clearly God is revealed to the mind, the more it will hate Him; and also, that there is nothing in the Gospel at all adapted to win the mind, but that the character of God as there presented is adapted only to repel the soul. He maintains this on the ground that the soul of the sinner is, in its very substance, enmity against God. But this must be a great mistake.

2. The carnal mind must be a voluntary state. If you have Bibles with marginal references and readings, you will observe that in the margin it is written, "the minding of the flesh." The carnal mind is the fleshly mind, or the mind in a state of committal to the indulgence of the appetites, passions, and propensities.

3. It is that state of mind into which Adam fell. It appears that, for a time, Adam preferred the will of God to his own, the pleasure of God to his own, and the interests of God to his own. But a temptation of a peculiar nature was presented to him through Eve. The wily serpent addressed Eve: "Yea, hath God said, Ye shall not eat of every tree of the garden?" She answered: "We may eat of the fruit of the trees of the garden: but of the fruit of the tree which is in the midst of the garden, God hath said, Ye shall not eat of it, neither shall ye touch it, lest ye die. And the serpent said unto the woman, Ye shall not surely die: for God doth know, that in the day ye eat thereof, then your eyes shall be opened; and ye shall be as gods, knowing good and evil. And when the woman saw that the tree was good for food, and that it was pleasant to the eyes, and a tree to be desired to make one wise, she took of the fruit thereof, and did eat; and gave also unto her husband with her, and he did eat."

Here two constitutional propensities, innocent in themselves, were strongly excited by this appeal of the tempter. The desire for knowledge

---

*Edward Dorr Griffin (1770-1837) was Pastor of Park Street Church, Boston, from 1811-1815, and published *Lectures Delivered in the Park Street Church*: Boston, 1813. He also wrote *The Extent of the Atonement*: New York, 1819.

is constitutional: the appetite for food is constitutional: These appetites are not wrong in themselves, nor is it morally wrong that they should be in an excited state. But the question, as put by the tempter, amounted to a proposal to Eve and to Adam to gratify their appetites, *although* it involved disobedience to God. This question was really fundamental to their moral character. They could not yield to this temptation without preferring their own self-gratification to the will of God, and their own pleasure to God's pleasure. To yield to this temptation would be to revolt from the government of God. It would break off their allegiance to Him. In the very act they must decide to seek their own pleasure in their own way as their supreme good. This would really be a change of the supreme ultimate end of life. Instead of loving God supremely, they now love themselves supremely. They reject God's authority, God's rights, God's happiness and His glory, and make them subordinate to their own gratification. You will observe that the temptation was not merely to put forth a single volition to secure some good, without any reference to the ultimate end in view. It was nothing else than a proposal from the tempter to set aside God as the great end for which they should live, and set up self-gratification as the supreme object of life. Yielding to this temptation plunged them into a state of choice—a settled state of voluntary preference of self-interest above all other good.

A voluntary state as distinguished from a voluntary act is a matter familiar to us all. We all know what is meant by choosing a partner for life, and abiding in that choice; and we know that when that choice is settled and abiding, the volitions and the outward life flow from it. The abiding choice gives direction to all the subsequent life.

Just so of this choice made by Adam. It became a fixed state of mind. He lapsed into a state of supreme selfishness; which is nothing else than a strong committal of the will, and consequently of the whole being, to self-gratification.

4. This carnal mind, or state of minding the flesh, reveals itself in fulfilling the desires of the flesh and of the mind. As is said in Eph. 2:1-3—"And you hath He quickened who were dead in trespasses and sins; wherein in time past ye walked according to the course of this world, according to the prince of the power of the air, the spirit that now worketh in the children of disobedience: Among whom also we all had our conversation in times past in the lusts of our flesh, fulfilling the desires of the flesh and of the mind; and were by nature the children of wrath, even as others."

The mind being settled in its great ultimate aim and end, the supreme choice being to gratify the deepest desires and propensities, it will of course reveal itself in all the myriad ways of self-indulgence in which unconverted sinners actually live.

5. The carnal mind has all the attributes of moral depravity. It is directly contrary to moral law. It is utterly sinful. It deserves punishment. It *ought* to be instantly abandoned. It *can* be instantly abandoned. To abandon it would mean a change of heart.

IV. *The "carnal mind" is a state of enmity against God.* I say a *state*; that is, *an abiding choice.*

It is enmity against God:

1. Because it is the exact opposite of what His law requires. His law requires us to love Him supremely and to make His glory, pleasure, will and interests, the supreme object of our lives. But this minding of the flesh is making self-indulgence the supreme object of our lives. This is not only a refusal to obey His law, but a state of mind the direct opposite of it.

2. This minding of the flesh is directly opposite to the whole character of God.

3. It is a state of voluntary alienation from God, and is of intense committal against Him. It is the wicked heart. It is so treated in the Bible itself. It is spoken of in the chapter of our text as being "in the flesh," and a state of mind in which it is impossible to please God. Furthermore, in this same chapter it is affirmed to be a state of death in sin: "To be carnally minded is death." Also, in Eph. 2:1-3, this carnal mind is represented as a state of spiritual death, of bondage to the flesh, of enmity against God.

4. I observe again that this carnal mind is a state of total moral depravity. As is said in verse 8: "So then they that are in the flesh cannot see God."

5. This carnal mind reveals itself in the neglect of God. This is the reason why sinners neglect worship, prayer, and communion with God, and why they do not love to think of Him or speak of Him.

6. The carnal mind reveals itself also in contempt for God's authority. The Psalmist enquires: "Wherefore do the wicked contemn God?" I answer, "Just because they are wicked. And their wickedness consists in this carnal-mindedness."

But, perhaps you will say: "I do not contemn the authority of God."

But how much do you care for this authority? Do you, in fact, treat it as if it were of the slightest importance? You will set aside the authority of God for the most trifling indulgence. See that young man smoking that cigar. Do you think, young man, that that is right? Do you think God wants you to smoke that cigar? Do you believe He is pleased with it? You know He is not; and yet, you care less for God's authority than you do for smoking that cigar. Every day you live you gratify yourself in ways which you know to be unlawful, without the slightest regard to God's authority. What do you mean, then, by saying that you do not contemn the authority of God? Is there anything in the world that you treat as of less importance than the authority of God? Your daily conduct is equivalent to saying: "What do I care for the authority of God? Who is God that I should obey Him, or what profit should I have if I should pray unto Him?"

7. The carnal mind reveals itself in opposition to God's people and cause. Who does not know that unconverted sinners are always picking at God's people, and in a multitude of ways manifesting opposition to

them: magnifying their faults and publishing them as widely as possible, ridiculing their piety, accusing them of hypocrisy, and in every way manifesting opposition to them. Now this is not because they have received any injury from God's people; nor is it really because God's people are worse than other people; but it is because of their own enmity to God that they oppose Him in His people.

8. This carnal mind also reveals itself in a want of confidence in God. Sinners very well know that they have every reason to confide in Him, but they do not. They have not the slightest confidence in all His professions of love for them, nor are they at all inclined to trust Him.

9. This carnal mind reveals itself in a total want of sympathy with God. In every way, this state of mind shows itself to be the opposite of God's state of mind. His revealed will and way are an abomination to them, and their will and way are an abomination to Him. As He says: "They loathe Me, and I abhor them."

10. The carnal mind reveals itself in a whole life of rebellion against God. That unconverted men are in a state of rebellion against the authority of God is one of the plainest facts that lie on the face of society.

V. The "carnal mind" is a state of mortal enmity against God. By this I mean that the human mind is so firmly entrenched against God, and so utterly opposed to Him, that sooner than be governed by Him, it would take His life if this were possible. Rebellion against any government always implies this.

Again, the crucifixion of Christ demonstrated this fact so far as it is possible for human beings to make such demonstration. Christ was God manifest in the flesh. They slew His human nature, and, no doubt, they would have slain His divine, if they could. It does not answer this to say that it was only the Jews who were highly prejudiced against Him, that slew Him. Nor is it any answer to say that if the Jews had known that He was God, they would not have crucified Him. For, we see now on every side those who acknowledge Jesus to be God, yet reject His authority and give the most unmistakable evidence that they would oppose Him to the death sooner than be governed by Him.

VI. The "carnal mind" is a state of supreme opposition to God; that is, it is more deeply set in opposition to God than to any other being in the universe. God is infinitely holy, and the carnal mind is in a state of entire sinfulness. These two things are infinitely opposed, the one to the other. There is nothing in the universe to which the sinner is so much opposed as real holiness, and there is nothing in heaven to which he is so much opposed as to infinite holiness.

Again, it is seen that all other enmities besides this can be subdued by a change of circumstances, without the interposition of the Holy Spirit. But so intensified is the enmity of the carnal mind against God, that sinners complain that it is utterly impossible for them to love God unless the Holy Ghost induces them to do so. I do not admit that it is impossi-

ble, as they pretend; *but I do admit that without divine influence they never will love Him;* whatever the consequences might be of their refusal.

Remarks

1. The human mind is manifestly in a *physically diseased state.* By this I mean that sin has deranged its development insomuch that there are various tendencies in the constitution that result in selfishness. But, let it be remembered that this is a physical and not a moral depravity. To illustrate this: Many persons come into being with depraved appetites—a strong natural appetite, say, for strong drink, or some other sensual enjoyment. Now, these appetites, although in a diseased state, yet being constitutional, are not in themselves sinful. It is only their unlawful indulgence that is sinful. In fact, no appetite of man can be sinful that is strictly constitutional and normal, nor can it become in itself sinful by being in an unhealthy or depraved condition. The *sin must consist in its unlawful indulgence.* Adam and Eve had constitutional appetites for knowledge and for food. These were not sinful; not even when they were strongly aroused by the temptation to indulgence. *It was only the consent of the mind to indulge them in a prohibited manner that constituted their sin.*

2. *It has been very common to confuse temptation with sin.* None of the constitutional appetites or propensities can be in themselves sinful, because they are involuntary and are a part of our nature. Nevertheless, these appetites and propensities, when aroused, are of course temptations to seek their indulgence. It must be their unlawful indulgence and this only that constitutes sin. But it has been very common to speak of their very existence, and especially of their excited state, as sin.

Now, *unless the soul, by an act of will, indulges the temptation, there can be no sin.* If the mind resists the excitement, suppresses it so far as possible, and refuses to gratify it, there can be no sin. Indeed, when the appetite is strongly aroused, but yet resisted, we cannot possibly deny that the virtue is the higher, as the temptation is the greater, and the mind more strongly and perseveringly resists it.

3. It is a great mistake to confound physical depravity with moral. It is very curious to see how the Bible has been interpreted on the question of constitutional sinfulness. It seems to me that men often interpret it without the least reference to any sound principles of biblical criticism. For example, one of these principles is that no passage is to be so interpreted as flatly to contradict human reason, unless it is so irresistibly plain that it can bear no other interpretation.

4. Now, I have not time to examine all the passages that have been misinterpreted on this subject. But take one, generally made very prominent in the attempt to prove from Scripture that the human constitution is *morally* depraved, to wit: Ps. 51:5.

"Behold, I was shapen in iniquity, and in sin did my mother conceive me."

What is this text quoted to prove?

That the human constitution, or, in other words, the very nature of all men, is morally depraved.

But this dogma is certainly contrary to human reason. If by moral depravity we mean something *sinful*, it is certainly inconceivable by reason that *that* should be morally blameworthy over which the man never had any control—a thing that belongs to his very constitution as he came from the hand of his Maker. That any human soul should be blameworthy for such a constitution, should be guilty of moral wrong for possessing it, is certainly as contrary as possible to human reason.

Now remember, *we are never to interpret any passage of Scripture so as to make it teach a doctrine palpably contrary to human reason, if it will bear any other interpretation. I say contrary to human reason, and not merely above its reach.*

Now, the doctrine that the human constitution is in itself sinful, blameworthy, morally wrong, morally depraved, is not so much above reason as opposite to the irresistible decisions of the human reason. It cannot therefore be proved, unless from passages unequivocally clear, explicit, and incapable of any other interpretation.

Let us now apply these remarks to the passage above quoted. What does it say?

(1) The verse is quoted to prove that moral depravity is in our nature and universal; that moral depravity is constitutional and pertains to the entire human race. *But this verse affirms no universal proposition whatever.* "Behold, I was shapen in iniquity, and in sin did my mother conceive me." Surely *this affirms nothing of mankind in general*, and we are not to extend and torture the passage to make it teach so absurd a doctrine.

(2) In this verse, the Psalmist does not even affirm his own sin. *If he accused anyone of sin, it was his mother.* "Behold, I was shapen in iniquity, and in sin did my mother conceive me."

(3) This is the language of poetry. The Psalmist was smarting bitterly, and was deeply moved under a sense of his great sin in the matter of Bathsheba and Uriah. As is natural in such cases, he has expressed himself in a highly figurative and poetic manner, and undoubtedly had a strong sense of his great sinfulness, and meant to say that he had been a sinner ever since he was capable of being so. Now, surely, to make such a passage teach so monstrous a dogma as the universal sinfulness of human nature, is a flagrant perversion of God's Word. It cannot be made to teach any such thing without greatly over-straining what is really said in the passage. But most surely no passage should be over-strained to make it teach an unreasonable dogma. You must not force strong poetical expressions to mean more than they really say, when this super-addition is contrary to reason.

(4) The usual interpretation of this passage totally perverts the real meaning of the Psalmist. He was greatly agonized in view of his own sinfulness, and was confessing his own sin to God. He was far from being in a state to accuse anybody else, or to make any apology for his own sin. But, the usual interpretation would represent him as searching for some excuse for his sin, and really charging the blame upon God, as if he had said: "O Lord, thou hast given me a sinful nature, and how am I to blame for my sin?"

This is a gross misrepresentation of the meaning of the passage, and of the spirit of its author.

Eph. 2:3 is another passage extensively quoted to prove that nature is itself sinful:

"Among whom also we all had our conversation in times past in the lusts of our flesh, fulfilling the desires of the flesh and of the mind; and were by nature the children of wrath, even as others."

Upon this verse I remark,

(1) The apostle represents the sinfulness of men as consisting in *fulfilling* the desires of the flesh and of the mind, *and not in the desires themselves*. This is the same view of moral depravity that I have given in this discourse. Paul does not represent these desires as being in themselves wrong; it is only their sinful indulgence which makes men children of wrath.

(2) Another remark is due here to show why Paul uses the words "by nature."

Suppose a child were born with a natural appetite for strong drink. This natural appetite does not make him a drunkard *before* he indulges it. But suppose he grows up to manhood, does indulge himself, and becomes a drunkard. Now, looking to the *occasion* of his fall, we should naturally say, he was a drunkard *"by nature."*

The same is true with those who have a natural propensity (as some have) to lie and steal. If they were born with a natural tendency in those directions, and we knew it, we should speak of them as liars or thieves "by nature." By this language we should not mean that they were actually guilty of any of these crimes *before* they had indulged these physically depraved propensities; much less should we assume that these inherited propensities were sins of their own.

There is no doubt in my mind that this is the real meaning of the apostle in this passage. The constitutional desires (*Epithumiai*, Greek) were natural to man, and in this sense men are "by nature children of wrath." The appetites are constitutional to man in his physically depraved state. It is quite natural to speak of him as being by nature a sinner, when really *we* can *mean* no more than that *he inherits the temptation to sin*, and *not that the temptation is itself sin*. The desires are natural to him; the fulfilling or indulging of them is voluntary; and therefore, sinful.

is is all that this passage can be made to mean by a fair interpretation. I say of this and of all the passages that are quoted to prove the doctrine of constitutional sinfulness, as I have said of Psalm 51:5, that they have not been soberly interpreted. They have been made to teach a most irrational doctrine by straining them and making them mean even more than they say. They naturally mean no more than that men inherit a *physically* depraved constitution. Certainly none of them asserts that human nature is itself sinful. I have quoted the two strongest passages on this point that are to be found (as I suppose) in the Bible, and surely it requires no great ingenuity to show that these passages naturally admit a very different interpretation from that which has been generally given them.

5. You can see from this subject why men need regeneration, and also what regeneration is. It is the giving up of the carnal mind, a ceasing to mind the flesh, and giving up the whole mind to obey God. It is a change from being committed to self-gratification, to the committal of the whole soul to obedience to God.

6. From what has been said, it is evident that each one is and must be the author of his own moral depravity. For it consists, as has been shown, in committing the mind, voluntarily, to self-indulgence. No one can do this for another.

7. *Physical depravity*, or a diseased state of the constitution, *is no doubt the occasion* (not the *cause*) *of moral depravity.* The propensities are no doubt depraved. They act as a temptation, to which, as a matter of fact, mankind at first universally yields.

8. Many persons who think they are the friends of God are deceived. They have never been converted. It is a great mistake; and they need only die to discover this. It were far better to learn it and correct it here, where they can repent and come to Christian faith.

9

LICENSE, BONDAGE, AND LIBERTY*

Romans 8:15

"For ye have not received the spirit of bondage again to fear; but ye have received the Spirit of adoption, whereby we cry, Abba, Father."

In a sermon preached recently, I said that the Lord had three classes of servants: bondsmen; mercenaries; and those who serve Him in love. I wish now to make another threefold distinction. Persons may be classified according to their *spirit*. Some have a spirit of license; others a spirit of bondage; and others a spirit of true Christian liberty. Into one or the other of these classes all moral agents, who have any knowledge of God, must necessarily fall. It will be my present object to develop the prominent characteristics of each class:

    I. *The spirit of license,*
    II. *The spirit of bondage,*
    III. *The spirit of true Christian liberty.*

I. *The first class have what I call the spirit of license.*
License differs essentially from liberty. License is selfishness unrestrained by moral considerations—a state in which men do as they wish, with no fear of God before their eyes, and follow out their own selfish ends without moral restraint.

Its characteristics are:

An undeveloped conscience. They have had so little moral training that their views on moral questions are yet immature, or merely negative, and not infrequently erroneous. To this class I once belonged. Many things which I have since come to regard as gross sins gave me then no trouble. My conscience was undeveloped. Nothing had then transpired to develop it. Some of my earliest impressions of moral restraint were produced by seeing my mother weep because my father would let his sons go to the lake fishing on the Sabbath. Her tears reminded me forcibly that there was something wrong in this. I was then old enough to know all about such matters of duty, but not having my attention turned to these subjects, I remained practically as if I had no conscience.

The Oberlin Evangelist: Vol. XVI; May 24, 1854.

Others have only a seared conscience. These go on much as if they had no conscience at all, although they may have had a conscience very considerably developed. They can recollect when they could not lie or swear. Tempted, they were often obliged to refrain by the demands of conscience. Now they are inclined perhaps to smile over their former notions.

Others are not restrained, although ever so much upbraided. They have no faith in the great things revealed of God. Indeed, they act as if there were no God; for although they admit His existence, they allow Him to have no practical influence on their minds. They have no practical regard for what is morally right. Having no vivid sense of moral obligation, their minds are wholly open to the impulses of selfishness. If they forbear to cheat, lie, or steal, it is not through any moral consideration, but under the influence of some form of selfishness. They manifest the spirit of license, because conscience has no practical control over them. The desire to do good has no influence. They do not care to do any good, although they know they have the power and the opportunity.

Here let me stop and ask how it is with you in this respect? What testimony does your heart and life bear when tried by such tests as these? Are you living as you know you ought not to live? Are you doing what your conscience condemns? Are you going on in your own way, despite what God may require, under a spirit of moral recklessness? Let this matter be inquired into. You may not be reckless as to other considerations; but if you are so as to *moral* considerations, the fact ought to alarm you. If the motives which ought to control you fail to do so, your heart must be fearfully wrong. If your condition is such that others, in order to influence you, must appeal to something besides conscience and the sense of duty, you may know that you are far gone in moral recklessness and ruin.

It is curious to see how this downward tendency acts on the moral nature. The perception of moral principles grows dim; moral relations seem to fade away gradually from the mind. The man will tell you he doubts whether such and such things are sinful at all. He does not quite see how there need be any wrong in them. If you try to point out to him their moral qualities and relations, you are amazed to find that his perceptions on such questions are so dull that you cannot make him see a sin. This is naturally the state of all those who have the spirit of license. For if persons have clear, sharp, moral perceptions, they will fall into one of the two latter classes. The men of license you will find have but few moral principles. Singularly, you will see that these principles have dropped out of their mind until there is little of that sort left. They can now laugh over the commission of sins which once made them sweat with agony. All moral principles become lax in their minds. Things once deemed wrong they learn to excuse. They look back on their former scruples as superstitious and foolish; and they talk largely of their *"progress"*—little thinking, alas, that their way of progress is towards hell.

Persons in youth, having the spirit of license, will manifest it in their pleasure-loving tendencies, and in their passion for dress. Amusement is often their chief delight, and of course their spirit of license develops itself in this direction. "What," they say, "were we not made that we might enjoy ourselves? Does not God like to see us happy?" But if you search carefully into their state of mind you will see that they are "lovers of pleasure more than lovers of God;" that they care little as to what will please God, but much for what will please themselves. They know how to excuse anything which it pleases them to do.

Developments of the same reckless spirit vary according to age and tastes. As to the young, they are pleasure-loving; the middle-aged are covetous and money-loving (or perhaps they aspire after distinction in their professions). Whither the heart goes, in that direction, you will find the spirit of license in sin developing itself. Under such a state of moral feeling, men will be sure to leave a broad margin for deviations from moral right. They can justify a great many dishonest ways of getting gain, or of promoting their favorite schemes of ambition.

It is striking and sad to see how their worldly-mindedness can deface and even efface all their notions of right and wrong. How they will plead for sin; defend various forms of sin and indulgence; roll their sin as a sweet morsel under the tongue—unscrupulously violate the sabbath—allow themselves almost any amount of latitude in this direction, especially if among strangers; take a little strong drink and say, "What's the harm if nobody knows it and it brings no disgrace?" In business, what will they not do if they can escape detection? If there is danger of detection, they will call it a mistake and rectify it—a thing they never do for the sake of the moral principle. In political life, they manage to subserve their ends—their object being, never the general good, but always their own personal interests. In whatever form of self-seeking, they care not for the eye of God, nor for the dictates of conscience.

The law of progress with all men of this class is from bad to worse. If you notice where they started and trace along their secret history, you will see this distinctly and fearfully illustrated. You, young men, who yield yourselves to sin, do you not see that your law of progress is from bad to worse? And you, young women, if you give yourselves up to license in sin?

Some of you have been almost surfeited with religious instruction. You have heard prayers enough and have seen tears enough to melt any heart but yours. Where will you be when once removed forever from these restraints and given up to the full sweep of that fearful law of downward progress!

For those whose conscience has been rightly developed, I have great hope. How many have we seen here who, when they first came among us, had hardly conscience enough to make them appear decent in the house of God; but not having been hardened, they began to listen, and as they listened began to feel and think. Soon you meet them in the inquiry meeting; and then soon, at the feet of Jesus.

On the other hand, some go the other way. Already hardened fearfully, they wince under the truth; their hearts rebel against it; they fall into some low form of skepticism—cast off God and His truth, and with fearful strides rush downward, downward, to the depths of hell!

Where, young men, are you? And you of every age and of all conditions professing or not professing piety, let me ask you to apply these tests to your own heart and life. Where are you? Have you the spirit of license? And more than all, let me ask, "Have you that most fearful of all symptoms of being far gone in the way of death; that, knowing your state to be as bad as it can be, yet you *do not care?*"

II. *I must next speak with some detail of those who have the spirit of bondage.*

Very commonly, yet improperly, those who have this spirit are called *conscientious Christians.* They get this name especially because they differ so widely from those who have the spirit of license. It is true; this class differs very much from that. Their conscience is not seared, but tender; it is not undeveloped or inactive, but wakeful and efficient in certain directions. Yet, they are not properly *conscientious*, because they do not go deep enough. Their conscience reaches only to the exterior of life—not to the interior. It restrains them from external conduct which they deem wrong, but does not control the heart. It is a conscience without either faith or love. Hence, their life is not spontaneously after the will of God. They are in bondage in the sense that they are not at liberty to do what they would like. Since their heart does not sympathize with God, all His ways are irksome and all their own ways are pleasant. And of course all their religious duties must come hard. Now if their hearts were truly given to God, they would be filled with the Spirit, and nothing could so please them as the things that please God. In such a state, they can serve God without bondage.

"'Tis love that makes our cheerful feet,
    In swift obedience move—"

And this obedience is the highest freedom and the purest blessedness. When the heart is right, it asks nothing wrong, and men have only to go according to their heart; or more strictly, they have only to follow the Lord, and to this the heart makes no resistance but yields with the utmost delight.

But those whose hearts are yet in sin, yet who do a bond-service—for God as they suppose, but really, for self—they would fain lessen their religious services if they might. They would stay away from religious meetings, if they could. They lust for the fleshpots of Egypt, and would return thither if they dared. They are in bondage to their consciences. For the sake of peace with their conscience, they conform to its dictates in part, in the way of compromise, pleading to be let off as much as possible, and making the best turns they can as men are wont to do with a hard master.

Again, this class are in bondage *to God*, serving Him, (so far as they render Him any service) in the spirit of slaves, not of sons. They think they *must* be religious, or do worse, and they are afraid of the worse alternative. They would do many things which God forbids, but they dare not. Thence they submit, yet the heart yields only the *form* of service.

They are in bondage to the *church*. They are afraid of censure. To have Christians watch over them is about equivalent to having spies environing their path. So far from rejoicing to have the kind and watchful eye of brethren and sisters on them, they feel this to be an unwelcome restraint.

Now, beloved, how does this test apply to your heart?

This class abound in resolutions. These constitute their principal Christian exercises. To make resolutions and to break them; to endeavor, yet to fail; to perform; to resolve and resolve, yet to go on as ever—this is their religious history. The reason is, they never break up the deep foundations of selfishness and let their souls settle down into the great depths of benevolence.

They are often greatly pressed with conviction. A deep sense of sin troubles them. Conscience upbraids. They say, or omit to say, many things for which they condemn themselves; and hence, they feel exceedingly uneasy. If they are students, they scarcely get a lesson. In fact, they are simply convicted sinners, not converted saints.

Again, their knowledge of their own case controls the judgment they form of others; and hence, they judge others harshly. They cannot conceive how a Christian can smile without sin. They do not understand that buoyancy of spirit which is so congenial to the peaceful Christian. Always dissatisfied with themselves, how can they be satisfied with others? Always conscious of doing wrong, how can they, naturally, judge otherwise of their friends? Their own mind screwed up under a feeling of bondage and a sense of constraint, they give no credit for honest piety to those who walk peacefully and calmly in the light of the Saviour's presence. Spontaneously forming harsh judgments, first of themselves, and next of others, they have no idea what a change would come over these judgments of others if once they were to come themselves into gospel liberty. Set these bond-servants to the work of Christian discipline; they almost never reclaim or reform the offender. It is quite beyond their power to *love him* down—for the love is not in them.

Or let another commence discipline in the church; and you will find them almost surely throwing themselves in the way. Their sympathies will be on the side of the wrong-doer. They will treat everything as persecution which is intended to reform and subdue.

Commonly they are strict and punctual in their religious duties, yet not willingly and joyful, but of constraint. Take the constraint away, and no such duties would be done.

In these religious duties, they get no real comfort. The true child of God gets real comfort without seeking it; this class seek it much and long, but in vain. They value it highly; they want somebody to give them comfort, and they applaud the ministers who speak comfortably to them; but, not complying with the conditions of comfort, they must fail to find it.

They have but little hope, and that is unsettled and hard to keep and of little practical worth. Anxious, unhappy, an annoyance to others, they are prone to be sour, morose and censorious. It is natural that they should misunderstand those who pass into real peace by submission to God. When they see such persons enter a state of gospel light and liberty, they are alarmed, and say, "How can he be so cheerful? What can make him so lighthearted? There must be something wrong." Now persons under the spirit of bondage have not gone far enough even to see where the peaceful Christian stands.

They are also characterized by a religious zeal and a sanctimoniousness which must needs *put on* something, and which to a discerning eye will have the air of something *put on*, and not spontaneous. It is not a natural solemnity, but a constrained formality.

Their prayers amount to this; they pray that they may be converted. But they do not so understand it, for they think they have been converted, perhaps long ago; yet, their convictions lead them to pray for just what would, if granted, be conversion. The amount of their prayer is that God would give them repentance, a new heart, gospel faith; in short, would make them Christians. They struggle earnestly, in their way, but going perpetually about to establish their own righteousness, they come not into gospel rest.

With them religion seems a hard business—as it always must seem to be, while the heart is wrong. "What," they say, "How can a man love God with all his heart? How can one love his neighbor as himself?" The best they can do is to struggle on and find no peace. One perpetual round of tasked "duty-doing" makes up their religion. In it all, there is no real service done for God from a heart devoted lovingly to His character and service. Such have only the spirit of bondage again to fear.

III. *I am next to consider the case of those who have the spirit of liberty.*

Some understand Christian liberty to be the privilege of doing as they please, right or wrong. But they greatly mistake; for this is only *license.*

Liberty, psychologically considered, is the power to do the contrary—the free ability to choose and to act otherwise than the actual choice. But, considered in reference to the Christian life, it may be better defined as the *spirit of doing right spontaneously.* The heart is united to God by thoroughly choosing His ends; and hence, it is unified with Him in sympathy and interest, even as the Son with the Father whom He respects and loves.

The Bible (here in our context) speaks of Christians as being "sons of God." It represents them as becoming "sons" both by being begotten of His Spirit in regeneration and by adoption. Indeed, the Spirit of God dwells in them, takes up His abode in their hearts; and hence, creates a living union between their souls and His. They come to have the same great reason for action—the same radical purpose and aim—that God Himself has. They have chosen the same great end and have adopted the same views. They have submitted their heart to the control and guidance of His truth and Spirit so that genuine benevolence issues from their very hearts, spontaneously. Hence, a harmony with God in their ends, aims, and affections, becomes an established, settled state; and they are really no more in bondage than Christ himself was. You need not appeal to their conscience to prick them on to duty. They have a conscience, to be sure, but it is to them a *guide*, not a *goad*: a very important distinction. Their conscience is not a goad, under which they move along, stung, wincing, bleeding; but a guide—given of God to lead their way and point out moral relations. When cordially accepted as a guide, it has no sting; it comes not to lacerate, any more than if it were wrapped in the softest silk. As soon as the heart settles and sinks sweetly into the will of God, conscience needs no rod—no scorpion sting—not even a word of command; it has only to say—"This is the way. Here you are to go—this is the will of your Father in heaven."

Persons not in this state, and strangers to it, may suppose that your conscience has fallen away and dropped out. It was said of a wife: "She is dutiful, but has no love." But suppose this woman is married to one she tenderly loves, to whom her heart is bound with bonds stronger than death. She might then say: "It seems to me that my conscience has fallen away; it seems as if I had no conscience. Formerly it was compelled to be as a goad, and not merely a guide; but now it has no such work to do as before; the heart needs only to know the way and it rejoices with great joy to walk therein."

This is a spirit of spontaneous co-operation with God. It is love acting itself out and manifesting itself in a way natural and easy. Everything is done as is supposed will please God. The mind acts on high principles. The law of love and of God is written on the heart. All obedience is natural and free, because it is spontaneous and in harmony with the supreme choice. This is the full idea of Christian liberty: acting as we please when our pleasure is to act only right; taking the right course because this pleases God, and nothing can please us but what pleases Him. The mind entrusts all its own interests and destinies with God. To Him is committed the future, otherwise all unknown and untried. To Him the mind commends the present with its toils and interests. And to Him, the past in the hope of free forgiveness through a Redeemer. Hence, the soul is free and at ease. It is conscientious in the true sense. Its state and acts are so entirely in harmony with an enlightened conscience that it comes into no collision with its dictates. "All is right," says the conscience. And of course there is peace as long as religious feeling and duty are spontaneous.

Remarks

It is hardly necessary to say that the first class which I have described—having the spirit of license—are spiritually blind and dead.

This is abundantly obvious. The second class—men in bondage—are regarded as very exemplary Christians, but they are in fact only convicted sinners. That they are not saved is very evident from the fact that they are constantly praying for salvation; that is, when they are stirred up to any religious exercise. You may try to get them to pray and to labor for others; you cannot. They fall right back to praying for themselves. After preaching one evening, I went into the library room of the church, and at the door a young lady met me, and said she wanted to speak with me. She wanted to ask me what she should do to be saved. Her father, long a leading man in the church, came by; so, after talking awhile with the daughter, I said, "Let us pray for this dear child of yours." He seemed as one confounded. I observed his strange appearance, yet thought it best to press on our work. Therefore I said: "You lead first in prayer for your daughter, and I will follow." He prayed awhile, yet for himself only. He had not the face to say even once: "Lord, have mercy on my daughter." He could only say: "Lord have mercy on *me*." Not one word could he say for her, though we were under such circumstances of heart-thrilling interest.

It is of no use to try to drive a person out of this rut; they will forever slump back into it. But as soon as they come into the liberty of the gospel, it becomes as natural as their breath to pray for sinners. A forcible illustration of this occurred in a meeting for inquiry in which I had no assistance. I spoke to them for awhile to try to lead them to Christ, and then I proposed to pray. Before I commenced, I said to them: "After I close, if any of you want to pray, just open your mouth and your heart freely." After I stopped, one of them began; prayed a minute for himself; seemed really to come in humble faith to Christ; and then immediately began to pray for the one next to him. When he stopped, this next one began in the same way, first for himself; then coming to Christ, he launched out in most earnest prayer for his next neighbor. So the thing went on for a long time, each one praying first for himself, and until his heart committed itself to Jesus; and then pouring out his prayer for sinners. It was a most affecting season, and especially instructive for showing how naturally the heart that has laid itself over upon the arms of the Saviour prays for those yet in their sins.

Those who are really in bondage often remain so through pride. They are not humble enough to disclose their real state. When a full pouring out of their souls in confession would do them good and would honor the gospel, they refrain, too proud to take their place before God and man as humbled penitents. Especially is the danger extreme when those who have held a prominent position in the church get into bondage. Often such persons never get out: I could tell you of many cases that would surprise you. They are prone to say: "If I confess, I shall stumble others. Who will believe I am converted, or will have any confidence in me, if I confess the real truth of myself?" Hence, Satan shuts them in all round about, and few persons of any class are in so great a danger of losing their souls.

Persons in bondage often seem to themselves to have a much deeper sense of sin than those who are in gospel liberty. They think so, but they are entirely mistaken. Those who are free in the gospel have altogether the keenest sense of sin. Yet the bones broken under the law are set and healed, and God has caused rejoicing where only pains were before. But if persons from this state were to fall into sin, you would see their conscience wake to a searching and a fearful retribution.

Young men, who have not associated with those Christians who were in gospel liberty and acting under the impulses of love, will almost always have false conceptions of religion. Their idea of it will lack the amenities and the charities of the true Gospel life.They do not see how anybody can be in such a state so as not to lust after the fleshpots of selfishness. They have no conception of that state in which the soul rises to a new class of aspirations and sympathies—in which it ascends far above the murky and foul atmosphere of earth, and bathes itself in the love and the light of heaven. They need to come into close communion with Christians, who are in this state, before they can properly appreciate the idea of religion.

Do you, my hearers, lack this glorious gospel light and liberty? How is it with you today? Those of you who are not professors; what attitude will you take? Is it not time that you should set your face towards your Father's house, saying, "From this day, my whole heart is Thine?" What do you say to this! Is it not time that you should get out of darkness?

Think of your bondage. Is it not time that you should awake and accept the offered boon of freedom? Jesus Christ has proclaimed you free, if you will; and is it not time that you should accept it? Will you longer remain of choice a slave?

In some of the southern states, the emancipation of a slave is so great a matter that it is done only by means of special forms and by a solemn public transaction. The master brings his slave before the court and there in a special form makes out and subscribes his papers, and thus gives the slave his freedom.

A far more wonderful transaction has taken place in another quarter; a far higher court has been in session; nay, the Supreme Executive of the universe has come forth to act in this great emancipation, and has made out true papers for giving gospel liberty to a race of lost, enslaved sinners. Have you heard of this? The thing was done many years ago, but the business still lingers unfinished. In fact, there have not been messengers enough to carry the glad news yet to every creature; and what is worse, very many to whom it has come cannot be persuaded to accept the boon. Hence, much time has been lost and the work still lingers. And now what will you do with this proposal? It comes to you; what will you do with it? Do you say, "I am not a slave"? Ah, but you are, and you *know it!* Do you say, "If I were only sure that I could get such a religion—one of true gospel liberty—I would have it?" Let me tell you *there is no other true religion*—none. All other is counterfeit. You can have this if you will.

Suppose a young man here should say: "If you can tell me what to do, I will do it. Anything I can do, I am ready to do." This would be hopeful and right; and nothing less than this can be right. How many of you will pledge yourselves to do your duty, if you should be told what it is? If you are willing to do what God requires you to do to be saved, even to the cutting off a right hand, then you can be readily directed to Christ and you may surely come and find life and peace. But many sinners come and ask what they shall do, and then, having heard, they refuse to do it. They come to the door and knock; but when bidden to come in, they say: "Oh no, I had no thought of coming in!" They turn coolly, or it may be scornfully, away. Alas, "the turning away of the simple shall slay them!" They cannot many times repel the Gospel from their hearts and dash salvation's offered cup from their lips, and yet be welcomed in, when they shall have pressing occasion to call in fearful earnest for admission.

10

ALL EVENTS RUINOUS TO THE SINNER*

Romans 8:28

"And we know that all things work together for good to them that love God, to them who are the called according to His purpose."

In my further discussion of this subject, I shall attempt to show that *all events conspire to ruin the obstinate and finally impenitent sinner.*

This is not directly taught in the text, but is implied in it, and is abundantly taught us in the Bible.

It will be my object.

    I. *To show that this is and must be a universal truth.*

    II. *To point out some particulars that will illustrate it.*

    III. *To show that we really know this to be true, even as we know its opposite to be true of the people of God.*

I. *To show that this is and must be a universal truth.*

It may be shown to be a universal truth in a great many ways. For example, moral obligation is conditioned upon knowledge, and is always equal to knowledge. Whatever, therefore, increases knowledge increases guilt, if the obligation is not complied with but the individual continues to resist the light and its claims.

Increasing guilt augments the sinner's ruin. The more guilty, the greater his punishment. Hence, whatever augments his guilt conspires and conduces to aggravate his ruin.

It cannot be doubted a moment that all events that fall under the sinner's observation, or become known to him by any means whatever in this life, will increase his knowledge of God and of course his duty and obligation. All these will consequently conspire at once to augment his guilt and damnation.

All those events that remain unknown to the sinner during his present life may become known to him in the future life, and then may work out their legitimate results—*increased knowledge—augmented guilt—more aggravated doom.*

The Oberlin Evangelist: Vol. IX; January 20, 1847. The companion sermon is in *Principles of Victory,* pp. 128-136: "All Things for Good to Those That Love God."

II. *This whole point may be rendered more plain and practical by some detail of illustration.*

All the gifts of providence conspire to work out the sinner's ruin.

Of these gifts; the first is the gift of *existence.* The existence which God gives the sinner is a blessing to him if he uses it rightly, but a fearful curse to him if he abuses it. But he does abuse it in the worst possible manner as long as he lives in sin. As long as he devotes the existence which God gives him to rebellion against his Maker—and what can be a greater and fouler abuse of existence than this—there is a fearful curse upon him. Every moment of life spent in sin must prove a curse to the sinner. It goes to aggravate his guilt and, of course, his ruin.

And no sinner can avoid this fearful result, if he will persist in sinning. Exist he must—he cannot prevent it—cannot put an end to his existence—for death only changes its *place* and mode and does not bring it to an end. *Live,* then, each sinner must, and if he will go on in sin, he must go on augmenting his guilt and consequent ruin.

Reason is another gift of providence—a precious blessing if devoted to God—if used legitimately and faithfully according to its nature and design. But if trampled down, abused, set at naught—if its demands for right and for God are all repelled and denied—how fearful the guilt which its possession and abuse involves!

In what respect do you differ from the lower orders of created beings? They have understanding; they have will; but they lack *reason.* This, then, is your preeminence above them. And will you abuse this and bring yourself quite down to a level with them in your conduct? How can you do so without awful, shameful, damning guilt?

Conscience is one of the functions of the reason. Did your conscience ever stand up and accuse you? Did it ever set your sins in order before your eyes and make you see and feel their perfect guilt? If so, then you know something of that deathless worm of your future cup; you have had a little foretaste of the horrors of self-accusation and self-condemnation. Oh, there is nothing in your existence so terrible as this! If you allow yourself to trample down this law of God developed in your reason, you will arouse against your own soul a fearful power within your own bosom that you can never resist or appease! It will be heard—that dreadful tone of self-accusation and self-reproach. What can ever allay the pungency and anguish of its tortures!

Next, look at what are most commonly intended by the gifts and bounties of providence—the things on which you are wont to lay much stress. Suppose you have health and wealth, friends and education; what are they? Are they working together for your good—your real, highest, eternal good? This turns entirely on the question of whether they lead you to repentance, gratitude, and love to God; or whether they only yield you the pleasure of sin for a season, augment your mercies, your ingratitude, your guilt, and consequent damnation. You may call these things *good,* and if you would use them in serving God and let them lead your heart to Him in love and gratitude and sweet obedience, they would be truly a *good* to you. But, if you remain a sinner, you are of course the greater sinner for having received and abused these greater mercies, and they can only work out for you a far more exceeding and eternal weight of damnation. You let the Lord load you down with His blessings here, and then abuse them so that they shall become only as millstones about your neck in the lake that burneth with fire forever. You know it must be so, and cannot be otherwise.

So it will be with all those things by which you amuse yourself and seek to augment your enjoyment in sin. You count yourself most happy if you can secure these things. But, oh! Your final disappointment will be when you shall see how they are converted into curses to your soul! These very amusements may have diverted your attention from saving your soul. They may have fanned and fed the fires of unhallowed passions. They may have made you tenfold more the child of hell than otherwise you could have been, and thus they may have exceedingly augmented your final ruin.

Again, what you deem your good forture results in the same augmentation of guilt and damnation. You deem yourself most fortunate if you can secure earthly good. But, oh! How do these things—abused—work out your deeper damnation! How they help to treasure up wrath against the day of wrath! Your Father sent that good forture to turn your eye toward His kind hand, to touch your heart with gratitude, and to lead you to repentance. You abuse and pervert every thing, and swell the fearful measure of your awful doom!

Let the wicked go on his way according to his heart's desire, filling his cup with earthly joy, and finding all things prospering in his hand; yet, saith the Word of Jehovah, "Say ye to the wicked, it shall be ill with him; for the reward of his hands shall be given him."

Yet again, the trials and the curses that fall to the sinner's lot shall all have the same result. You complain of these things as if they worked out only evil, and as if God designed them for no other end; but in this you altogether fail to comprehend the gracious designs of your Heavenly Father. He sends you earthly good to melt your heart, and you abuse it and wax more hard in sin. Why should He not change His hand and at least make trial, if possibly reverses and disappointments will not bring you to reflection; or to see whether He cannot tear you away from your idols and make you search for the living God. He does so, but all is of no avail. You only fret and complain. Not so do Christians. If God sends them mercies, they are grateful. If He sends chastisements, they are submissive. But how different is it with you! If God sends you mercies, you are thankless. You sit every day at the table which your Heavenly Father spreads and loads down for you, but you do it each day with a heart as cold as a stone. It seems to be entirely out of the question for you to think of recognizing your Father's hand, or of your own augmented obligation to serve and please Him.

If, on the other hand, He sends afflictions upon you, you complain and harden your heart. You do not humble yourself under His chastising hand. Oh, you ought to understand that these trials are a part of the discipline with which God seeks to subdue your soul to His scepter. And you ought to know that if His efforts fail, it is all evil to you, utterly and infinitely evil. Oh, indeed! If all the resources of infinite power, wisdom, and love, fail to change you, what can be more desperate than your case or more guilty than your heart?

Your whole life of impenitence is filled up with such results. Does the Lord take away your friend? Then you repine; you feel that there never was a case so aggravated as yours, and you will not bow under the hand that chastises you. How unlike the Christian, who when smitten, looks up to his own Father's hand and bows beneath it; smiles, loves, trusts, adores. But not so do you accept the punishment of your iniquity. Every effort the Lord makes to reclaim you renders you only more hardened, more guilty, more fitted for destruction.

It is indeed grievous beyond expression to see how these things work, and what results are produced by all the varied discipline which the Lord employs to save your soul. It is painful to see that all these efforts only serve to harden your heart; until the Lord is forced to say of you as in Isaiah 1, of the ancient Jews: "Why should ye be stricken any more? Ye will revolt more and more. The whole head is sick, and the whole heart faint. From the sole of the foot even unto the head, *there is* no soundness in it; *but* wounds, and bruises, and putrifying sores." The original in this passage seems to convey the idea that they had been chastised till from the crown of the head to the soles of the feet there was no longer a sound spot where another blow could be inflicted. The resources of chastisement were exhausted, and still no good result followed. So it sometimes happens that a parent will chastise his child until he has no hope that mere chastisement can do any good. This seems to be the state of mind which the Lord expresses respecting the Jews. And He often has occasion for this state of feeling towards impenitent sinners. He watches all around their path and searches out all the avenues to their heart; He tries now mercies and then afflictions, and follows up the alternations perhaps year after year through a long life—but all in vain. Ah, worse, often infinitely worse than in vain, for it only serves to augment the sinner's fearful guilt and final condemnation. Strange that sinners do not see that this is true and in the nature of the case must be. Strange that you do not see that sickness, losses, and judgments of every kind are designed to subdue your refractory spirit; and of course, if they only serve to make you the more refractory, the result can be nothing less than a fearful aggravation of your guilt and ruin.

Thus all your sins, instead of being overruled for your good, serve only to heap up a mountain load of guilt, and swell the miseries of your doom.

Again, the deeds of others, good or bad, only enhance your guilt. I beg of you to look a moment at this fact. You live among professed Christians. If they are faithful to God and to your soul, and adorn the Gospel by their life, this only hardens your heart; for you resist all the influences of their entreaties, prayers, tears, and godly life. On the other hand, if they dishonor the gospel, you take offence—you stumble over them, and become the more bold and hardened in your sins.

Now you know it would not be thus in either case with Christians. If they fell in with truly pious brethren, their hearts would be refreshed and their piety quickened; if with bad professors, the result would be to quicken them to pray, to revive their own love for Zion, and to increase their sympathy for the cause of Jesus Christ.

So also, if Christians are persecuted, it only works good to them, because it teaches them forbearance and forgiveness of injuries and trains them to love their enemies and bless those that curse them.

Far otherwise with you, sinners! In fact, you never know what it is to be benefited by any conduct, good or bad, of your fellow-beings. Everything works only evil to you. Indeed, everything works out evil and only evil to you. The law of God and the Gospel of God, the smiles of providence or its frowns, all possible conduct of your fellowmen and all possible varieties in the course of the Lord towards you; rain or sunshine, storm or calm, prosperity or adversity, each and all serve only the one dreadful end with you—that of augmenting your guilt and of course your final doom of misery.

Dreadful consideration! That your character should be such that all possible events work evil only to your soul! If you had a full and a just view of your case as it is, you might truly say, "Whatever happens is all evil to me. Whatever the times are—times of revival, or times of declension—all is evil to me: times of plenty, or times of famine—all is evil to me; times of health, or times of pestilence—all is evil to me. All conspire to fill up the measure of my guilt and aggravate my eternal doom."

Often in looking at this, I have felt as if I should sink—the view is so saddening, so awful. Sinners seem so stubborn and so refractory, and it is so obvious and sure that everything that occurs to the sinner must work evil and evil only to his guilty soul.

Again, all those providential circumstances that befall others result alike in evil to the sinner. If his neighbors are sick or if they are well, this sinner will abuse the warning voice of God through His providence. Perhaps the sinner thinks that such things as these are not going to affect his own case, but they surely will, and inevitably must. They are the voice of God to him, and he must hear or refuse God. Continuing in sin, he does the latter, and of course augments his own guilt and damnation.

It matters not how these events may affect your neighbor, whether for good or for evil; they are in either case evil and only evil to you. The same event may work good to another; yet, it shall be only evil to you. That funeral we attended this morning when a dead child of God was laid in the grave of the saints; that may have touched your sympathies, and you may have been moved to pity over so early a death, but you might much more reasonably pity yourself. When I see sinners at a funeral, I know they are often saying to themselves: "I am glad that I am not there in the place of the dead!" And yet, it may be better far that you should die now than that you should be spared any longer. Beyond all question, it is better for you to die and to be laid in the grave in the place of the first death that occurs, rather than that you should live longer to make every death you hear of only an augmented curse to yourself. Oh, how horrible this is!

So also, to live in a land of Bibles and Sabbaths and enjoy instruction and choice influences enough to make you an angel of light; and yet, abusing and perverting them all, you convert them into the worst form of curses. All the means God uses to save you are working evil to you. God means them for good, but you will curse yourself by the very means He uses for blessing you. He would fain make all the events of His providence work out for you a far more exceeding and eternal weight of glory, but despite of the endeavors of infinite love, you persist in working out of all these things your own deeper damnation.

III. *We know it to be true that all things work out evil to the sinner.* Though the text does not affirm this, yet the Bible does, and so does reason, and experience and observation. It is a truth that every man's reason must affirm. Every man knows that the occurring events of God's providence increase his knowledge of God, and hence his obligation to love and obey Him. Of course with this increase of light comes also increasing guilt in resisting its claims, and in the train of increasing guilt comes augmented ruin.

Now every sinner must know all this to be true. There is not a sinner in this house whose reason does not affirm each step in this process or argumentation to be true, and true as to himself.

This leads me to say that every man's own experience will testify that until he turns from sin by real repentance, all the course of divine providence serves only to harden his heart. He knows that the longer he resists and the more light he has to oppose, the more hardened he becomes.

So all our observation of others testifies. We see the sinner growing old in his sins, resisting one call of God after another, breaking through every restraint, setting at naught the repeated warnings of divine providence; and we always see such a sinner waxing fearfully hard of heart against God and the voice of his own conscience. I have often been shocked to see how fearfully hardened sinners sometimes become by resisting a long succession of means and influences adapted to bring them to repentance.

The truth we have been illustrating is evinced also by ample testimony from the Word of God. The Bible seems everywhere to assume that all things do and shall work evil to the sinner who will not repent. Being "often reproved and still hardening his neck, he shall be suddenly destroyed and that without remedy."

Remarks

1. I remarked in a previous sermon that Christians sometimes blame

themselves for things the occurrence of which upon the whole they do not regret; so wondrously will God overrule those evil deeds of theirs for great good. Thus God will not leave them to bitter and eternal regret over the *consequences* of their failures or their sins, though they must forever condemn their own sins and blame themselves for sinning. It is one of the great mercies of the Lord towards them that He does not leave them under the pang of everlasting regret in view of unmingled evil resulting from their misdeeds.

But sinners are left to the double anguish of everlasting self-blame and eternal regret over the utterly ruinous results to themselves of all their sins. Every event of their lives has been sin and only sin, and all have worked out the legitimate result of sinning—all evil to them and evil only and continually. Since they would not repent and would not open their hearts to the healing and restoring influences of God's providence and Spirit, the Lord could not counteract the natural tendency of sin on their heart to augment its moral hardness and consequently their own eternal ruin.

2. Sinners have never any good reason to rejoice respecting their own prospects. In fact, remaining in sin, they have nothing in which they can reasonably rejoice. Those very events of their lives in which they are most apt to rejoice will probably be those which above all others will fill them with anguish hereafter. Those very seasons of prosperity in which you rejoice most now may be your bitterest grounds for regret and sorrow when you shall come to see all their legitimate results upon your character and doom. So long then as you continue in sin, so long you have absolutely nothing to rejoice in. The more you rejoice and deem yourselves prosperous and happy in earthly good, the more will these very things pierce and sting your soul through all your future existence.

3. Others of you have no good reason to rejoice in anything that befalls you, as long as you remain an impenitent sinner. The only valuable hope you can have is that they may lead you to repentance. This failing, all will work for evil and only evil to the sinner.

It often happens that parents rejoice in events that befall their ungodly children. They rejoice perhaps to see them well settled in life or peculiarly fortunate in business. But none of these things are ever looked upon in their true light except through the medium of the great truth we are now considering. Whatever leaves them still in their sins works fearful ruin to their souls, and the more joy it seems to bring the more fearful will be its power to curse and embitter all their future being.

4. While it is true that no event, however grievous in itself, can befall a Christian which should make us grieve for him, it is equally true that no event can befall the sinner in which we are not compelled to grieve for its results upon him. Nothing can happen to him that will not fearfully curse him, if he still persists in sin. It may be ever so well adapted for his improvement, for his best good, for his happiness; yet, he shall pervert it all to the greatest of evils to his soul.

See that young man going to college. It might prove a blessing to him, but it will prove to him only a curse. It will increase his knowledge, and thus augment his guilt. It will give him greater preeminence and influence; but, if he improves this for greater sin and mischief, it will curse him at the last with tenfold destruction.

Another has married a wife—beautiful, accomplished, pious—so much the worse for him. It only serves to swell the sum of his guilt and ruin. He may live in a land of Sabbaths, and in the midst of revivals—so much the worse: he may have pious, praying parents—so much the worse.

5. Sinners need not stumble at the trials of the people of God. *No more or greater trials shall befall the Christian than are indispensable as means to work out for him a far more exceeding and eternal weight of glory. The truth is: God's people need these trials.* They must be carried through many a fiery ordeal. What then? Let them rejoice, for all shall work out for their good. Let them be made to weep; it shall work for their good. Let them be sick; it shall do them good. Let them lose their property; it shall be for their good. Let their friends die; all shall augment their good. Every Christian may say, "Whatever befalls me, the Lord will cause it to result in my greater good." Let a mighty wave dash over him, lifting high its crest and sweeping him along with torrent power; it does him good. Let another come with mighty force; it does him good. Another still; all is good. There he stands amid those mountain-waves, happy in his God, for he believes that all shall work out good to his soul. This is only the discipline his Father sends him, and why should it not cheer his soul to think how all shall work out his eternal good.

Right over against this, everything is occasion of grief and dismay to the sinner, no matter how joyous to his soul in its approach. "Whatever befalls me," he must say if he sees rightly, "all is evil to me. Be it storm or sunshine; whether I lie down in peace, or take my bed of pain and languishing, all is prospectively evil to my soul!"

How awful this condition! But it is even so; and the intelligence of every being in the universe affirms that these results are all right and as they should be.

6. All events to all eternity will make the impassable gulf between saints and sinners only the more deep and broad. *The fact is: these two classes are oppositely affected by all the providences of God, and doubtless will be so, by all that shall occur to them, throughout eternity.* God has so constituted the human mind that in its selfish state all right events shall work out only evil; while in its renewed state all shall work out good. *Difference of character lays the foundation for this wide contrast in the result. Only* the sinner himself is ultimately to blame that all things work evil to him. If he *will* do evil, then shall all things be converted into evil in their results to him.

7. It is infinite folly for men to estimate events only according to their present and most obvious bearings and relations. The result of this course is and always must be that men will constantly and fatally deceive themselves. If every sinner in this house could see all the final results of the events that are transpiring now, he would stand amazed and transfixed with horror. "What!" he would say, "Is untold anguish and

horror coming out of this cup of my earthly joy?" Oh, if sinners could clearly see these things, they would not so often bless themselves for their good fortune.

8. The arrangements of providence in respect to both saints and sinners are made with a design to illustrate the character of God. All the events of this life, and all that occur throughout eternity also, will all serve to illustrate the perfections of Jehovah. Not to have arranged all things for this end would have been a great mistake—but God never makes such mistakes. A wise and glorious end in view characterizes all he does.

9. It is the perverse course of the sinner, and nothing else but this, that makes the providences of God work out evil to him. Sinners are wont to pity themselves, and say, "Alas for me, for God has made my lot such that all things work only evil to me!" Let all sinners know that the fault is wholly and only their own, and that God has made the best possible arrangements for their good. It is only their perversion that makes the best things become to them the worst.

And sinners cannot help knowing this. After all their complaining and faultfinding, they know that they have no plea to make against God. You know, sinners, that it is all your own fault that every day is not a blessing to you—that every sun-rising and sun-setting does not come fraught with mercies to your soul. You know that you might place yourself in such an attitude towards God that all His providences should work out your real and highest good. You are now an enemy of God, but you know you may at once become His friend. I can make the appeal to every sinner's own conscience. You know that if you would not harden your own heart, all the events of divine providence would result in your good. They would bring admonitions that you would give heed to with the greatest profit to your soul, and would throw you into scenes of discipline which could not fail to prove a blessing to you. *Only yield your heart to the providences, the truth, and the Spirit of God, and you would become a child of God, and all things would work your good!*

I can well remember how it seemed to me before my conversion. I then saw most clearly that all was good to the Christian; if he was sick, all was well to him; or if in health, it was a real blessing. If he lived, it was to enjoy the friendship of God; if he died it was to enter upon his eternal reward. Being himself a friend of God, evil could no sooner befall him than it could befall his great friend, Jehovah. Nothing could be an evil to him, for if he were ever so much afflicted, it would only make him the more self-denying, meek, patient, and heavenly.

But right over against this, the opposite in every respect, is the case of the self-hardening sinner. He puts on an air of self-confidence and enjoyment; he would fain make you think that sinners are the only happy men on earth. He dances along his way for a brief season, but it is on slippery places; and suddenly his feet slide—and *he is in hell!* So transient is all the bliss that sin and Satan give! It is only a lure to endless woe.

If sinners only appreciated their real condition, they could not rest in sin one moment. All their levity would appear infinitely shocking to themselves. I recollect to have seen several cases in which sinners were in such a state of mind that they could not rejoice in any possible event. There is one lady among you who could tell you a great deal about this state of mind—a state of darkness, despair, and anguish, in which everything was clearly seen to be evil and only evil, and all things however apparently prosperous were working out evil and nothing else to her soul and her eternal state. If the sun shone sweetly, all was gloom, for that God who smiled through those sunbeams was her enemy. Each storm only reminded her of Jehovah's wrath against the sinner. If friends loved her and sympathized with her, all was evil; she had no friends above, and deserved none here below. So of everything that could occur. All was evil, undiluted and unassuaged.

But when her soul came into the light and glory of the Gospel, and found peace and joy in God, the whole scene was at once perfectly changed. Her husband has told me that he never knew her to fret or repine since that blessed hour. I asked her once what was the secret of her remarkable equanimity, she replied, "Once I escaped from the jaws of hell—from the dark iron castle of Giant Despair. Ever since I have looked upon myself as a miracle of grace, and I cannot regard any of the little troubles of life as anything to be compared with those indescribable agonies. I am often amazed to see how small a thing can disturb the equanimity of saints, or raise the mirth of sinners."

If sinners are going to continue in their sins, they may as well bid farewell at once to all peace and joy; and welcome anguish and black despair to their souls. Let them say at once, "All things are evil and nothing but evil to me." Let them give themselves up to universal mourning, no matter how soon, or how utterly. "Hail everlasting horrors, hail!"

But there is only one way of escape—open yet a moment longer. *Turn to God; yield your whole soul to Him; accept His Son as your Saviour, and His service as your choice for life*—then you are a child of God and His foe no longer. Then all things are yours, and you are Christ's, and Christ is God's. You are welcomed at once to the bosom of that glorious family above, and the possession of the riches and joys of heaven is all your own.

But if you remain in your sins, as from present appearances you are likely to do, all events and all agencies possible will work out your destruction. Every step you take brings you nearer the vortex of that awful whirlpool—the great Maelstrom of perdition. *"Your steps take hold of hell."*

11

MEN, IGNORANT OF GOD'S RIGHTEOUSNESS, WOULD FAIN ESTABLISH THEIR OWN*

Romans 10:3

"For they, being ignorant of God's righteousness, and going about to establish their own righteousness, have not submitted themselves unto the righteousness of God."

Paul states here three facts in respect to the Jews, viz.: that they were ignorant of God's righteousness, that they sought to establish their own, and that they did not submit to God's. This is a condensed statement of their religious condition. The fundamental difficulty with them was their ignorance of God's righteousness. On this rock the nation was wrecked. Not knowing Jesus, they were forever going about to establish their own righteousness—and forever unsuccessful.

What was true of the Jews is still true to an alarming extent of multitudes, both in and out of the Church, among all classes in Christian lands. It may be said that all do this who are not really Christians and receive Christ.

In discussing this subject, I inquire:

   I. *When one may be said to be ignorant of God's righteousness.*
  II. *When men may be said to go about to establish their own righteousness.*
 III. *What this righteousness of God is of which sinners are so ignorant.*
 IV. *Submission to God's righteousness is the condition of salvation.*

Let us proceed,

I. *When one may be said to be ignorant of God's righteousness.*
When he does not truly know God: particularly when he does not know Him as He reveals himself in the spirituality of His law. It was at this point the Jews failed. They did not see that the law called to the inmost heart and for perfect love there. Their carnal eye was attracted by the external and ceremonial, and the amount of visible *doing* in the Mosaic

---

*The Oberlin Evangelist: Vol. XVII; November 21, 1855.

129

system gratified their ambition for distinction and display, so that they quite overlooked those very explicit statements, everywhere frequent throughout their Scriptures, which were designed to call attention to the state of the heart as the only thing of real value in God's sight.

God's righteousness and perfect purity of character are revealed in His law, and are especially to be learned there.

Again, men are ignorant of God's righteousness when they do not understand His method of making sinners righteous. The Jews did not feel any need of such a system as the gospel. They supposed they should be accepted if they merely obeyed their ceremonial law. In this they made a grand and fatal mistake. God never gave that law for this purpose, but for another entirely different reason from this. It was only introductory to the real Gospel—intended to prepare the way for it. The ceremonial law hinted plainly at the true system, and aimed to illustrate the great principles upon which it reposes.

It is remarkable that sinners generally have no idea of God's plan of securing in them what He commands. They look no further than the precept and the penalty, and seem utterly unaware that the high aim of God is to bring them back to obedience and love. Hence God must bring them first under a felt sentence of death; but this does not make them righteous; it only prepares the way for bringing them to Christ.

Again, men are ignorant of God's righteousness when they fail to understand the conditions on which He can treat them as righteous; that is, can justify and save them. This was the mistake of the Jews and is the mistake of all sinners. They do not understand how it is that God proposes to make them righteous, and turn them from all their sin.

II. *I am next to inquire, When men may be said to go about to establish their own righteousness.*

First, what is meant by *establishing* one's own righteousness?

Suppose you see a man come into a court of justice. He is accused. He pleads *not guilty.* In some way he justifies his conduct. Perhaps he will even attempt to prove his own entire righteousness in the whole transaction, so that he can face the judge down and insist that in every particular he has done nothing wrong and only what is right. This would be going about to establish his own righteousness.

Sinners go about to establish their own righteousness when they bring in pleas of excuse for their sin. If a man can show his right under the circumstances to do as he does, this goes to establish his righteousness. So sinners go about to parry conviction—to bring in extenuating and justifying circumstances. Of this, God accuses them: "Wilt thou condemn Me, that thou mayest be righteous?"

Legitimately, the bearing of an excuse goes to arraign God. What do you mean, sinner? Do you think God can accept your apology, and admit himself to be wrong? If not, why do you present it? Why bring it up before your Almighty Judge, to insult Him to His very face, by impeaching His equity?

Every sinner who brings forward any form of excuse for his own sin, is really trying to establish his own righteousness.

Again, men are trying to establish their own righteousness when they depend on *doing* for acceptance with God. How often do they tell you they mean to do right, showing plainly by their manner, and by the use they make of this supposed intention, that they think hereby to secure favor with God. They turn off His claims with this plea, and do not at all believe they are in danger of being sent to hell. Now is this anything else but going about to establish their own righteousness?

The same must be said of those who depend on their own *reformation*. I often meet with young persons, who before they came here had been much more loose in many points of moral conduct, as for instance, the observance of the Sabbath, but coming here they attempt to *reform*, and this greatly relieves their consciences. Of course, now they are in a good way, and think themselves almost sure of heaven; whereas, this reform may be wholly due to their love of a fair reputation. Mingling here with people who themselves observe the Sabbath, and who have established this general usage, they are forced to conform, and do so, without any more regard for *God* than they had before.

Such persons I have seen pass through other stages of self-righteous endeavor. They become convicted of sin, and begin to pray perhaps. Still they are uneasy, and, therefore, resort to some forms of external reformation. How very common is this among the masses of awakened sinners! Many of you who are before me have had this sort of experience. How long it took you to understand that you were all wrong, and that nothing would avail for you short of a most radical change of heart!

In the same train of feeling, men depend on having done nothing worthy of condemnation. Indeed! What is this but going about to establish their own righteousness? They think they have done nothing that can justify God in sending them to hell. On this point, they take issue with God, assuming that they have done nothing very wrong. They must know that, in God's sight, sin deserves hell, else He would not have built hell, nor have made it the penalty of sin. How, then, should they dare to dispute this point with God, and arraign Him on the implied charge of injustice?

The same thing is seen, under a slightly different form, when men depend on their general integrity of character. They have been honest and kind, and, on the whole, so good that they think God cannot send them to hell, but will strike the balance in their favor. They have done a great many things that are right. On the whole, they have done more good than hurt, and, therefore, they are sure it cannot be right for God to send them to hell. Their life shows more obedience than disobedience—as they insist.

Indeed, sinner! What do you know of personal holiness? What experience have you of a pure heart—of real love to God—of sincere regard for His will? Surely, you are only going about to establish your own righteousness.

Again, sinners evince the same spirit when they hold on to the idea that they are about as good as professors of religion. Some they know of, who are not any better than they should be, and they think their own case might compare favorably with them. Such sinners are going about to establish their own righteousness.

Also, sinners depend on their religious observances. Many have learned better than to rely on their honesty or morality; so they resort to their religious observances. Even Protestants do this, and just as really make a merit in these observances, as the poor man who expects to go to heaven by kneeling before the holy altar, kissing the holy water, and saying his *Ave Marias*. This Protestant prays just like the Catholic; that is, with the same purpose, and the same state of heart; he reads his Bible on the same principle, and in the same way goes through what he calls his "religious duties."

This was the mistake of the Jews. They fasted twice in the week, and were greatly given to prayer and alms to the poor. In these services, their scribes, priests, and Pharisees, spent a great share of their time. Thrice a year they went up to Jerusalem to the solemn feasts. Religious duties absorbed a large share of their time and money. You would be appalled to learn how much their temple cost, and their religious worship, sacrifices, and offerings. On all these they placed the utmost dependence. But evermore, when men rely on other methods of salvation than God's, they are really going about to establish their own.

III. *I am next to inquire what this righteousness of God is, of which sinners are so ignorant.*

In general, God's righteousness is synonymous with His infinite moral purity; but, in such connections as this, it seems to mean more specifically His integrity as a moral Governor. He is bound to sustain the interests of His government in its relations both to the unfallen and to the fallen. Under the most solemn obligations to do His utmost to secure universal obedience as a necessary means to the highest happiness, He cannot suffer law to be broken, nor rebels to live—except on the ground of some satisfaction made that shall amply sustain the sanctity and honor of law. Of course, this quality of His character, as a moral Governor, determines the great features of His plan of saving sinners. It stands revealed in His law and in His Gospel. This righteousness of God renders it forever certain that no sinner can be accepted on the ground of any works of his own. God's claims are so high, and the sinner has fallen so low, that God can never accept any work of his hands. Even his prayers—out of Christ—and his best works are all odious to God. He is trying to put God off with something less than a perfect heart.

By the very terms and spirit of the law, it demands perfect obedience, and the exigencies of God's great kingdom require no less. The law, in both its precept and penalty, must be honored, or no sinner can be saved. I do not mean that God will insist that the utmost measure of the penalty shall be visited on the sinner's own person; but it must be this, or a substitute that will answer the one great end of fully sustaining the dignity, influence, and authority of His law. His throne must be infinitely removed from all supposable connivance with sin.

Hence, it became necessary that our Surety should honor the law, as to its penalty, by offering His humanity on the altar of His divinity. In His own person, too, He obeyed the law fully.

Hence, sinners, to be saved, must return to real obedience. God's righteousness requires this.

We can now apprehend God's method of making sinners personally righteous. First, He opens the way by giving His Son to honor the law, so that God can come down from heaven and enter into covenant with the sinner and draw him back to life and love. This is God's method—that Christ be received as the sinner's righteousness, having borne for him the curse of the law, obeying it perfectly, and then suffering in place of the penalty, which the sinner else must have suffered. The sinner, by faith accepting Christ, becomes, in the governmental respect, united to Christ, so that, for Christ's sake, God accepts them both. Families sometimes come into such a relation to government that the children stand in the stead of the parents, and are rewarded or forgiven for their parents' sake. Similar is the relation sustained by Christ and the believing sinner to the government of God. Christ is "set forth to be a propitiation for us through faith in His blood," in this sense, that the merits of His death are made over to us, on condition of our believing, and we have the full benefit of all that Christ has suffered and done to honor the law. We now abandon all hope of justification from personally obeying the law, and receive Christ as God's mode of making us right before the law. He is given to us as a Redeemer and Saviour. He is treated in this transaction as if He had been a sinner, we, as if we were righteous.

Thus we stand before God as if *in Christ*. Paul said, "If any other man thinketh he hath whereof he might trust in the flesh, I more; . . . touching the righteousness which is in the law blameless; but what things were gain to me, those I counted loss for Christ, that I may be found in him, not having mine own righteousness, which is of the law, but that which is through the faith of Christ—the righteousness which is of God by faith."

Thus by a governmental act, God merges in Christ the whole mass of believers—He having become our Surety, our Advocate, Mediator and King. In this wonderful arrangement, God turns the whole race around from looking to the law for justification, to looking unto Christ.

IV. *Submission to God's righteousness is the condition of salvation.*

So the apostle implies: "For they, being ignorant of God's righteousness, and going about to establish their own righteousness, have not submitted themselves unto the righteousness of God." Here you cannot fail to observe that this method of salvation is something to be *submitted* to. The will must yield its full assent to this plan.

The constant effort of sinners is to *do* something of their own—some work of some sort, or get up some experience. This is the great idea which they aim to realize as soon as they are convicted. Hence, they cannot have peace of mind, nor real pardon, because they do not meet God's plan. They struggle against God's Spirit, and resist His influence; they turn and shift in all possible ways to get up some righteousness of their own. The seventh chapter of Romans is only a picture of one who is struggling and floundering as in a spiritual quagmire—binding himself with promises and resolves, and yet finding them all of no avail. What masses of even professed Christians are in precisely this condition! They make not a prayer in which they do not feel condemned. Their state is one of conviction and despair; so deeply agonizing that they can have no peace. They are struggling to effect an impossibility—to establish, in some way, their own righteousness; and failing in this, they sink down into despair. Hence, it comes to pass that the last step a man takes before submission to God is usually a mighty effort to establish his own righteousness; which effort ends in despair, after which, he consents to submit to God's plan of being made righteous. How often have I seen this in professors who thought they knew what religion is, but in the clear light of these truths have seen their mistake. If they come really to despair of help in themselves, and then cast their souls on God through Christ, all is well. Probably most ministers find cases of this sort. Great numbers of them have fallen under my observation. How many have I seen who struggle and struggle, long, and without relief, because they struggle in a wrong direction. They are ignorant of God's righteousness, and therefore go about to establish a righteousness of their own. A striking case now occurs to me, of a lady, now on mission-ground, a lady of many noble traits of character, but before her conversion, strong in her self-righteousness. Hearing of the great revivals in Oneida County, some thirty years ago, she went to see them. Her object was to learn what this new and strange movement might be. She heard sermon after sermon, but writhed under their pointed truths, often finding fault with the preaching as being too personal, and as being full of wrong things. Conviction, however, sank deeper and yet deeper. Soon a friend with whom she was boarding said to me, "We have a dreadful case at our house. You must come and see her." I went. I found she had set herself to defend the idea that she did not deserve to be damned, for if she was a sinner, it was only because she was made so, and born so. Being cornered up on these points, and shown her error, she became more agonized; the struggle was fearful! At last she screamed at the top of her voice, and yielded! Then a change came over her—a charming, glorious change, which no language can describe. Almost her first words, as she broke silence again, were, "I'll be a missionary!" But few months passed ere this vow was fulfilled, and she has lived a missionary to this day. Her self-righteousness, like a mighty tower of strength, came down wonderfully; and when Jesus became her righteousness, she was a lamb at His feet. Such a change in the whole person, manifest in every aspect, is truly wonderful.

Often it happens that you see professors of religion moving heaven and earth by their self-righteous efforts to get up some righteousness of their own. You will be struck, in examining their religious system, to see how utterly Christ is left out of it, as a practical Saviour. They think of their good and right things—not of Christ—as really the ground of their hope before God.

This method of God's righteousness is exactly opposed to human pride. Pride loves to do the work and have the honor of it; but God's system has done all the meritorious work itself—leaving nothing for man to do that he can be proud of.

It is for this reason that conversion costs such a conflict. Often it seems indispensable that God should startle sinners with awful fears before they will yield. On Mt. Sinai and all around, the trump of God waxes louder and louder, the mountain is all ablaze, and rocks quake under Jehovah's mighty voice long and loud, till every nerve of the sinner trembles, and he sees nothing but darkness—until the atonement reveals a living Christ to his agonizing soul.

This gospel plan seems to sinners as deep and as dark as midnight, until the Holy Ghost reveals to him his self-righteousness, cleaves down that self-righteous spirit, knocks out his props, and he falls and dies! Then the cross reveals life, and he rejoices with exceeding joy in a salvation wrought of God through redeeming blood.

This righteousness of God must be *submitted to*. The sinner must submit "to that righteousness which has sentenced him to hell." He must admit it to be right and just. I often ask sinners, "Are you prepared to subscribe to that righteousness which dooms you to hell?" If I find him wavering on that point, I say to him, "You do not understand God's righteousness. You cannot be saved until you subscribe to God's righteousness in this, and until you fully admit its justness and propriety. You must yield also to His supreme authority and right to govern all His creatures, and consent to be saved wholly by grace—things which many fail to understand. In England, I found, to my surprise, that many ministers talked much of grace, yet did not believe that men deserve damnation for their sins. I said to them, "What do you mean by this? You talk largely of grace, yet deny all need of it! For, grace is the antithesis of justice. How can there be grace shown the sinner, if it be not just to punish him?"

The point of greatest struggle with the sinner is in laying aside as worthless his own righteousness. You recollect the case of the poor Indian and his rich white neighbor, both awakened and convicted at the same time, but the Indian came at once to Jesus, while the white man remained a long time in extremest darkness and distress. At last, he asked the Indian how it happened that he had found Christ so soon, while himself had sought so long in vain. The Indian stammered his reply, "Indian poor; white man rich; poor Indian no clothes; white man good clothes, fine clothes; Indian throw his old rags right away, take Christ's robe at once; white man can't throw away his fine clothes."

You recollect, also, the case of the poor woman in the gospels. Christ had been invited to a rich man's table; they sat reclined at their meal, with their feet somewhat extended behind them, when this woman came up gently, clasped His sacred feet, bathed them with her tears, and wiped them with her hair. of her head. Blessed woman! She knew her position as a lost sinner, and she had tasted the grace that forgives freely. What an act was that! She did not seem to know or care if the whole world saw her! Her humility of spirit charms us, and we read in her case the feeling of those who discard all righteousness of their own, and come to understand the righteousness of God.

Remarks

The ignorance of the Jews came from their great pride, and is not at all to be ascribed to the obscurity of the subject itself. The ignorance of sinners now, even under the Gospel, is amazing. I have recently seen one who had been well instructed in the letter of these things, yet when he became deeply hungry for gospel life, seemed scarcely to know how to use one of the plainest truths it embraces. It was affecting to see him drink in a few of the simplest gospel truths, saying, "I am sure I never heard of that before—never thought of that." How common it is for sinners, under the Spirit's light, to say, "All this is new to me; I wonder, I was never told of this before!"

Many feel the need of becoming truly religious; they mean to be, and they set themselves to work for it in some way. Perhaps they set themselves to serve God, but have no right idea of what it is to be truly religious. Hence, we find so few who seem, in their own experience, to know the deep power of that Gospel. Ah, the deep foundations of their selfishness are not broken up. They have never been made conformable to Christ's death. Hence, the difference between this class, and those who are utterly cut down and slain by the law and then raised from the dead to a new life in Christ.

When the sinner is truly convicted of sin, the way is open before him, and the first conditions are fulfilled for his free pardon. Now, he has new apprehensions of God's law—of its great spirituality. But it is not enough to know this; another lesson yet remains. I am glad to see you cut down under thorough conviction, but you must also learn not to fly in the face of that fiery law for salvation! Sinner, professed Christian, do you know *how* you are to be saved? You need not make any atonement; you need not suffer and toil to work up an atonement; no need of this at all. In my own first convictions, I said, under my great sorrow, "I shall have to bear a great deal of this, I have been a sinner so long; I shall have to be nearly killed before I can be saved." Ah, how mistaken! God wants no such atonement—no such suffering of you. *The atonement is all made, ready to your hands!* Do you understand that no works, or prayers, or tears of your own can do anything for you towards an atonement, and towards constituting a ground of your acceptance before

God? God Himself has provided the Lamb for the offering. Now come, as the ancient Jew came, and lay your hand on that dear sacrifice, and there confess your sins. The veil of the great temple is rent away, and you may enter the inner sanctuary; may come quite to the mercy-seat and lay your own hand on the head of the victim that takes away the sin of the world. *Will you come?*

12

THE WAY TO BE HOLY*

Romans 10:4

"For Christ is the end of the law for righteousness to everyone that believeth."

In this discussion I am to show,

    I. *What is not intended by the assertion that Christ is the end of the law for righteousness.*

    II. *What is intended by this assertion.*

    III. *How Christ becomes the end of the law for righteousness.*

I. *What is not intended by the assertion that Christ is the end of the law for righteousness.*

1. Not that He abolishes the law in respect to believers. I am aware that some antinomians in the Church affirm this, but it cannot be true for the following reasons.

(1.) *The moral law is not founded in the arbitrary will of God,* for if it were He would have no rule of conduct, nothing with which to compare His own actions. But every moral agent must have some rule by which to act. Character implies moral obligation, and moral obligation implies moral law. Again, unless the law is obligatory on Him, benevolence in Him is not virtue, for virtue must be compliance with obligation. Nor should we have any standard with which to compare His actions, and by which to judge of them, so that we could know whether He is holy or unholy. Moreover, if He is capable of benevolence, it is impossible that He should not be under a moral obligation to be so; and if so, the law cannot, of course, be founded in His arbitrary will. Furthermore, He could, if the law were founded in His arbitrary will, by willing it, make benevolence vice and malevolence virtue, right wrong and wrong right. But this is absurd and impossible.

(2.) *The moral law is founded in God's self-existent nature.* He never made His own nature; and consequently, never made the law, and it must therefore be obligatory upon Him by virtue of His own nature which imposes it. It is as really obligatory on Him as on us.

(3.) He requires benevolence of us, because it is naturally obligatory on us. He made us in His own image; that is, with a nature like His own.

The Oberlin Evangelist: Vol. V; March 29, 1843.

Therefore, He could not discharge us from obligation to keep the law if He would, because our own reason would still reveal and impose it on us. We should perceive its obligation.

(4.) If He could and should abolish the moral law, then we could have no moral character. We could neither be sinful nor holy any more than brutes can. Observe then, Christ cannot be the end of the law in the sense that He abolishes it.

2. It is not intended that He abolishes the penalty with respect to believers so that they can sin without actual condemnation. Some have this view of justification; that at the first act of faith God sets aside the penalty and it can never afterwards attach to the individual no matter what he does. But this cannot be, for:

(1.) If the penalty is set aside, then the law is repealed, for law consists of precept and penalty.

(2.) If the penalty were so set aside, then Christians when they sinned would not need pardon; and they could not without folly and even wickedness pray for forgiveness. It would be nothing else but sheer unbelief in their own doctrine. But every Christian knows that when he sins he is condemned, and must be pardoned or damned. Christ, therefore, is not the end of the law in this sense.

3. Nor is He the end of the law for justification merely, for He does not obtain for them a legal justification. Legal justification is the act of pronouncing one just in the estimation of law. This Christ cannot do in respect to any transgressor. Gospel justification is pardon and acceptance. But it never was the end or object of the law to pardon sinners. In this sense, then, it is impossible that Christ should be the end of the law, for *the law never aimed at pardoning transgressors.* The word righteousness sometimes means justification, but it cannot mean that here because Christ never aimed at legal justification, nor did the law aim at pardon. He cannot, of course, be the end of the law in this sense.

4. Nor is He the end of the law in the sense of procuring a pardon for those that believe, for this was never the end *proposed by the law.* The law knows nothing of pardon.

5. Nor is it intended that He imputes His own righteousness or obedience to them. Some suppose that Christ was under no obligation to obey the law Himself, and that He can; therefore, impute His obedience to believers. But,

(1.) The *law never aimed at imputation.* This was no part of its object. *Did the law require Christ's righteousness or personal holiness to be imputed?*

(2.) The doctrine of imputed righteousness is founded on the absurd assumption that Christ owed no obedience to the law. But how can this be? Was He under no obligation to be benevolent? If not, then His benevolence was not virtue. He certainly was just as much bound to love God with all His heart, and soul, and strength, and mind, and His neighbor as Himself, as you are. How holy should God be? As holy as He can be. That is, He should be perfectly benevolent as the Bible says He is.

(3.) This doctrine assumes that Christ's works were works of super-erogation. Is this what the Apostle means when he says, "For such a High Priest became us, who is holy, harmless, undefiled, separate from sinners?"

(4.) This doctrine is a mere dogma of Popery; born, bred, and supported amid its darkness and superstitions. The sufferings and death of Christ were for us and constitute the atonement. His obedience was necessary to His making an atonement, *as a condition,* since none but a Holy Being could make it. Holiness is benevolence, and Christ must of necessity have been benevolent in order to make the atonement, which is a work of benevolence.

(5.) The doctrine of imputed righteousnes represents God as requiring,

(a) That Christ should render a perfect obedience for us.

(b) Then that He should die just as if no such obedience had been rendered.

(c) That, notwithstanding, the debt is thus paid twice over by our substitute; we must repent as though it were unpaid.

(d) Then that we must be forgiven.

(e) And after all this, that we must ourselves obey, or be personally holy.

(f) And finally, that we must count it all grace.

What a jumble of nonsense is this! Is this the Gospel of the blessed God? Impossible!

(6.) The doctrine of imputation utterly sets aside the true idea of the Gospel. The true idea of pardon does not enter into it. It is rather a five-fold satisfaction of justice. We are not restored to the favor of God according to this doctrine by a free pardon, but by imputed righteousnes. It is not at all amazing that thinking men, when they hear such slang as this, say, "Oh, nonsense! If that be the Gospel, we can have nothing to do with it."

(7.) Imputation is not, and never was, the end or object of the law. The end which it seeks is righteousness or true obedience.

II. *What is intended by the assertion that Christ is the end of the law for righteousness.*

The text affirms that He is the end of the law *for righteousness.* Righteousness is obedience to the law. He is, then, the end of the law for obedience. He secures the very end aimed at by the law; that is, He makes Christians holy; as it is said, "There is therefore now no condemnation to them which are in Christ Jesus, who walk not after the flesh, but after the Spirit. For the law of the spirit of life in Christ Jesus hath made me free from the law of sin and death. For what the law could not do in that it was weak through the flesh, God sending His own Son in the likeness of sinful flesh, and for sin, condemned sin in the flesh, that the righteousness of the law might be fulfilled in us, who walk not after the flesh, but after the Spirit." What have we here? Why, an express assertion of the Apostle, that Christ by His atonement and indwelling Spirit had secured in Christians the very obedience which the law required.

III. *How Christ becomes the end of the law for righteousness or obedience.*

1. Confidence or faith is essential to all hearty obedience to *any* law. An *outward* conformity to its requirements may be secured by fear.

2. Christ, then, must secure love or true righteousness by inspiring confidence in the character and government of God. God had been slandered by Satan, and the world believed the slander. Satan represented to our first parents that God was insincere in forbidding them to eat of the tree of knowledge, and that the result of their eating of it would be just the reverse of what God had threatened. Said he, "God doth know that in the day ye eat thereof, then your eyes shall be opened, and ye shall be as God,knowing good and evil!" This was a most taking temptation! "And when the woman saw that the tree was good for food, and that it was pleasant to the eyes, and a tree to be desired to make one wise, she took of the fruit thereof, and did eat." Now the thing to be done is to remove this prejudice which has existed in all ages. How shall it be effected?

3. Christ came to reveal the true God and the true character of His government for this express purpose. He came not only to teach, but, by His example, to give an illustration of what the law meant; and to possess the human mind of the idea that God is love. He knew very well that confidence was the thing needed; and that He had to reveal the character of God so as to beget confidence. He must hold it out in strong relief in a life of love before them. There was a greater necessity for this, because many of the dispensations of God towards mankind appeared severe. He had poured out the waters of the flood upon the old world and destroyed it. He had frowned upon the cities of the plain and sent them down to hell. In many other instances, He had been obliged to resort to such measures as were calculated, in the circumstances,to beget a dread and slavish fear, rather than to inspire confidence and love. It was, therefore, necessary to adopt measures of a different nature adapted to beget faith.

4. The nature of faith renders obedience certain, so far as it is implicit. A wife, for example, is always perfectly under the influence of her husband, insofar as she has confidence in him. Suppose he is a businessman; if she has confidence in his business talents, she does not concern herself at all in his business transactions. So, if they are going on a journey and she knows him to be careful and attentive to his affairs, then she will not fret. She will never ask whether he has taken care of their baggage and whether he has procured tickets and accommodations. She expects all this, as a matter of course, and is happy in her reliance on him. But suppose she had no confidence in his character. If he is a man of business, and she lacks confidence in his judgment, then she will be all

the time in distress for fear he will take some step which will ruin their affairs. If they are going on a journey, then she will, perhaps, fear that he will start off without his wallet, or forget some of his baggage, or that he will lose them on the way. It is easy to see that, so far as this lack of confidence extends, its tendency is to diminish her affection; and if it extends to his whole character, then she cannot love him. I might illustrate this in a thousand ways. If you call in a physician, and you have confidence in him, then you will take any medicine which he may prescribe. I recollect a case which perhaps some of you are familiar with. A certain king was sick, and he sent for a physician. The physician examined his symptoms and found his disease a dangerous one requiring a particular treatment. He told the king he would go home and prepare a certain medicine which would make him very sick while in its operation, but would remove the disease. While he was gone, the king received a letter warning him against the physician as though he designed to poison him. When the physician returned and presented him the medicine, he immediately swallowed it, and then handed his physician the letter which he had received. That was faith; and it placed him entirely under the control of his physician. It is easy, therefore, to see that if Christ could only restore faith among men, then He would, of course, secure obedience.

5. Faith in God's character is the foundation of faith in His promises. Many people seem to go the wrong way to faith. They try to exercise faith in the promises along with faith in His general character. But Christ takes the *opposite course;* revealing the true character of God as the foundation of faith in His promises.

6. He baptizes them by His Spirit and actually works in them to will and to do. How wonderfully Christ seems to work to get the control of believers. Unless He can get into their confidence He cannot do this, but as soon as He can inspire faith He has them under His control. We see the same law among men. See a human pair, by securing mutual confidence, wind imperishable cords around each other's hearts. Then, for one to know the will of the other is to do it. They do not need to be bound down nor driven by the force of penalties. This is the way of the seducer who can "smile and smile and be a villain still." He lays his foundation deep in the confidence of his victim until he may laugh at all that her parents may say and do against him. He gains such an ascendency so as to control the will more absolutely than if he could wield it by his hand. Such is the natural result of getting *into* the confidence of another. They will and do at our bidding. Thus Christ gains the heart, and works in us to will and to do of His good pleasure.

7. The way to be holy, then, is to believe. "Then said they unto Him, what shall we do, that we might work the works of God? Jesus said unto them, this is the work of God, that ye believe on Him whom He hath sent." "That they may receive forgiveness of sins, and inheritance among them which are sanctified by faith that is in Me." "This only would I learn of you; received ye the Spirit by the works of the law or by

the hearing of faith? Are ye so foolish? Having begun in the Spirit, are ye now made perfect by the flesh? Have ye suffered so many things in vain? if it be yet in vain. He therefore that ministereth to you the Spirit, and worketh miracles among you, doeth He it by the works of the law, or by the hearing of faith? Even as Abraham believed God, and it was accounted to him for righteousness. Know ye therefore that they which are of faith, the same are the children of Abraham. And the scripture, foreseeing that God would justify the heathen through faith, preached before the gospel unto Abraham, saying, In thee shall all nations be blessed. So then they which be of faith are blessed with faithful Abraham. For as many as are of the works of the law, are under the curse: for it is written, Cursed is every one that continueth not in all things which are written in the book of the law to do them. But that no man is justified by the law in the sight of God, it is evident: for, The just shall live by faith. And the law is not of faith: but, the man that doeth them shall live in them. Christ hath redeemed us from the curse of the law, being made a curse for us: for it is written, Cursed is every one that hangeth on a tree: that the blessing of Abraham might come on the Gentiles through Jesus Christ; that we might receive the promise of the Spirit through faith." "What shall we say, then? That the Gentiles which followed not after righteousness, have attained to righteousness, even the righteousness which is of faith; But Israel which followed after the law of righteousness, hath not attained to the law of righteousness. Wherefore? Because they sought it not by faith, but as it were by the law: for they stumbled at that stumbling-stone. As it is written, behold I lay in Zion a stumbling-stone, and rock of offense, and whosoever believeth on Him shall not be ashamed." In Christ, then, the believer is complete; that is, He is all we need. His offices and relations meet all our necessities, and by faith we receive their redeeming influences.

Remarks

1. From this subject, we may see why the Gospel lays so much stress on faith. It is the only way of salvation.

2. This method of saving men is perfectly philosophical. And, as we have seen, Christ thus works Himself into the very heart of believers.

3. It is the only possible way, in the very nature of the case, to secure love. God might command and back up the command with threatenings, but this would only fill the selfish mind with terror, leaving its selfishness unbroken, and even grasping at its objects amid the roar of its thunders. In the very *nature* of mind, then, to secure obedience, He must secure confidence. Why, look at Eve. The moment she doubted, she fell. And so would all heaven fall if they should lose confidence in God. Yes, they would *fall!* They would no more retain their obedience, than the planets would retain their places, if the power of gravitation were broken. Everyone knows that if the power of attraction were destroyed, suns, stars, and planets would run lawless through the universe

and desolation would drive her ploughshare through creation. So, break the power of confidence in heaven, and every angel there would fall like Lucifer, and universal anarchy prevail.

4. What I have said does not represent virtue or holiness as consisting in mere emotions of complacency or in loving God merely for His favors; but the exhibition of His character in Christ begets in us real benevolence. It shows us what benevolence is, and stimulates us to exercise it. Nearly all preachers and writers of the present day confound religion with mere complacency in God for His favors. Both gratitude and complacency may, and often do, exist in the impenitent mind. It must, therefore, be a fundamental mistake to confound these with true religion.

5. Christ, by exhibiting His benevolence, begets His own image in them that believe; that is, they are naturally led to yield themselves up to the transforming tendency of this view of His character. This, the law could never secure in a selfish mind.

6. I said the doctrine of imputed righteousness is another Gospel or no Gospel at all. And here I would ask, "Is not this quite another way of salvation?" According to this way, instead of imputing righteousness to them, God makes them righteous.

7. The Gospel is not an evasion of the law. It comes in as an auxiliary to accomplish what the law aims at, but cannot effect, because it is "weak through the flesh."

8. We see who are true believers. Those who love God supremely and their neighbor as themselves; and unless your faith begets obedience, it is not the faith of the Gospel.

9. We can see the sustaining power of faith. This is not well considered by many. If the head of a family secures its confidence, he controls it easily; but if not, there is a perpetual tendency to resist him. The same principle operates in state governments. They are firm insofar and no farther than they are based upon the confidence of their subjects. So it is in the business world. Everything is prosperous as long as confidence is secured. When confidence goes, the tide immediately sets forth the other way. Why are so many houses in this country, which were once supposed to be perfectly stable, tumbling down around the heads of the merchants? Because confidence is destroyed. Restore that, and immediately things will assume a different aspect. Every merchant in New York will feel the impulse, and ships from abroad will come freighted down with merchandise. This principle is equally efficient and necessary in the divine government. This, the devil well understood. Hence his first effort was directed to its overthrow. But ministers too often put it in the back-ground, and hence the reason of so much failure in the work of reforming the world. Christ, on the other hand, always put it foremost, and His declaration, "He that believeth shall be saved," is the unalterable law of His governement.

10. Unbelievers cannot be saved for their want of confidence necessarily keeps the soul from hearty obedience.

11. Do you ask, "How can I believe?" I turn on you, and ask, "How can you help believing?" Christ has died for you to win your confidence. He stands at your door offering blessings, and assuring you of His good will. And you can't believe! What! And the Son of God at the door! But perhaps you stand back, and say, "Christians can believe, but how can I a poor, guilty wretch?" And why not you? Come, let your anchor down upon the character of God, and then if the winds blow, let them blow. If the ocean tosses itself, and yawns till it lays bare its very bottom, you are secure for God rules the winds and the waves. But I hear someone say, "I am such a backslider." Yes, and you are likely to be. Unless you believe, you will continue to go right away from God. Come, instantly, and believe. Come, all you professors; come, all you sinners; come now, and He will write His law in your hearts; and it will no longer be to you a law on tables of stone. Can't you believe it? Yes; Oh, yes. Then let us come around the throne of grace, and receive Christ as the end of the law for righteousness.

13

HOW TO PREVENT OUR EMPLOYMENTS FROM INJURING OUR SOULS*

Romans 12:11

"Not slothful in business; fervent in spirit; serving the Lord."

In remarking upon this subject, I design to show:
I. *That idleness is inconsistent with religion.*
II. *That all persons are bound to pursue some lawful employment.*
III. *That they are to be diligent in their calling whatever it is.*
IV. *How to prevent employments, either secular or spiritual, from becoming a snare to the soul.*

I. *Idleness is inconsistent with religion.*
1. Because it is wholly inconsistent with love to God. Whoever loves God with all his heart will certainly set himself to do the will of God and will no more be idle than God will be idle.
2. It is wholly inconsistent with love to man. The love of our race will certainly lead us to exert ourselves to promote man's happiness.
3. Idleness can result only from selfishness. A man must love his own ease supremely to be idle in a world like this.
4. Idleness is sponging out of the community in which we live. A man that does not earn his bread, who does not contribute as much to the happiness and good things of the world as he consumes, who lives upon the common stock without contributing his share, is a drone. If he is not engaged in some employment that promotes the well-being of man, he is subtracting continually from the common stock of blessings and sponging from the universe of God.
5. Idleness is injustice. This follows from what has just been said. A man has no more right to live by sponging than he has to live by stealing. Indeed it involves the same principle.
6. It is absolute and downright disobedience to God. God as much forbids idleness as He does theft or murder; and a man or a woman can

---

The Oberlin Evangelist: Vol. I; November 6, 1839. Also, *The Promise of the Spirit,* pp. 231-239.

no more be religious without pursuing some employment by which God may be glorified and the world benefited than a habitual drunkard can be religious.

II. *All persons are bound to pursue some lawful employment.*
This is a plain inference from what has already been said. But what is a lawful employment? This is an all-important question, in answer to which I observe,

1. To be lawful, an employment must not be injurious to our own best interests or the best interests of mankind.

2. Speculation is not a lawful employment. To embark in uncertain speculations involves in it the principle of gambling and is eminently *the spirit* of gambling. It is a game of chance, where one of the parties must gain and the other lose and where selfishness stalks abroad naked to grasp every man's wealth without blushing.

3. To be lawful an employment must not be selfish. All selfishness is sin. And every employment, however lawful it may be in itself, is rendered unlawful by being selfishly pursued.

4. To be lawful there must not be too much or too little of it. A business lawful in itself may become unlawful when too much is undertaken or too little is performed, so that on the one hand a man is crushed or on the other he is idle; but,

5. To be lawful a business must be useful, that is, it must be such an employment as is calculated in its nature to benefit mankind.

6. To be lawful a business must be suited to your capacity. You cannot lawfully employ yourself in that for which you are not fitted. By this I do not mean that you are to be perfectly qualified for the transaction of any business before you can lawfully engage in it, but that you should be as well or better fitted for that particular employment than for any other.

7. To be lawful it must be that employment to which you are called of God. You are to be wholly the Lord's and to consult His will in all things, and never to be engaged in any employment to please yourself or promote your own separate or private interest. You are bound therefore to submit yourself to the direction of the Lord in all things and to select no employment for life or for any length of time but under the direction of God.

It is generally admitted that ministers are to be especially called of God to the work of the ministry. But all men are to be equally devoted to God, and all employments are to be pursued equally for the glory of God. Every faculty and every day and every moment of all men are to be devoted to the Lord. And all men are equally bound to consult the will of God in the selection and pursuit of their employments. And no man can give himself up to employments to which he is not called of God, or to which he does not really believe himself to be called of God, without thereby apostatizing from the service of God. Now every one of you would say that if a minister should select the ministry to please himself he would lose his soul. This is equally true of every other employment.

8. To be lawfully employed you must engage in that in which you can be most useful. It is not enough that you render yourself useful in some degree: you are bound to be engaged in that employment in which you can, all things considered, do the most good. A man might render himself useful as a peddler, but if he can be more useful in some other employment he is bound to prefer it.

9. That only is a lawful employment which can honestly and reasonably be pursued for the glory of God. Every kind and degree of business that cannot, with an enlightened conscience, be solemnly engaged in and transacted for the glory of God carries its own condemnation on its very front.

10. No business is lawful that is not, *as a matter of fact*, engaged in and pursued with the supreme desire to know and glorify God therein.

11. No business is lawful which is inconsistent with the highest degree of spirituality. I mean that only which consists with entire holiness of heart and life is a lawful employment. Anything that Jesus Christ or an apostle would not engage in under the circumstances is really unlawful for everybody else.

III. *Men are to be diligent in their calling.*

1. This is implied in the text. The text is commonly quoted as if it read, "Be diligent in business." This is not the way in which it reads, though this is plainly implied in it and is in its real meaning.

2. It is also plainly implied in the law of God.

3. The necessities of the world require it. There is enough for every man to do. And no man has any right to be idle or dilatory in his calling.

4. Every degree of slothfulness is injurious to yourself in many ways.

5. It is also injurious to those with whom you are immediately connected. They have a right to expect the diligent use of your powers in promoting their common interests.

6. Every degree of slothfulness in you is injurious to the world at large and to the universe, inasmuch as there is just so much less of real good in the universe for every moment's idleness in which you indulge.

7. It is a bad example in you to be idle for a day or an hour or to be in any manner negligent or slothful in your employment. Its tendency is to produce universal idleness, which would ruin the universe.

8. You are bound to do all the good you can in every way, both to the bodies and souls of men; and this obligation is entirely inconsistent with any degree of slothfulness.

IV. *How to prevent secular or spiritual employments from being a snare to the soul.*

It has come to be a subject of almost universal complaint that our employments lead us away from God. Men complain of their cares and of having so much business on their hands as to secularize their spirit, blunt the edge of devotional feeling, and more or less insensibly but certainly to draw off their hearts from God. And those who are engaged in intellectual and even spiritual occupations, such as teachers of science and teachers of religion, are by their employments apt to fall into an intellectual and hardened frame of mind and to wander far from God. It seems to be understood that there is a kind of necessity in the case, and that we are naturally unable to attend to the various duties and callings incidental to our relations in this world, without secularizing our spirit and annihilating a devotional state of mind. Now to suppose there is any necessity for this result is to charge God foolishly. He has never placed us here surrounded with these necessities to be a snare and a curse to us. On the contrary, all the employments that are strictly lawful, instead of being a snare, are indispensable to the highest development of our powers and to the growth and consummation of our piety.

The whole difficulty lies in the abuse of a thing eminently wise and good. That the facts are according to the general complaint cannot be doubted. Men really are ensnared by their employments. But why? Many seem to suppose that the only way to maintain a spiritual frame of mind is by a total abstraction from those employments in which it seems to be necessary for men to engage in this world. It was this conceit that led to the establishment of nunneries and monasteries and to all those fanatical and odious seclusions from society that have abounded among the Papists.

The truth is that the right discharge of our duties to God and man, as things are, is indispensable to holiness. And voluntary seclusion from human society and abstracting ourselves from those employments by which man may be benefited are wholly inconsistent with the principles and spirit of the Christian religion. See Christ and the apostles! They were eminently active, zealous, and useful in promoting the glory of God and the good of man in every way in their power. It is a desideratum, therefore, in religion to understand the secret of making our employments, whatever they are, the means of increasing instead of destroying our spirituality. A great deal needs to be said upon this subject. I can now only say the following things and may at a future time, if God permit, resume the subject.

1. If you would not that your employment should be a snare to your soul, see to it that it is not unlawful; that is, see to it that it is not an injurious employment, the natural tendency of which is to injure yourself or your fellowmen.

2. See to it that you do not introduce some unlawful ingredient into a business otherwise lawful, and thus vitiate the whole and render it a curse to you and those around you. For example, consider a man who is an innkeeper. To keep a house of public entertainment is, in itself, lawful and useful. But if a man to increase his profits or to please all classes of people will sell ardent spirits, this is absolutely unlawful and an abomination in the sight of God, and it introduces an element into his business which vitiates the whole and renders his business a curse to mankind.

A merchant perhaps does the same thing. In order to increase his profits or to please his customers, he sells tobacco and other fashionable but injurious narcotics. And while he deals in many things that are useful and important, he does not hesitate to buy and sell almost anything upon which he can make a profit. Now if he admits into his business any ingredient that is injurious to the interests of mankind, he renders the whole an unlawful business. It demonstrates that he is not and cannot be pursuing his employment from right motives. And it is impossible that he should pursue a business of this kind in a manner that shall be acceptable to God. In other words, his business itself is an apostasy from God. God has said, "Whosoever shall keep the whole law, and yet offend in one point, he is guilty of all."

Now the principle involved here is that while a man admits any form of sin whatever to be habitual in his employment, it is rendering all obedience for the time being wholly impossible. He is in the exercise of a spirit which is in itself disobedience to the whole law and a setting aside of the authority of God.

3. Be sure that you do nothing selfishly. If you allow selfishness in any of its forms to come in and to have a place in your employments, you are already departed from God, and your business, whether spiritual, intellectual or whatever it may be, has become an abomination to God.

4. See that your business is strictly and properly a lawful one. If it be not in the most proper sense a lawful employment it will, if persevered in, certainly ruin your soul. To be lawful, I have already said, it must be some employment that is useful, suited to your capacity, that to which you are called of God, that in which you can become useful, that which can be truly and honestly and solemnly dedicated to God and performed for Him, that which as a matter of fact is thus dedicated to and performed for God, that which is consistent with the highest degree of spirituality (with perfect holiness of heart and life), and such as Christ and the apostles would engage in under the same circumstances.

5. See that your eye is single, that you have but one great leading motive, and that to glorify God and serve your generation.

6. Consult God at every step of your employment. Do everything with prayer. Let every day and every hour bear witness that you are transacting everything for God and consulting Him at every step of your progress. You would no doubt feel shocked should you know that a minister went about his preparation for the pulpit without prayer to God. Should he not, on going out to visit his people, pray for divine direction, and when he returned from such visits should he not spread the whole matter and what he had done before the Lord—in short should he not take counsel of God in all the departments of his employment—you would feel shocked. And should he become exceedingly hardened and reprobate in his work and should his employment be the snare and ruin of his soul, you would not wonder; for this would be the very result that under the circumstances you would anticipate. And it is to be feared that this is the very course and the very result with multitudes of

ministers. Now as eveyrthing is God's and every man is His and every employment is to be pursued as much for His glory as the employment of a minister, it follows of course that every person is bound to have as single an eye to consult God at every step, and to make His employment a subject of daily prayer, just as a minister is. And if he does not, he will surely apostatize from God.

7. Be sure to do everything in a spirit of entire consecration to God. Maintain perpetually, in everything, a spirit of as entire consecration as you know and feel that you ought to maintain in the exercises of the Sabbath day. It is impossible that men should ever pursue their employment without ensnaring their souls, until they understand that the business of every day is to be as sacredly devoted to God and performed in a spirit of as entire consecration to His service as the holy exercises of the Sabbath. This must not only be understood in theory but must be reduced to practice. The Sabbath must be distinguished from other days only in the peculiarity of its employments. You must cease to suppose that the Sabbath is God's day and that the week days are yours, that you may serve God one day and yourself six days in the week. The Sabbath has its specific and appropriate duties. And so have other days. But every day and every hour, and every employment and every thought, are to be wholly consecrated to God. And until you have habituated yourself to go to your farms, to your shops, or to your merchandise, as to a business that belongs wholly to God and is to be performed in a spirit of as true devotion as are the duties of your closet or of the sanctuary, your whole employment will be an everlasting snare and the final ruin of your soul.

8. In short, do nothing, be nothing, buy nothing, sell nothing, possess nothing, do not marry nor decline marriage, do not study nor refrain from study, but in a spirit of entire devotion to God. Consecrate your sleep, your rest, your exercise, your all to God. Learn to do this, *practice this*, or your employment, whatever it may be, will be the snare and ruin of your soul.

9. But that without which all else will be in vain is yet to be mentioned. And mark what I say. *You must abide in Christ*. "Without me," says Christ, "ye can do nothing." Only as you abide in Him by faith, and He in you, will you do any one of the things that have been mentioned in a right spirit. He is your life. He is the bread and water of life. Faith in Him is the grand and universal condition of all true virtue and obedience to God.

Remarks

1. God calls you to no employment in kind or amount that is inconsistent with entire holiness of heart and life. Whenever you find, therefore, that your employment really prevents your walking wholly with God, something is certainly wrong. Either your employment is unlawful in itself or, if in itself it is a lawful one, it is that to which you are not

called, or you have taken too much upon yourself, or too little, or your motives have become wrong. There is utterly some fault in you. Make a solemn pause then, as on the very brink of eternity, and inquire after and remove the stumbling blocks out of the way. If it be a right hand or a right eye give it up in a moment, as you love the ways and dread the wrath of God.

2. God never calls you to any business and then withholds the necessary grace for the perfect discharge of your obligations. If grace be sought as it ought to be, and constantly will be while your motives are right, it will not be withheld.

3. But if God calls you to a business and you become selfish in it, it is no longer acceptable to Him; and your pursuing it with a selfish heart is an utter abomination to Him. I fear it is not an uncommon thing for young men, who suppose themselves to be called to the gospel ministry, in the course of their preparation, to become cold and ambitious and anything but holy. And yet they persevere, because they dare not go back and relinquish their course. They are sensible that they are away from God; but believing themselves to have been called to the work of the ministry, they feel as if they must go forward, partly lest they should lose their reputation with men and partly because they fear the displeasure of God, while they know that as a matter of fact their hearts are not right with Him. And thus they go through their classical studies hoping that when they enter upon theology their studies will be of such a character as to make them holy. But coming as they do in such a state of heart to the study of theology, they are only hardened more rapidly than before. But finding this to be the case does not deter them from going forward. They think that now they must make up their opinion on various points of doctrine, and that when they have settled all these things and entered upon the active duties of the ministry, then they shall be aroused to a better state of feeling. But the hardening process still goes on. So that by the time they are through their course their hearts are like the nether millstone. They are all head and no heart, all intellect and no emotion. In this state they come to the active duties of the ministry; and woe to the church that shall employ one of them. They might as well place a skeleton in their pulpit, for he is but the shadow of a minister and not the substance. He has the bones but not the marrow and life and spirit of the Gospel.*

4. No man has a right to undertake so much business, for any compensation whatever, as to interfere with his hours of devotion. In cases where persons labor by the day or month or year, allowance should always be made in the prices they receive for sufficient time and opportunity for devotional exercises. They have no right to exact or receive such wages as to render it necessary for them to give up all their time to

---

*See Charles G. Finney, *Principles of Victory*, compiled and edited by Louis Gifford Parkhurst, Jr. (Minneapolis: Bethany House Publishers, 1981), "Letter to a Young Seminarian on Preaching," pp. 23, 24.

labor; nor ought their employers to expect them to encroach, under any pretense whatever, upon those hours appointed to secret communion with God.

5. There is great danger of a diligence in business which is inconsistent with fervency of spirit in serving the Lord.

6. From my own observation, I am persuaded that there is a great error in requiring too much study of young men who are preparing for the ministry. There is such a great cry for a learned ministry—so much stress is laid upon a thorough education—and so much competition among colleges and seminaries as to present a great temptation to instructors to push the intellectual pursuits of young men to the utmost and even beyond the utmost limit of endurance.

Now while I am in favor of a thorough education, I do not and cannot believe, with the facts as they exist before me, that the great difference in the usefulness of ministers depends on their being learned men in the common acceptation of that term. Human science by itself never made a useful minister; and wherever human science is pushed beyond its proper limit and made to encroach upon the hours and spirit of devotion, wherever the spirit of human science instead of the Spirit of God comes to be that fountain at which a man drinks, he may become in the language of men a great man but he will never be a good minister. Until there is a great change upon this subject—until the great effort of the teachers is to make their pupils pious as well as learned, and they are more anxious and take more pains to effect the former than the latter— our seminaries can never send out efficient ministers. To require diligence in study without requiring fervency of spirit; to concern ourselves more that our students have their lessons than that they walk with God, that they commune with Cicero, Horace, and Demosthenes, rather than with God; for us to satisfy ourselves every day in relation to their intellectual progress and pay little or no attention to the state of their hearts—is an utter abomination. And teachers who do so, whatever other qualifications they may have, are unfit to have the care of young men.

7. When you find yourselves proceeding in any employment without prayer for direction, support, and guidance, you may rest assured that you are selfish; and however diligent you may be, you may know that you are not fervent in spirit serving the Lord.

8. The speculations of the last few years have so secularized the Church as to annihilate her power with God. She has in reality been engaged in gambling under the pretense of making money for God. In doing this multitudes of leading church members have involved themselves and the cause of Christ in great embarrassment and disgrace. And it does seem as if they were deranged in their spasmodic efforts to enrich themselves.

9. No amount of money can save or even benefit the world in the hands of a secular church. If professors of religion had made all the money they have endeavored to make and did they possess a universe of gold,

it would do nothing towards converting the world, while the very spirit and life of the church is secular, earthly, sensual, and devilish.

10. No idle person can enjoy communion with God for the plain reason that his idleness is perpetual disobedience to God.

11. The Apostle has commanded that they who will not work (that is, who are idle) shall not eat. If persons are able to pursue and can find any employment by which they can benefit mankind and are idle, it is no enlightened charity to feed them.

12. If idle persons eat they cannot digest their food. It is an unalterable law of God that men shall perform some kind of labor. This is essential to the well-being of their body and mind. Idleness is as inconsistent with health as it is with good morals. So that if men will be idle, they must suffer the penalty of both physical and moral law.

13. You see from this subject the great importance of training children to habits of industry and of early imbibing their minds with the spirit of continually doing something that is useful.

14. Everyone can do something to glorify God and in some way benefit mankind. He can labor with his hands or his head or his heart. He can work or teach or pray, or do something to contribute his share to the common stock of good in the universe. It is the language of a sluggard to complain that you can do no good. The truth is, if you have a spirit to do good, you will certainly be trying to do good.

15. If we do what we can, however little, it is just as acceptable to God as if we could do a thousand times as much. "If there be first a willing mind, it is accepted according to what a man hath and not according to what he hath not." Christ said of the poor widow who cast in her two mites, she has cast in more than the rich, who of their abundance cast in much. It is well if you have a heart to do a great deal more than you are able to do. It is that which you really would do for which Christ gives you credit, and not for that which you are really able to do. It is according to the largeness of your heart and not according to the weakness of your hands that God will reward you.

16. Not one of the employments that are essential to the highest good of mankind has any natural and necessary tendency to alienate the heart from God. By this, I do not mean that the perverted state of the human heart is not such that it is natural for it, being in a state of selfishness, to take occasion to depart from God in these employments. But I do mean that the real tendency of all these employments, to a mind not given up to selfishness, is to increase and perpetuate the deepest communion with God.

17. There is no excuse for a secular spirit. And, as I have already said, *whenever your spirit is secular your heart is selfish.*

18. If you have been called of God to any employment and have become selfish in it, it has become an abomination to God; and you are bound to abandon it instantly or to renounce your selfishness and diligently pursue your employment for God. By this, I do not mean that you would do right to abandon the employment to which God has called you;

but that, if you will not repent and be "fervent in spirit serving the Lord," you are as far as possible from pleasing Him in pursuing your business selfishly. If God be not with you in any employment, whether it be study, the ministry, merchandise, farming or anything else, if God does not go with you in it, you are certainly out of the way, are bound to reform, to turn instantly and wholly to the Lord, and to go not a step forward until you have evidence of the divine acceptance.

19. Lastly, let me ask you solemnly, beloved, have you some employment in which you are endeavoring honestly and fervently to glorify God? What is your employment, in what manner do you pursue it, with what design, in what spirit, and what is its effect? Do you as a matter of fact find yourself walking with God and does the peace of God rule in your heart? Or is there some ingredient in your business that vitiates the whole? Are you dealing in some article of death? Are you poisoning your fellowmen for the glory of God? Are you pursuing some scandalous traffic for some selfish purpose?

Oh, that the Lord may search you and pour the gaze of His eye through and through your inmost soul. And if your hands are clean, may the blessing of the Lord that maketh rich and addeth no sorrow be multiplied to you a thousandfold. But if you are out of the way, may He lay His reclaiming, sanctifying hand upon you and not suffer you to rest till all you have and are are wholly devoted to the Lord.

14

BEING IN DEBT*

Romans 13:8

"Owe no man anything."

In discussing this subject, I design to show:
I. *The meaning of the text.*
II. *That to be in debt is sin.*
III. *The duty of those who are in debt.*

I. *I am to show the meaning of the text.*
The meaning of this text, like most others, is to be learned from a careful examination of the verses in its connection. The Apostle begins the chapter by enforcing the duty of obedience to civil magistrates.

Let every soul be subject unto the higher powers. For there is no power but of God: the powers that be are ordained of God. Whosoever therefore resisteth the power, resisteth the ordinance of God: and they that resist shall receive unto themselves damnation. For rulers are not a terror to good works, but to the evil. Wilt thou then not be afraid of the power? Do that which is good, and thou shalt have praise of the same: for he is the minister of God unto thee for good. But if thou do that which is evil, be afraid; for he beareth not the sword in vain: for he is the minister of God, a revenger to execute wrath upon him that doeth evil. Wherefore ye must be subject, not only for wrath, but also for conscience sake. For for this cause pay ye tribute also: for they are God's ministers, attending continually upon this very thing.

They are the servants of God, employed for your benefit. You are, therefore, to pay them tribute, that is, give them the support which their circumstances require.

In the light of this and various other passages of Scripture, I have often wondered how it was possible that any person could call in question the duty of obeying civil magistrates, or how they could call in question the right and duty of magistrates to inflict civil penalties, and even capital

The Oberlin Evangelist: Vol. I; July 13, 1839. Also, *The Promise of the Spirit*, pp. 175-184.

punishment where the nature of the case demands it.* Certainly this passage recognizes their right and their duty "to execute wrath" upon transgressors, as the servants and executioners of God's vengence.

Render therefore to all their dues: tribute to whom tribute is due; custom to whom custom; fear to whom fear; honour to whom honour. Owe no man any thing, but to love one another; for he that loveth another hath fulfilled the law. For this, Thou shalt not commit adultery, Thou shalt not kill, Thou shalt not bear false witness, Thou shalt not covet; and if there be any other commandment, it is briefly comprehended in this saying, namely, Thou shalt love thy neighbour as thyself. Love worketh no ill to his neighbour: therefore love is the fulfilling of the law.

From this connection it is evident that the Apostle designed to teach that whenever we come to owe a man, we should immediately pay him and not suffer any debt or obligation to rest upon us undischarged. "Owe no man any thing, but to love one another." Here the Apostle recognizes the truth that love is of perpetual obligation, and that this obligation can never be so canceled or discharged as to be no longer binding. He recognizes no other obligation except love with its natural fruits as being, in its own nature, of perpetual obligation. In respect to this obligation, all that we can do is to fulfill it every moment, without the possibility of so fulfilling it as to set aside the continued obligation to love.

But we are to owe no man anything else but love. We are to "render to all their dues, tribute to whom tribute is due, honour to whom honour." I understand the text then simply to mean, let no obligation but that of love with its natural fruits, which is from its very nature a perpetual obligation, rest upon you undischarged. I am aware that some modern critics maintain that this passage should have been rendered indicatively. But such men as Doddridge and Henry, Barnes and Prof. Stuart, are of the opinion that its imperative rendering is correct.** And all are agreed that the doctrine of this text, as it stands, is plainly a doctrine of the Bible.

---

*See *The Heart of Truth* and *Systematic Theology* for Finney's more complete views on "Human Government," and the right of revolution.

** 1) Philip Doddridge (1702-1751) was a nonconformist theologian, who began an academy in 1729 to train students for the ministry. Born in London, he died in Lisbon.

2) Matthew Henry (1662-1714) a Presbyterian minister, who began his famous *Commentary on the Bible* in 1704, and whose work has made a decided impact on the evangelical ministry.

3) Albert Barnes (1798-1870) a Presbyterian minister and commentator, who has become best known for his *Notes on the New Testament*. One of the best studies on the atonement is his: *The Atonement* (Minneapolis: Bethany House Publishers 1860 reprint, n.d.)

4) Moses Stuart (1780-1852) was Professor of biblical studies at Andover, who in 1819 prophesied that Unitarianism was a halfway house on the road to infidelity.

Here the question arises, *what is it to owe a man in the sense of this text?* I answer,

1. If you *employ* a laborer and do not stipulate the time and terms of payment, it is taken for granted that he is to be paid when his work is done and to have the money. If you hire him for a day and nothing is said to the contrary, he cannot demand his pay till his day's work is done; till then you owe him nothing. The same is true if you hire him for a week or a month or a year. When the time which he is to labor is stipulated and nothing is said about the time and terms of payment, you owe him nothing, that is, nothing is due till his time has expired. But if the time was not specified which he was to labor, he may break off at any time and demand pay for what he has done. Or if the time of payment was expressed or understood, whenever it arrives you then owe him and are bound to pay him agreeably to the understanding.

2. The same is true if you hire a horse or any other piece of property. If you hire it for a specified time and nothing is said of the conditions of payment, the understanding is that you are to pay when the time for which the property was hired has expired. It then becomes a debt. Then you are to pay, and pay the money. If there were any other understanding fixing the time and terms of payment, you do not owe the man until the specified conditions are complied with.

3. The same is true if you *purchase* any piece of property. If nothing is stipulated to the contrary, the understanding is that you are to pay the cash at the time you receive the property. At that time, and neither before nor after, you are expected to pay the purchase money.

We do not properly owe an individual until we are under an obligation to pay him. Whenever he has a right to demand the pay we have no right to withhold it. There may be such a thing as contracting a prospective debt, giving your obligation to become due at a certain time. But then you do not properly owe because you are under no obligation to pay till it becomes due. But whenever it becomes due you are bound immediately to pay it.

II. *I am to show that it is a sin to be in debt.*

1. Because it is a *direct violation of the command of God*. This text is just as binding as any command of the decalogue. And a violation of it is a setting aside of the command of God, as much as to commit adultery or murder. It is not to be regarded merely as a piece of advice given by the Apostle, but as a direct and positive and authoritative command of God.

2. It is *unjust to be in debt.* If your creditor has a right to demand payment, you certainly have no right to withhold it. If it is due it is a contradiction to say that it is not unjust for you not to pay. It is a contradiction, both in *terms* and in *fact*, to say that you owe a man, and at the same time are guilty of no injustice in refusing or neglecting to pay him. It is as much injustice as *stealing* and involves the same principle. The *sin* of stealing consists in the appropriating to ourselves that which

properly belongs to another. Therefore whenever you withhold from any man his due, you are guilty of as absolute an injustice as if you stole his property.

3. It is sin *because it is falsehood.* I have already shown that you do not properly owe a man till it becomes due. It becomes due when and because there is a promise on your part expressed or implied that you will pay it at that time. Now you cannot violate this promise without being guilty of falsehood.

4. If what has just been said is true, it follows that men should *meet their contracts* as they would avoid the grossest sin. They are bound to avoid being in debt, to meet and fulfill their engagements, as much as they are bound to avoid blasphemy, idolatry, murder or any other sin. And a man who does not pay his debts is no more to be accounted an honest man than he who is guilty of any other heinous crime.

5. If a professor of religion is in debt, he is a *moral delinquent* and should be accounted and treated as a subject of church discipline.

OBJECTION. It may be said, I cannot avoid being in debt. I answer to this,

That if you cannot pay you could have avoided contracting the debt and were bound to do so.

Do you reply, I really needed the thing which I purchased?

I ask, were your necessities so great that you would have been justified in your estimation in lying or stealing to supply them? If not, why have you resorted to fraud? The same authority that prohibits lying or stealing prohibits your owing a man. Why then do you violate this commandment of God any more than the other? Is it not because a corrupt public sentiment has rendered the violation of this commandment less disgraceful than to violate these other commands of God? Why did you not resort to begging instead of running in debt? Better far to beg than to run in debt. Begging is not prohibited by any command of God but being in debt is prohibited. True, it is disgraceful to beg. But a God-dishonoring public sentiment has rendered it far less so to be in debt. And does not this account for your shameless violation of this command of God?

Do you say again, I have been disappointed. I expected to have had the money. I made the contract in good faith and expected to meet it at the time; but others owe me and do not pay me, therefore I am unable to pay my debts. To this I reply,

You should have contracted with that expressed condition. You should have made known your circumstances and the ground of your expectation in regard to being able to pay at the time appointed. In that case, if your creditor was willing to run the risk of your being disappointed, the fault is not yours, as you have practiced no injustice or deception. But if your contract was without condition, you have taken upon yourself the risk of disappointment and are not guiltless.

But here it may be said again, nearly the whole Church is in debt, and if subject to discipline, who shall cast the first stone? I reply,

(1) If it be true that the Church is so extensively in debt, no wonder

that the curse of God is upon her.

(2) Again, it may be true that a church may be so generally involved in any given sin as to make that sin a difficult subject of discipline. But when this is true of any church, it is a shameless abomination for the members of that church to attempt to hide themselves under the admitted fact that nearly all the Church is involved in the guilt of it. Now rest assured that when any sin becomes so prevalent that it cannot and is not made, in that church, a subject of discipline, then God himself will sooner or later take up the rod and find means to discipline, and that effectually, such a church.

III. *I am to state the duty of those who are in debt.*

1. They are bound to make any *sacrifice* of property or time, and indeed *any sacrifice* that it is possible for them to make, to pay their debts.

Here it may be asked again, does the law of love permit my creditor to demand a sacrifice of me? If he loves me as he does himself, why should he require or even allow me to make a sacrifice of property to pay what I owe him? I reply:

(1) If anyone is to make a sacrifice or suffer loss, it is the debtor and not the creditor. It will almost certainly be some damage to him to be disappointed in not receiving his due. It may so disarrange his affairs and break in upon his calculations as to occasion him great damage. Of this he is to be the judge.

(2) Your sacrifice may be necessary not only to prevent his *loss* but to enable him to meet his contracts, and thus prevent his *sin*. His confidence in your veracity may have led him to contract prospective debts, and by not paying him you not only sin yourself but cause him to sin.

(3) The refusal of one to make a sacrifice to pay his debts may involve many others in both *loss* and *sin*. A owes B, B owes C and C owes D, and so on in a long chain of mutual dependencies. Now if there be a failure in the first or any other link of this chain, all below it are involved in loss and sin. Now where shall this evil be arrested?

Suppose you hold the place of C. A refuses to make a sacrifice to pay B, and B to pay you. Shall you sin because they do, and involve your creditor in loss and sin? No. Whatever others may do, you are bound to pay your debts. And unless your creditor voluntarily consents to defer the time of payment, you are bound to pay him at any sacrifice.

2. Persons that are in debt should not *contract new debts* to pay old ones. It is the practice of some, when they get involved, to keep up their credit by borrowing from one to pay another. Their meeting and canceling the last debt depends altogether upon the presumption that they shall be able to borrow the money from somebody else. When they have borrowed from one they will keep him out of his pay as long as possible without losing their credit. And then, instead of making a sacrifice of property sufficient to discharge the obligation, they borrow from B to pay A and from C to pay B and thus, perhaps, disappoint and disoblige

a dozen men by not paying them exactly at the time agreed, instead of at once stopping short and parting with what they have, at any sacrifice, to pay the debt.

I do not say that a man should not in any case borrow of one man to pay another. But this I say, that as a general thing such practices are highly reprehensible. Still, if a debt becomes due and you have not the money at hand but are certain that at a given time you shall have it, I do not suppose it wrong for you to borrow and pay this debt, with the understanding that you pay this borrowed money at the time specified. But to borrow money with no other prospect of an ultimate payment than that you can borrow again, and thus keep up your credit from time to time, is wicked.

3. Those who are in debt have no right *to give away* the money which they owe. If you are in debt the money in your hands belongs to your creditor and not to you. You have no right, therefore, "to be generous till you are just." You have strictly no more right to give that money away than you have to steal money to give away.

But here it should be particularly understood what *is* and what *is not* to be accounted as giving money away; for example, it is not giving away your money to pay the current expenses of the congregation to which you are attached. Your proportion of the current expenses of the congregation or church to which you belong is impliedly if not expressly contracted by you. You cannot withhold it any more than the payment of any other debt. The same may be said of the support of ministers and foreign missionaries and all for whose support the faith of the church is pledged. It seems to be a common but erroneous understanding of professors of religion that what are more generally called their secular debts or obligations are binding and are to be discharged of course, but that their obligations, expressed or implied, to religious institutions are not so absolutely binding; and of course they can *give* nothing, as they express it, to these objects until their debts are paid.

Now beloved, you ought to know that to the support of the institutions of religion, you are pledged, both virtually and actually, by your profession, and that these are your most sacred debts and are thus to be considered and discharged by you. I beseech you not to consider the meeting and canceling of such demands as these in the light of a *gift*, as if you were making God a present instead of discharging a solemn debt. I have been astonished to find that the pecuniary embarrassments of the few past years have so far crippled the movements of the great benevolent societies for want of funds, and that missionaries, for whose support the faith and honor of the church were pledged, should be so far cut short of their necessary supplies, under the pretense that the church must pay her secular debts before she could discharge her high and sacred obligations to them and the work in which they are engaged.

4. A person who is in debt has no right to purchase for himself or family things not absolutely essential for their subsistence. Things that might lawfully be purchased and used under other circumstances be-

come unlawful when you are in debt. A creditor has no right to deprive you of necessary food and indispensable raiment, or of your liberty. To do so would put it out of your power ever to pay. But you have no right to indulge in any thing more than the necessaries of life while your debts are unpaid. To do so is as unlawful as it would be to steal to purchase unnecessary articles.

Remarks

1. From what has been said it is plain that the whole credit system, if not absolutely sinful, is nevertheless so highly dangerous that no Christian should embark in it.

Since the preaching of this sermon, this remark has been censured as a rash one. A rash remark! Let the present history and experience of the church say whether the credit system is not so highly dangerous that the man who will venture to embark in it is guilty of rashness and presumption. When has religion for centuries been so generally disgraced as by the bankruptcy of its professors within the last few years? And how many millions of dollars are now due from church members to ungodly men that will never be paid? Rash! Why, this is the very plea of the Church, that they can do nothing for the support of the Gospel because they are so much in debt. Is there no danger of any man's getting in debt who attempts to trade upon a borrowed capital? Indeed it is highly dangerous, as universal experience shows.

And what is the necessity, I pray, for Christians to embark in so dangerous an enterprise, and one that so highly jeopardizes the honor of religion? Is it because the institutions of religion demand it? Religion sustains a greater loss through the debts and bankruptcies of Christians than it ever gains by their prosperity.

But the credit system, as it now prevails and has prevailed, is useless and worse than useless. For example, suppose the consumers of merchandise, instead of anticipating their yearly crops and yearly income and running in debt with the expectation of paying from these, were to take a little pain to reverse this order of things and be a year beforehand, paying down for what they purchase and having the income of each year beforehand, so as to contract no debts. In this case the country merchants, giving no credit but receiving ready pay, would be able to pay down on the purchase of their goods from the wholesale dealer, the wholesale dealer would pay down to the importer, the importer to the manufacturer, and the manufacturer to the producer.

Now any man can see that many millions a year would be saved to this country in this way. The manufacturer could afford an article cheaper for ready pay, and so could the importer and the wholesale dealer and each one in his turn, down to the consumer. Everyone could sell cheaper for ready pay as no risk would be run, and business could be done with much greater convenience and safety. Thus an entire rejection of the credit system in its present form and an adoption of the system of ready pay would afford to the consumer every article so much cheaper as to save millions of dollars every year. And I do not apprehend that there is in reality any serious difficulty in so reversing the whole order of business.

At another time I may more particularly examine the credit system in its foundation and various ramifications, and the nature and tendencies of the prevailing system of doing business on borrowed capital. But at present I can only say, as I have said, that waiving the question whether it is absolutely sinful in itself, it is too highly dangerous to be embarked in by those who feel a tender solicitude for the honor and cause of Christ.

2. That if in any case the present payment of debts is impossible, your duty is to regard your indebtedness as a sin against God and your neighbor, to repent, and set yourself with all practicable self-denial to pay as fast as you can. And unless you are laying yourself out to pay your debts, do not imagine that you repent either of your indebtedness or any other sin. For you are impenitent and a shameless hypocrite rather than a Christian, if you suffer yourself to be in debt and are not making all practicable efforts to do justice to your creditors.

3. If payment is *possible* by any sacrifice of property on your part, sin is upon you till you do pay. There is a wicked custom among men, and to a considerable amount in the church, of putting property out of their hands to avoid a sacrifice in the payment of their debts. As an instance take the elder whom I mentioned in a former lecture, who confessed to me that "he was avoiding the sacrifice of his property in the payment of his debts by *finesse* of law."

4. The lax notions and practices of the world and of the Church upon this subject are truly abominable. It has come to pass that a man may not only be considered a respectable citizen but a respectable member of the church, who resorts not only "to *finesse* of law to avoid the payment of his debts" but who practices the most palpable frauds against both God and man by putting his property out of his hands to avoid meeting his just responsibilities. Oh, shame on the Church and on these professors of religion! Some of them will even go to an unconverted lawyer for advice in this iniquitous business and lay open before his unconverted heart their shameless iniquity. Alas, how many lawyers are thus led to call in question the whole truth of the Christian religion, and over these dishonest professors they stumble into hell. And until the Church will rise up and wash her hands and cleanse her garments from this iniquity, by banishing such persons from her communion, the cause of Christ will not cease to bleed at every pore.

5. Some persons take the ground that not to meet their contracts and pay their debts when they become due is not sinful, on account of the general understanding of businessmen upon such subjects. To this I answer,

(1) There is no understanding among businessmen that debts are not to be paid when they become due. Among that class of men the nonpay-

ment of a debt always involves a disgrace and a wrong, even in their own estimation.

(2) Let the public sentiment be what it might among businessmen, still the law of God cannot be altered; and by this unchanging law it is a sin to be in debt. And as "sin is a disgrace to any people," it is both a *sin* and a *shame* to be in debt.

6. The rule laid down in this text is applicable not only to individuals but to corporations and nations and all bodies of men assuming pecuniary responsibilities.

7. It is *dishonest* and *dishonorable* to hire or purchase an article and say nothing about payment till afterwards.

8. The violation of this law is working immense mischief in the Church and in the world. It is truly shocking to see to what an extent the Church is involved in debt and church members are engaged in collecting debts of each other by force of law. The heart-burnings and bitterness that exist among church members on account of the nonpayment of their debts to each other are awfully great and alarming. Besides all this, in what light does the Church appear before the world—as a mass of money-makers and speculators and bankrupts, shuffling and managing through *finesse* of law to avoid the payment of their debts? I could relate facts within my own knowledge, and many of them too, that would cause the cheek of piety to blush. Alas for the rage and madness of a speculating, money-making, fraudulent church!

9. There is great reason to believe that many young men in the course of their education involve themselves in debts that so far eat up their piety as to render them nearly useless all their days. I would sooner be twenty-five years in getting an education, and paying my way, than involve myself in debt to the Education Society or in any other way. How many young men there are who are in debt to the Education Society and who are dealing very loosely with their consciences on the subject of payment. Because the Education Society does not press them right up, they let the matter lie along from time to time and increase their expenditures as their income may increase, instead of practicing self-denial and honestly discharging their obligations to the Society.

10. I cannot have *confidence* in the piety of any man who is not *conscientious* in the payment of his debts. I know some men who are in debt and who spend their time and their property in a manner wholly inconsistent with their circumstances, and still make great pretensions to piety. They are active in prayer meetings, take a conspicuous place at the communion table, and even hold a responsible office in the Church of Christ; and yet they seem to have no conscience about paying their debts.

I believe it is right and the duty of all churches and ministers to exclude such persons from the communion of the church. And were it generally done it would go far to wipe away the stains that have been brought by such persons upon the religion of Jesus Christ. I do not see why they should be suffered to come to the communion table any more than whoremongers or murderers or drunkards or Sabbath breakers or slaveholders.

11. There must be a great reformation in the Church upon this subject before the business class of ungodly men will have much confidence in religion. This reformation should begin immediately and begin where it ought to begin, among the leading members of the Church of Christ. Ministers and church judicatories should speak out upon the subject, should "cry aloud and spare not, but lift up their voice like a trumpet and show Israel his transgressions and the house of Jacob their sins."

And now, beloved, are any of you in debt? Then sin is upon you. Rise up and show yourselves clean in this matter, I beseech you. Make every effort to meet and discharge your responsibilities. And beware that in attempting to pay your debts you do not resort to means that are as highly reprehensible as to be in debt.

12. Let no one complain and say that instead of preaching the Gospel I am discussing mere business transactions of the world. *Religion is to regulate the business transactions of the world. Religion is a practical thing.* It does not consist in austerities, prayers and masses and monkish superstitions, as Papists vainly dream. If religion does not take hold of a man's business operations, if it does not reform his daily life and habits, of what avail is it? Until in these respects your practice is right, you cannot expect to enjoy the influences of the Holy Spirit. *You cannot grow in holiness any further than you reform your practice.*

The preceptive part of the Gospel, therefore, is to be spread out in all its detail before you. And when you find it "convinces you of sin," I beg of you not to turn around and say that this is preaching about business and not about religion. What is business but a part of religion? A man that does not consider it so in practice has no religion at all.

And now, dearly beloved, instead of suffering your heart to rise up and resist what I have said, will you now as I have often requested go down upon your knees and spread this whole subject before the Lord? Will you not inquire wherein you have erred and sinned, and make haste to repent and reform your lives?

15

LOVE WORKETH NO ILL*

Romans 13:10

"Love worketh no ill to his neighbor: therefore love is the fulfilling of the law."

In discussing this subject I shall show:
I. *What the love that constitutes true religion is not.*
II. *What it is.*
III. *Who is to be regarded as our neighbor.*
IV. *Why love worketh no ill to our neighbor.*

I. *What the love that constitutes true religion is not.*

1. The love that constitutes true religion is not natural affection, or the love of one's relatives. This needs no comment. The absence of natural affection, as mentioned in the Bible, is evidence of a high degree of depravity; but its exercise is not holiness.

2. It is not the love that exists between the sexes. This is only a modification of natural affection.

3. It is not the love of complacency. Complacency is an emotion of delight in its object. It is an involuntary state of mind, and exists naturally and often necessarily, when an object calculated to excite emotions of complacency is present to the mind. Being an involuntary state of mind, it often has no moral character at all, and when any degree of moral character is to be ascribed to complacency, it is because the emotions are indirectly under the influence of the will. Emotions are consequent upon thoughts, and arise spontaneously in the mind, when the attention is directed to the deep consideration of any subject. And as the will controls the attention, it indirectly controls the emotions. And emotions of complacency or displacency have moral character only as they are indirectly produced by the action of the will. Complacency may respect a great many different objects:

(1.) Personal beauty. We are so constituted that the presence of beautiful objects naturally excites emotions of complacency or delight in its object. The presence of a beautiful human being naturally and certainly excites emotions of delight, where no feeling of prejudice, envy,

---

The Oberlin Evangelist: Vol. III; March 3, 1841. The companion sermon is in *Principles of Victory*, pp. 172-182: "Love Is the Whole of Religion."

or other selfish consideration, begets an opposite state of emotion.

(2.) Complacency may respect other physical accomplishments, such as an elegant form, dignified deportment, elegant manners, good breeding, and multitudes of similar things. In such things we naturally take delight, and emotions of complacency naturally and certainly exist in the mind, under the consideration of such objects, unless some selfish or envious reason prevents.

(3.) It may respect intellectual endowments, a towering intellect, a lofty imagination, great learning, great eloquence; and innumerable such things may naturally excite emotions of complacency in their objects.

(4.) It may respect benefits received or expected. We naturally feel emotions of complacency in those who befriend us, or grant us great favors; and therefore, men may exercise very strong *emotions* of love to God on account of favors received or expected from Him, without one particle of true religion. Just as naturally as similar emotions of complacency might be exercised towards any other benefactor, without reference to any other feature of his character than that which is made by the bestowment of the particular favors which excite gratitude and complacency.

(5.) Complacency may respect and be founded in a similarity of views and intentions. Every man knows it to be true; he naturally feels complacency in those whose views, aims, and objects of pursuit correspond with his own, unless it be in cases where a similarity of aims produce a clashing of interests, as is sometimes the case with competitors in business. We see men of the same political creed having complacency in each other; and so we often see among professing Christians and members of the same sect. They often exercise a strong affection for or complacency in each other, solely on account of the fact of a similarity of views and prejudices. But in this there is not a particle of true piety.

(6.) Or, complacency may be a mere reciprocation, a mere loving of those who love us, and because they love us. But there is no piety in this. The Saviour says, "If ye love those that love you, what thank have ye? Do not even sinners love those that love them?"

(7.) Or it may respect character, whether good or bad. We often see individuals exercising a high degree of complacency in each other, because they are associated in vice. On the other hand, we often see persons exercising a high degree of complacency in each other on account of their virtues. Men are so constituted that they never can conscientiously approve of a wicked character; but on the contrary, they must always approve of right character. And all moral beings in the absence of selfish reasons for a contrary feeling will naturally experience emotions of delight in right character, when it is the subject of contemplation. But emotions of love or delight in right character do not constitute piety. Nor are they any certain evidence of piety. There is not a moral agent in the universe who knows what the character of God is, who does not approve it. Nor one who may not, and perhaps does not, when viewing the character of God in the abstract, experience strong emotions of delight in the moral beauty of His character, upon the same principles that he would feel emotions of delight in personal beauty.

(8.) It may respect the natural attributes of a being. Thus the wickedest of men may experience the strongest emotions of admiration and delight, in view of the natural attributes of God, as manifested in the works of creation, without a particle of that love to God that constitutes true religion.

4. It is not a fondness of a particular person. The love that constitutes the essence of true religion does not respect moral character at all. Nor is it complacency in particular individuals, or a feeling of love of any kind for particular individuals, to the neglect of others. God's holiness consists in universal benevolence to all beings, irrespective of their moral character; and for this reason, it led Him to give His only begotten Son to die for His enemies.

5. Nor is this love an emotion or mere feeling of any kind.

6. It is not a mere experience, or something in which we seem to ourselves to be passive, as we do in the exercise of emotions. A false philosophy has confounded emotions with true religion, under the name of religious affections. And it is astonishing and alarming to witness the extent to which this mistake and delusion is entertained by mankind. Hence, they speak of *experiencing* religion, and speak of religion as something in which they are passive, something springing up in their own minds involuntarily. They speak of *experiencing* such and such state of mind, and regard religion as something to be *experienced,* rather than as something to be done. Indeed, the mistake seems to be almost universal; the belief that religion belongs to the emotions, or feelings, rather than to the actings of the will. Hence, complacency in God and in Christians because they are holy is generally regarded, not only as evidence of piety, but as constituting the very essence of piety itself. And multitudes of professors of religion are supposing themselves to be highly spiritual, simply because they are in the exercise of lively emotions of gratitude for favors received, of complacency in God, on account of benefits conferred, and of complacency in Christians because they are Christians. Now let me say that these emotions may be the *result* of a right state of the will, or of the exercise of that love which constitutes true religion, or they may not. They do not in any case constitute the essence of true religion, and may often exist without it. And what ungodly man, who has ever been in the habit of intense thinking upon religious subjects, cannot testify to the truth of this from his own experience. The fact is that religion is something to be done, and not merely to be *experienced*; religion is something in which man is voluntarily active, and not passive. Indeed, the foundation of all true religion consists in voluntary action, and not in emotion. By voluntary action I mean, of course, the actings of the voluntary power or of the will.

II. *What the love that constitutes true religion is.*

1. I have just said, it always belongs to the will; that is , it consists in acts of the will.

2. It is a *state* of the will, in opposition to a single or a series of volitions. There is an important distinction to be here noticed, between
choice and volition. Choice is the mind's election or selection of an end.
Volition consists in those efforts or actions of the will which are put forth
to accomplish the end chosen. A man chooses to be a merchant. In obedience to this choice his will puts forth all those volitions that put his
body and mind in motion, and that are necessary to accomplish the object chosen. Choice, then, is a state of mind in opposition to those volitions that are exercised for obtaining the end chosen.

3. The love, then, that constitutes true religion, is a fixed, permanent choice, or state of the will. It should be understood that it is a *state,*
abiding choice, or preference; and from the very laws of the mind has a
controlling influence. If you choose to go to the city of New York, this
choice will naturally and certainly beget those volitions and states of
mind, and actions of the body that will accomplish this end, if it is within your power.

4. The love that constitutes true religion is the choice of a supreme
end or object of pursuit, or a selection of the great and ultimate end of
existence. It is a supreme, permanent, controlling preference or choice of
the mind.

It is benevolence or good-willing; the exact opposite of selfishness.
Selfishness is the supreme preference or choice of self-gratification as the
grand end of life. It is a choosing or willing our own gratification. This is
the foundation of all sin, and the carryings out of this consist in those
volitions, states of mind, emotions, and bodily actions that make up the
history of wicked men. The love mentioned in the text, and that constitutes true religion, is that state of mind demanded by the law of God.
Hence, it is said in the text, that "love is the fulfillment of the law." It is
the mind's supreme election or choice of the universal good of being as
the supreme end of existence. And it respects the good of all beings
capable of doing or enjoying good. This supremely respects the Being of
God, since He is capable of doing and enjoying infinitely more good than
all other beings. True religion therefore, prefers His good, happiness,
and glory, to all other things in the universe. Remember, it is benevolence toward God, and not complacency in God, that constitutes the
foundation of all true religion. Complacency in God is virtue when it is
produced by a virtuous state of the will, but not otherwise. Complacency
in the character of God is often mentioned in the Bible as constituting
virtue; but it should always be remembered that emotions of complacency in God and other holy beings, when they are virtuous at all, instead of constituting the foundation and essence of virtue, are virtue
only in its lower form. I repeat it; the foundation of all virtue is benevolence to God and to the universe. It is good *willing* and *doing,* in opposition to mere good *feeling.* I wish to get this idea distinctly before your
minds, because there are so many mistakes upon this subject.

5. But here let me say that the love which constitutes true religion is
disinterested love. And here again let me beg you not to misunderstand

me. For oftentimes, when we speak of disinterested love, it is manifest that we are understood to mean disinterested good emotions, rather than disinterested good willing. When it is said that disinterested love consists in loving God for what He really is, it often seems to be meant that we are to exercise complacency in God on account of His character. And this complacency is represented as disinterested love; but this is a grand mistake. To love God for what He is, and with that love which constitutes true religion, is to love Him with the love of benevolence, to will His good, His glory, and His happiness. Now complacency in His character will naturally and certainly exist where there is true benevolence toward Him, and as I have already said, it may exist where there is no benevolence at all, when His character is viewed as it may be, as a mere abstraction. But let it be forever remembered that true religion consists in benevolence to God and to men and to all beings capable of loving or receiving good. This benevolence does not respect personal character, but regards the good of every moral and every sentient being, whether sinful or holy, in proportion to its relative value as that is apprehended by the *mind*. It longs for the salvation of the wicked as much as for the salvation of the righteous. This is manifestly the temper and spirit of God. This is the spirit of Christ, and this is the essence and substance of true godliness wherever it exists. It would not wantonly injure a fly nor tread upon a worm. It regards happiness as a real good. It longs for the diffusion of universal holiness among all moral agents and of universal enjoyment among all sentient beings. God delights himself in the happiness of the little chirping birds, and bounding lambs, and leaping fishes, and all the multitudes of animal existences with which the universe is teeming. So every benevolent mind has chosen the promotion of universal good as the supreme end of life. Consequently its volitions, thoughts, and actions are in deep harmony and sympathy with God, and directed to the same end to which He directs His efforts.

III. *Who is to be regarded as our neighbor.*

1. We are to regard all moral beings as our neighbors, in whatever country or in whatever world they may exist. We are to regard their interests and happiness according to their relative value. This cannot reasonably, and probably will not, be doubted.

2. All sentient beings are to be regarded as our neighbors; all are connected with us in the great chain of being. And the good of mere animals is to be regarded and treated by us according to its relative value. The beasts of the field, the fowls of the air, the fishes of the sea, everything that has life and breath, all are to be regarded as our neighbors.

3. Our neighbors are especially those moral beings most immediately within our reach, and who are the most naturally and certainly affected by our influence, those whose geographical proximity to us brings them within our immediate neighborhood, in a most emphatic sense. Our families, and those whose habitations are most contiguous to ours, who live in the same town, country, state, or nation—these are to be

regarded as especially our neighbors, but not to the neglect or annihilation of our relation to the human family and to the universe. But to those more within our reach we are under special obligation, whether they be men or mere animals. Every sentient being within our reach is to be regarded as emphatically our neighbor.

IV. *Why this love worketh no ill.*

1. Because this love belongs to the will and therefore it naturally controls the actions of both body and mind; it will work no ill to its neighbor. As it directs the thoughts, it will not think evil of a neighbor. As it consists in choice, and therefore directs the volitions, it will not suffer volitions that shall work ill to its neighbor. As it controls the attention, and therefore the emotions, it will neither beget nor suffer emotions or desires that work ill to its neighbor. As through the volitions it controls the outward actions, it cannot work ill to its neighbor.

2. Because love has no tendency to work ill to our neighbor:

(1.) Love respects a neighbor's rights, and aims at securing them instead of trampling upon them.

(2.) Love respects a neighbor's piety, and endeavors by all possible means to make him holy as a means of making him happy. It regards his holiness and happiness as a great good, and is not reckless of the influence it exerts, either to promote or destroy a neighbor's piety.

(3.) Love regards the interests and well-being of a neighbor in all respects.

(4.) Especially does love respect the rights, piety, and happiness of those with whom we are most nearly in contact, and who for this reason are more immediately under our influence.

(5.) Benevolence omits no known duty, whereby our neighbor's interest may suffer, and therefore does not by omission work ill to its neighbor.

(6.) Love does not omit any duty, whereby our neighbor is stumbled, and led through imitation of our example or in other ways to fall into sin.

(7.) As love consists in good-willing, or in choosing the universal good of being as the supreme end of life, it will of course beget those volitions and actions, that will promote the good of all around us, and especially of those who are near, and most immediately affected by our conduct. In the 13th chapter of First Corinthians, the Apostle describes this love as the foundation and sum of all virtue; and after asserting in the strongest language that no faith or work is of any value without it, he mentions several of its predominent characteristics with the manifest design of distinguishing that which constitutes true religion from everything else. Our translation calls it charity. The original work is the same as that which is rendered love in this text. The same word is uniformly used in the original for that state of mind that constitutes true religion, or the love required by the law of God. This love, he says, is "patient and long suffering." And who does not know that we are naturally very patient and long suffering towards those whose happiness is very dear to us, and toward whom we feel truly benevolent. Mere complacency is fitful and evanescent, and depends so much upon the particular exhibition made to our mind at the time that it is transitory from its very nature. See the complacency that parents have in their children. When they are sweet and smiling and lovely, the parent is exceedingly delighted with them. But if they become ill-natured and hateful, here another exhibition is made to the mind, which, instead of exciting complacency, begets impatience and fretfulness. Just so a mere complacency in God will often be exceedingly fitful and of short duration, as the ever varying course of His providence exhibits Him to our minds as robed in smiles or clothed with frowns. But benevolence is not subject to these changes, because it has not its foundations in the moral character, in the naturally pleasing or displeasing manifestations that are made to the mind, but it is good-willing. Love is a patient, persevering, and supreme disposition to promote the good of its object.

A second characteristic named by the Apostle is kindness. "Charity suffereth long and is kind." This is of course a characteristic of benevolence or of good-will.

A third characteristic is that it "envieth not." Envy is an emotion of unhappiness in view of the prosperity of others. Now as the love that constitutes true religion consists in benevolence, it is impossible that it should consist also with envy. Benevolence cannot be disturbed and made unhappy by the prosperity of its object. Envy is, therefore, the very opposite of true religion, and is the offspring of hell. An envious man is "of his father the devil, and the lusts of his father he will do."

A fourth characteristic of this love is that it "vaunteth not itself," or, as rendered in the margin, it is not rash. It is mild and amiable, and not rough and headstrong.

A fifth characteristic of this love is that it "is not puffed up." It is not swelling and pompous and showy and Pharisaical and ostentatious and proud, but is exactly the reverse of all this.

A sixth characteristic is that it "doth not behave itself unseemly." True politeness consists in the practice of benevolence. And when wicked men affect to be truly polite, they affect to be truly benevolent. They are, to be sure, hypocritical in this; but still, it remains a truth, that true politeness manifests itself in a disposition to make everybody happy. So that one of the characteristics of true religion is true politeness. It "doth not behave itself unseemly." There is a natural urbanity and courteousness that is always a characteristic of true benevolence. True religion does not need the polish of a dancing school, or need to ape the manners of nobility or the most refined classes of society in order to exhibit genuine politeness. Who doubts that Jesus Christ was truly polite? His benevolence led Him to seek the comfort and happiness of all around Him. He sought both their temporal and their spiritual good. When at a feast, He chose not the chief seat for Himself; but gave others preference. His benevolence exhibited itself in making as little trouble as possible wherever He went; and consequently when in the house of

Martha and Mary, He manifested no disposition to have the sisters give up their time to preparing good dishes for His entertainment. But He commended Mary for listening to His instructions, and reproved Martha for giving herself up to carefulness for His entertainment. Take any person you please, and let him be filled with the love of God, and he will naturally and certainly exhibit a lovely exterior instead of that which is unseemly. If riding in a stage coach, if in a steamboat, a railroad car, at a public house, at home, or abroad, in public, or in the family circle, he will exhibit a disposition to accommodate, to prevent all unhappiness and all sin, and to make everybody comfortable and holy and happy. He will not be boorish and unmannerly, rough, outrageous, and unseemly; but will exhibit that wisdom that cometh down from heaven, which is "first pure, then peaceable, gentle, and easy to be entreated, full of mercy and good fruits, without partiality, and without hypocrisy."

A seventh characteristic is that it "seeketh not her own." Its supreme object is the promotion of the universal good and happiness of all. Of course, it will not be selfish, but will manifest itself in the most assiduous endeavors, to make all around as comfortable and as happy and as holy as possible.

An eighth characteristic is, it "is not easily provoked." Of course benevolence will not easily quarrel with its object. It is not quickly impatient and ready to scold, but is extremely calm and forbearing.

A ninth characteristic is that love "thinketh no evil." It not only does not meditate any evil, but does not surmise or suspect evil where all appearances are right. A selfish mind is always suspecting hypocrisy in others, because it is conscious of hypocrisy in itself. A hypocrite, a liar, a knave, or dishonest man, is apt of course to suspect others, because he naturally judges others by himself. But an honest, upright, benevolent mind, thinketh no evil, unless there is some appearance of evil.

A tenth characteristic is that love "speaketh no evil." This is not especially mentioned by the Apostle in this connection, but it is a doctrine abundantly taught in the Bible. And if it were not, the very nature of true benevolence renders it certain that love speaketh no evil. Speaking evil is speaking either truth or falsehood which is prejudicial to the character of anyone with a selfish intention, and when the circumstances of the case do not demand such speaking as a dictate of benevolence. Now benevolence is the choice of the universal good of being. It is therefore impossible that benevolence should be guilty of evil speaking. Love is tender of every man's reputation as of the apple of its own eye, and would as soon pluck out its own eyes as to inflict a needless wound upon the character of anyone.

Another characteristic is that love "rejoiceth not in iniquity, but rejoiceth in the truth." As all iniquity is injurious to the universe, benevolence must deplore it of course, and cannot rejoice in it. But as truth is the instrument of universal good, benevolence must of course rejoice in the truth.

The Apostle goes on to say, love "Beareth all things, believeth all things, hopeth all things, endureth all things." I cannot enlarge upon these particulars. He concludes by saying, charity or love "never faileth;" that is, it abideth. From its very nature, it is a *state* of mind, and is not fitful and evanescent like emotions. The emotions of the mind are naturally like an effervescence, thrown into an excitement, and then naturally and quickly subside. On the contrary, "charity never faileth." It is the supreme and deliberate choice of the mind, or abiding and permanent state of the will; instead of that feverish excitement which people talk of *experiencing,* and which they falsely dominate true religion.

Remarks

1. From this subject we learn the delusion of an Antinomian religion. Vast multitudes of professors of religion suppose religion to consist in frames and feelings instead of good-willing. They can relate what they call a good experience. They can talk of their views and raptures and peace of mind; and in these things they manifestly suppose true religion to consist. Now, I have already said, and wish here to repeat it, that as these frames consist in emotions, and are only indirectly under the power of the will, they are the very lowest forms of virtue, and doubtless may exist where there is no true religion at all. They may arise solely out of a mistaken view of God's character and relations, and of our own character and relations. The Universalist doubtless exercises the love of complacency toward the God which he worships. The Antinomian feels complacency in God, as he understands His character. Thus every form of enthusiasm, fanaticism, and delusion, may be united with complacency in an imaginary God. Indeed, it is very easy to see that almost any possible or conceivable state of the emotions, or mere feelings, may be produced by mistaken views of things. Now as the mere feelings or emotions of the mind depend upon the views and opinions which are entertained by the mind, very little dependence can be placed upon them, even as evidences of true piety consists in them. Many persons are carried away with dreams and entertain the strangest and most absurd opinions on religious subjects, but their emotions will be found to correspond with their views thoughts and opinions. And these emotions will sometimes be exceedingly deep and overpowering, and it matters not at all whether these opinions are true or false. Persons will feel just as deeply in a dream, in view of the most absurd and ridiculous things that a dreaming mind can imagine, as if those things were actual realities. Now it would be strange indeed if the reality and depth of these emotions should be depended upon as evidence of the reality of their objects. The solemn fact is that there is a great and very common, but ruinous, mistake upon this subject in making religion to consist in emotions, and what are very commonly termed affections, instead of consisting, as it really does, in the state and actions of the will.

It appears to me that President Edwards has committed a sad mistake upon this subject in confounding the *sensibility with the* *will,* and has laid a foundation for a vast amount of delusion.*

And here let me be understood. Emotions, or frames, or feelings are the certain and necessary results of a right state of the will, or of the benevolence or good-willing that constitutes true religion. *If the will is right, it will direct the attention of the mind to the consideration of those subjects that will naturally and necessarily beget lively and deep emotions of gratitude, complacency, godly sorrow, and all those states of mind of which Christians speak, and which they are so apt to conceive as constituting true religion. But these constitute the happiness, rather than the virtue of the mind. They are rather the reward of holiness than holiness itself.* To be sure, they are virtuous so far as they are indirectly under the influence of the will. But they are only virtuous on that account, and are so, therefore, in no other sense than thoughts and the decisions of conscience may be virtuous. Thought is the spontaneous and necessary acting of mind when the will directs the attention to an object of thought. The decisions of conscience are the necessary decisions of reason when the attention of the mind is directed by the will to a consideration of conscience. Both the thoughts and the decisions of conscience are necessary when the attention of the mind is thus employed by the will. And whenever any state of mind, or motion of the body, is under the control of the will, there is a sense in which these actions have moral character. But separate them from the actions of the will, and they have no moral character at all. Now if the will be right, there is a sense in which the thoughts and the decisions of conscience and the outward actions may be virtuous; and if the will be wrong, there is a sense in which they are all vicious.

It should, however, be borne continually in mind that the praise or blame-worthiness lies in the voluntary actions of the mind, or in the decisions of the will; and, properly speaking, in the decisions of the will alone.

2. From this subject it is easy to see that where there is true religion there must of necessity be a corresponding life. The emotions do not control the actions of body or mind. Consequently, if religion consisted in emotion, it might exist in the mind in its reality and strength without being evinced in the outward conduct. For we know that men often exercise the deepest feelings and emotions on subjects, while they refuse or neglect to act in conformity with their feelings. But the same cannot be said of the actions of the will. Men always act outwardly in conformity with their volitions. Their outward actions are connected with the actings of their will by a natural necessity. Good-willing, therefore, or true religion, always manifests itself in a holy life. Inaction and supineness in religion are absurd and impossible, where true religion exists.

---

*Jonathan Edward (1703-1758) was an American Calvinist philosopher and minister, whose greatest work was probably *Freedom of the Will* (1754); see Jonathan Edwards, *Freedom of the Will,* edited by Paul Ramsey (New Haven: Yale University Press, 1957).

Benevolence, or good-willing, must produce action and good action by a natural necessity. It is therefore absurd and ridiculous to say that a man has true religion and yet is not employed in doing good, where he is able to act at all. Remember, I beseech you, that religion is benevolence or good-willing, and not mere feeling or emotion; and because it is good-willing, it necessarily produces good acting. So that the very essence of religion is activity, exertion, or effort of heart and life, to promote universal good. A religion of supineness is, therefore, not the religion of Christ. Antinomian inaction is as opposite to true religion as light is to darkness. And a person can no more be truly religious, and give himself up to inaction and ecstasy and peace and joy than he can do anything else that involves a contradiction. Religion consists in the state or actings of the heart, or will; and is, therefore, in its very nature, essentially activity. I mean as I say. Religion is activity itself. It is the mind willing the good of universal being.

3. You see also the great delusion of making religion to consist in a complacent love of God and of Christians. I have already said that complacency is an emotion, and where the will or heart is right it will always be exercised towards God. But it is the effect, rather than the essence of true religion. It appears to me that many mistake in supposing that the love of the brethren, which is so largely insisted on in the Bible, is complacency rather than benevolence. But a little consideration will show that the love of the brethren and Christians insisted upon by Christ and his Apostles is benevolence, and not complacency. It is spoken of as the same kind of love with which Christ loved us. Hence, it is said, that "as Christ laid down his life for us, we should be ready to lay down our lives for the brethren." But the love of God and of Christ for the world was benevolence, and not complacency. It was a love exercised to enemies, and not to those that were holy; and consequently, it must have been benevolence.

4. We see the mistake of those who excuse themselves for the want of love to the brethren, because they say they do not see in them the image of Christ. The love that we exercise to the image of Christ is complacency. And this excuse shows that those who make it suppose the love required of them to be complacency and not benevolence; and that, consequently, where there is no holiness manifest, there is no obligation to exercise love. Now this is a ruinous mistake. For the love which we are required to exercise to the brethren is good-will, or benevolence, and therefore does not respect their moral character. So that a true Christian exercises deep and permanent affection for the brethren, whatever may be their spiritual state. There are many persons who seem to give themselves up to the most censorious and denunciatory speaking of heartless professors of religion, and seem to think that this is all well enough, because they are all backsliders or hypocrites. Now, I would humbly ask, is this benevolence? Is this love?

To this benevolence the love of complacency is added, where there is a foundation for it, or a manifestation of holy character. And complacency will render it still more certain, that he who exercises it will avoid all evil speaking. But benevolence itself, where there is no manifestation of holy character, as I have already shown, will naturally avoid speaking evil, or "working ill to our neighbor."

5. You see from this subject the delusion of those who profess to be religious and yet transact business upon selfish principles. Selfishness and benevolence are exact and eternal opposites. Said a professional man to me, not long ago, "I have been surprised that the religion of those who have been long religious does not do more to overcome their selfishness." This is just the same thing as to express surprise that those who have long professed to be religious have no religion. The fact is that the very beginning of religion, or the new birth itself, is the overthrowing of selfishness as the reigning principle of the mind. It is the establishment in the mind, as a permanent state of the will, of the antagonist principle of benevolence. Hence, it is said that "whatsoever is born of God overcometh the world," and that "he who is born of God cannot sin, for his seed remaineth in him, so that he cannot sin, because he is born of God." By this I do not understand the Apostle to mean that a soul that is born of God cannot be seduced into occasional sins by the power of temptation; but I do understand him to say that *he cannot live in sin. He cannot transact his daily business upon selfish principles,* which are the essence of all sin. It is, therefore, absurd and impossible that a benevolent or truly religious mind should transact business upon selfish principles.

6. Love, or benevolence, and its necessary fruits, is the whole of religion. I say *necessary* fruits, because the actions of the mind and body are connected with the actions of the will by a natural necessity; so that the fruits of holiness are the necessary products of a right state of the heart or will.

7. Where there are no fruits there is no true religion. It is in vain for unfruitful souls, Antinomians, and persons who sit down in inaction to pretend to be pious. They talk in vain of their views, their experience, and their raptures. Unless the fruits of benevolence, or good-willing, are upon them; unless, like Christ, they go about doing good, when they are able to go about at all, it is a delusion and nonsense for them to suppose that they are truly religious.

8. We see from this subject the delusion of those individuals and churches and ecclesiastical bodies, who seem to be given up in a great measure to censoriousness and vituperation, engaged in little else than watching for the haltings and the errors of their brethren, and who seem to be abandoned to a spirit of fretfulness rather than of love or good-willing. In this remark, I do not of course mean to accuse the whole Church of believing in this state, but speak of those who really are in this state.

9. You see the delusion of those editors of newspapers, whose columns savor of gabble rather than of the sweet benevolence of God. Look into their pages: is that the "love that worketh no ill to his neighbor"? Why, instead of working no ill to his neighbor, it would work the ruin of

the world if people had any confidence in what they read in such periodicals. No thanks to some of the editors of the present day, if their pages do not work unlimited mischief. It will only be because the readers have ceased to confide in them. I do not of course design this remark to be of universal application, but that there are lamentable cases to attest the truth of this remark will be acknowledged with sorrow by those who truly love the Lord.

10. We see the delusion of those whose religion consists in *desiring* the happiness of those who are at a distance, while it neglects the happiness of those in its immediate neighborhood. Multitudes of individuals will go to the Monthly Concert and pray for the heathen, will give money to send the Gospel or the Bible to the heathen, but their prayers seem always to overlook those right around them, and who are more immediately and necessarily affected by their conduct. Their own domestics or clerks or laborers, are perhaps daily rendered unhappy by their malevolence and peevishness. They are left in a great measure unprayed for, unwarned, unblessed by them. They seem to be engaged in anything but promoting the happiness of those within their reach, and yet suppose themselves to be truly religious. But herein is a great delusion. It is the religion of the imagination and desires. It is like the piety of a man who contemplates going on a foreign mission: he feels deeply, as he says, for the heathen, but never bestirs himself to save the souls of men at home. He can go through with his education as lazily as a drone. He can let his own classmates and perhaps his own roommate go down to death and hell around him, and yet imagine himself to feel truly benevolent and to long for the salvation of the heathen. He never promotes piety and revivals of religion at home, and yet works himself into the belief that he shall do it abroad. But again, I say this is the religion of the imagination, and a deep and ruinous delusion. Let such a man go to heathen ground and be surrounded with the naked and cold realities of heathenism; and he will find at last his sad mistake; and were it not for his pride of character and fear of the loss of reputation, he would soon find his way back to Christian lands, and the repose and indolence of a contemplative life. How many there are who are in the constant neglect of the happiness of all in their immediate neighborhood, whose prayers and efforts seem always to overleap the heads of all within their reach, and light down upon distant and unknown lands. Now true benevolence embosoms all mankind, but it always concerns itself for the time being to secure the well-being of those most immediately within its reach. Those that compose the domestic circle are the objects upon which it necessarily and primarily exerts itself. Through these it flows abroad to all that are near, especially, and ceases not till it reaches those that are afar off. In this sense it is true that "charity begins at home," but not in the sense in which this is generally understood. This saying is generally supposed to mean that charity regards self-interest first and most, but the very fact that the term charity is used which is synonymous with benevolence shows that the true meaning of this saying is that benevolence begins by

seeking the happiness of those in its immediate neighborhood, and continues to extend itself until it reaches those that are afar off.

11. The kind of religion, or rather of irreligion, of which I have just been speaking would be of no benefit if the world were full of it. Suppose that all mankind had this kind of religion, each one desiring and praying for the happiness of those beyond his reach, but neglecting and trampling upon the happiness of all within his reach. Who then would be happy, if everyone were employed in making those immediately in contact with him unhappy, and were only seeking the happiness of those at a distance, who in their turn render themselves and those immediately around them unhappy while desiring and praying for the happiness of others at a distance. Such religion as this would leave the world in wretchedness if every man on earth possessed it.

12. You can see how real religion makes its possessor happy. There is a sweetness and a divine relish in the exercise of benevolence itself, and in addition to this the emotions of the mind will, ordinarily, be in accordance with the state of the will or heart. And thus true religion necessarily results in the happiness of its possessor.

13. You see what a truly religious family, neighborhood or universe would be, if everyone were employed in making those around him happy to the full extent of his power. A most divine religion this! Take but a single family, where benevolence is the law of every member. See the husband and wife, brothers and sisters, and all the members of the family, how careful they are not to injure each other's piety, or unnecessarily to wound each other's feelings—how kindly they watch over each other for good—how watchful they are to each other's interests and happiness—how pleased each one is to deny himself to promote the general good. The law of kindness dwells ever on their tongues. Such a family is a little picture of heaven. Wherever such a family is found, it is an oasis, or a little green spot in the midst of a vast wilderness of moral death.

14. You see the utter unreasonableness of infidelity. Infidels affect to disbelieve the necessity of a change of heart. But what do they mean? Do they not know by their own observation that mankind are by nature supremely selfish? And can they be happy without a radical change of heart? A world of selfish beings make up heaven! The idea is absurd and ridiculous. It is self-evident that without that change of heart which consists in a radical change of character from selfishness to benevolence, mankind can never be saved.

15. You see from this subject how to detect false hopes. False professors are either inactive in religion, or manifest a legal spirit in opposition to the spirit of love. There are two extremes that should always be well guarded in religion. The one is antinomianism, which satisfies itself with frames and feelings while it makes little or no exertion for the salvation of the world. The other is a legal zeal that bustles about often harshly and furiously and professes to be working for God, when there is a manifest dash of bitterness and misanthropy in the countenance and manner and life. This is not the love that worketh no ill to his neighbor.

It is not the benevolence and spirit of Christ; and all such religion is spurious however zealous, however active, and however apparently useful it may be.

16. Spurious conversions often throw the mind into a state of fermentation and deep feeling which of course soon subsides. But true conversion consists in a change of choice, and is of course an abiding state of mind. Where there are revivals of religion the chaff may be easily discovered from the wheat when the effervescence of excited emotion has passed by. You can then see whether the will is under the control of truth. While the emotions are strong they may induce a series of volitions which would lead for the time being to the conclusion that the will or heart is really changed, but as soon as these emotions subside, if the heart is not changed, the selfish preference will again resume its control; and just in proportion as the excitement ceases will it become apparent in the man's life and spirit and temper and especially in his business transactions, that his selfish heart or preference is not changed, and that he is still an unregenerate man. The fact that the emotions very often induce volition, and many times a series of volitions inconsistent with the governing preference of the will or heart, renders it impossible for us, in the midst of the excitement of a revival, to distinguish clearly between true and false conversion; but as the excitement subsides, if we are willing to be guided by the Word of God, we can clearly distinguish between those that are born again, and those that are not. And we are bound so to distinguish, and to deal faithfully, and promptly, and energetically with those who are seen still to remain in selfishness.

17. You see the vast importance of distinguishing that which constitutes true religion, and all those frames and feelings upon which so much stress is laid in many portions of the Church. Many are inactive in the cause of Christ, but they suppose themselves to be holy simply because they do not know what holiness is. They do not understand that their frames are the result of their views and opinions, and whether their opinions are right or wrong, cannot be known by their frames or emotions, but by the actings of their will. They may have love in the form of emotions, they may have peace, and joy, and even ecstasy in the form of emotions, without one particle of true religon. And if they are not really in a state of efficient good-willing—if they are not engaged in doing good, in promoting individual and general happiness to the extent of their power, it is absolutely certain that they are not truly religious. Oh, that this were understood! Oh, that it were known that religion is benevolence—the love that is willing to lay down its life for its neighbor! How much that is called religion is working continual ill to its neighbor! But blessed be God, true religion worketh no ill to its neighbor. Give me then religious neighbors, and I am content. Give me irreligious neighbors, and I will try to do them good. Let him hear that hath an ear to hear. Amen.

16

THE KINGDOM OF GOD IN CONSCIOUSNESS*

Romans 14:17

"The kingdom of God is not meat and drink, but righteousness, and peace, and joy in the Holy Ghost."

In speaking from these words, I inquire:
   I. *What is the kingdom of God?*
   II. *What are the three particulars which constitute this kingdom of God in our text, "righteousness, peace, and joy in the Holy Ghost"?*

I. *What is the kingdom of God?*
1. It is not an outward organization; it is not the visible church, or any ecclesiastical establishment whatever.
2. It is not any material or worldly good.
3. But it is the reign of Christ, the King, in the soul of man.

II. *I notice the three particulars which are here said to constitute this kingdom of God, "righteousness, peace, and joy in the Holy Ghost."*
1. What is righteousness?
Righteousness is moral uprightness. This is that love to God and man which the Bible requires. Righteousness does not belong strictly to muscular action, but to *the state of the heart.* And righteousness is really the spirit of the moral law existing and established in the heart. Christ promised that at a certain time He would "write His law upon the hearts of His people, and engrave it in their inward parts, and they should all know the Lord from the least of them unto the greatest of them." The spirit of this law, that which the law really requires in its meaning and intent, is supreme, perfect, disinterested love to God, and equal love to man.

It requires that God should be loved for His own sake, and supremely, because He is supremely and infinitely great and good; that man should be loved as we love ourselves; and that this love to God and man should be expressed in all appropriate ways in all the relations of life.

The Oberlin Evangelist: Vol. XXIII; April 24, 1861.

This love, with all its appropriate expressions in the temper, and life, and spirit, is righteousness. It is a *voluntary* love; and therefore, must reveal itself in uprightness of life in every relation in which we exist.

Righteousness is the opposite of unrighteousness. Unrighteousness is a withholding from God and man their due; a spirit of don't-care for God or man that condemns the rights, and feelings, and authority of God, and the rights of our neighbor. It is a want of conformity to the moral law, a voluntary withholding of obedience to it. Righteousness is the opposite of this. It is love positively exercised, with all its positive fruits. It is real active devotion to the whole mind of God, and also devotion to the interests and well-being of man.

Righteousness is a *state* of mind in which there is a continual offering of self in a confiding love-service to God. God is served diligently and with all the powers, and with respect to Him and not for pay. It is a cheerful and willing service; not because we *must*, but from a *supreme interest* in Him.

It always implies diligence, and industry, and study, to please God; it always implies the avoiding of everything that can *displease* Him; and in short, it consists in the heart's being fully committed to do and suffer all the will of God, and that readily and joyfully, for His own sake.

Righteousness also involves sincere devotion to the interests of man; a willingness to deny self when by so doing we can promote the greater good of others, and that from real regard to our fellowman as to a brother. It is in fact the spirit of universal brotherhood practically carried out.

This, then, is the righteousness which constitutes the great element or peculiarity of the kingdom of God in the soul.

It is Christ's righteousness imparted to the soul of man. It is Christ's law or will taking effect in the soul of man, and begetting His own righteousness in us; and thus we come to be partakers of the righteousness of God, not merely by imputation, but by actual experience, and active love and service. I pray you, let no one overlook the true end of righteousness. Do not forget that true righteousness is the very love in kind that is in Christ's own heart, and that led Him to do all He has done for mankind.

This love, it should be understood, must necessarily express itself in the life, because the connection between this love and outward action is a connection of necessity. This love consists in the will's devotion to God and to the good of man. It is consecration; it is making common cause with God and man, and *unifying* ourselves with God's state of mind.

2. The second element of the kingdom of God in the soul of man is said to be "peace."

Peace of mind is not apathy; a state of indifference to God, His claims, or service. Peace is the opposite of war, or strife, or friction, under the government of God. I say, it is the *opposite* of this; it is a state of *cordiality*, and of *conscious* cordiality, existing between the soul and God.

It does not consist merely in the soul's being reconciled to God, but also includes the fact that God is reconciled to man, and that this is revealed to us in consciousness. In this state of mind, we are aware that God has accepted us, and forgiven us, that our peace is made with Him.

Peace is a state of universal satisfaction of mind with God's will as expressed in creation and providence, His law and Gospel. I say *satisfaction* with His will, for if in anything we are not satisfied with God, we are restive, like an ungoverned child. If we *profess* to submit, we do it ungraciously, and not really. There cannot be peace between us and God as long as a particle of dissatisfaction with God's ways and will remains in the heart.

This peace is a state of mind in which there is a conscious yielding of everything that God claims. The mind is settled to do so; to make this the universal law of our activity; to accept all God's requirements, and yield, not merely of necessity, but willingly and cordially to all that He requires of us.

This state of mind is like the calm deep flow of a river. It is a calm deep flow of feeling in conscious harmony with God's state of mind. It is remarkable that in this state of mind we are conscious, not of the mind's lying still and being in a quiescent state, but the sensibility seems to be flowing as a deep current of the mind. And it all flows in one direction. Like a river, there is no conflicting of different currents, some flowing in one direction and some in another.

There may be ripplings in the current—there may be obstructions so that the waters in one place may dam up and boil over the obstructions, but there are no *counter* currents forcing their way upward and conflicting with the general stream, with the little eddyings here and there, and the obstructions, and boilings up, and flowings around the obstructing objects here and there. Upon the whole, the whole movement of the mind, the intellect, the sensibility, the will, all come flowing in one direction, and the flow is harmony; the flow is peace; the flow is a deep, broad river of life and love.

This peace is like the subdued, settled, satisfied state of a weaned child. As the Psalmist says, "Lord, my heart is not haughty, nor mine eyes lofty; neither do I exercise myself in great matters, or in things too high for me. Surely I have behaved and quieted myself as a child that is weaned of its mother; my soul is even as a weaned child."

Everyone knows that an unsubdued child, unsettled in obedience, is continually chafing under parental authority; and there can be no real peace between the parent and the child unless the child be actually and thoroughly subdued, so that he will accept the will of the parent as his law of life. And when the child is really and thoroughly subdued, so that he is cheerful and satisfied with his state of subjection; when this state becomes his chosen adopted state, and this subjection is preferred to following his own counsels and his own will, then there is peace between the parent and the child. Then the child himself has peace of mind; then the child himself can be happy. He is not restive, while keeping up a constant friction with parental authority. The same is true in the government of God. While the King is striving to set up His kingdom in the heart, and the sinner is resisting, there is conviction, remorse, dissatisfaction, struggling, evading, stubbornness, chafing, cavilling; and all the elements of disorder, of sin, of turmoil, are in the soul. In this state there can be no peace. This heart cannot be saved; it cannot, by any possibility, go to heaven. This mind can never have peace until it is completely, and joyfully, and universally subject to the will of God.

Now the peace of the gospel consists in this perfectly subdued, settled, confiding, joyful, quiescent state of mind, in respect to God, His government, character, requirements, and dealings.

This peace always implies and includes a state of mind the opposite of condemnation and remorse.

I say, the *opposite* of these; in other words, we are conscious, as I have already intimated, of our being accepted; not only of our being at peace with God, but of His being at peace with us. A state of forgiveness, of being restored to favor, of being on good terms with God through His abounding grace, is always involved in this peace.

This peace is the opposite of all unbelieving carefulness, and anxiety that could corrode, fret, or distress the mind.

When the kingdom of God is set up in the soul, not only is it true that God's *whole* will is accepted; but the soul has such confidence in God, such spirituality in regard to perceiving God in His universal providence, that, recognizing God in all the movements of His providence, unbelieving carefulness and corroding anxiety, that so much disturbs the world, is shut out from the mind.

3. I notice the third element which is involved in this kingdom of God, viz.: "joy in the Holy Ghost."

This is not a mere joy arising out of the supposition that we are safe. Although this consideration is a matter of joy, still this is not the joy here mentioned. It is joy in the Holy Ghost. From the union of spirit with God's Spirit, God's joy is really reproduced in us. Christ said to His disciples, "These things have I spoken unto you that my joy might remain in you, and that your joy might be full."

Joy, or rejoicing in God, is always an element of this kingdom of God in the soul. In this kingdom, God's joy, and righteousness, and peace, are so imparted to us by the Holy Ghost, that we are really conscious, not only of being partakers of His holiness and of His divine nature, but also of drinking of the river of His own pleasures or joys. Where righteousness and peace are, there religious joy, or joy in God, will be.

This joy is a rejoicing in God Himself. It is not rejoicing in ourselves, either that we are good, or that we are saved, or that we are going to heaven. God is the direct object in which we rejoice. The contemplation of God, communion with God, fills the soul with joy unspeakable; and there is in the soul of the Christian a joy deep, abiding, perennial, even amidst the trials of this life. We have always in God the same reason for rejoicing in Him; He is always the same glorious, loving, infinite object of joy. The mind that is in harmony with His will cannot but enjoy His peace, and rejoice in Him. Such a mind cannot be poor; such a mind cannot want the grounds and all the elements of rejoicing. Indeed, religious joy always will be where religion is. Since religion is supreme love to God and equal love to man, consisting in a cordial embracing of God's whole character, and will, and way, it can be that there shall always be joy. Even in the midst of sorrows, there will be a deep religious joy; in the midst of the trials of life, in the midst of temptations, in the midst of persecutions, and even in the article of death, there is joy, joy in God.

The mind that is devoted to God cannot be deprived of religious joy. Religious joy necessarily springs up in the very exercise of love, faith, and gratitude. It is the natural and certain result of a truly religious state of mind. Nay, it is an *element* of this state of mind; it essentially belongs to a truly devout state of mind.

Remarks

1. This, then, must be a matter of *consciousness*. A religion of which we could not be conscious could not be of much importance to *us*, at any rate. If we did not know whether we had it or not, surely it could not be *worth* having, so far as we are concerned.

But the fact is, if we can be conscious of anything, we can be, and must be, conscious of the kingdom of God existing within us.

Just think! the kingdom of God is righteousness, and peace, and joy in the Holy Ghost; and yet, I can remember the time when it was thought a very dark and suspicious circumstance if a person expressed great confidence that he was a Christian. It was gravely suspected, by even great divines, that such a one was not acquainted with his heart; but to express great doubts with respect to one's own conversion was regarded as an evidence of profound humility. And we would frequently hear the very excellent Mr. So and So, and Dr. Such a One, spoken of as having so many doubts as to whether they were Christians. Now we might earnestly and prayerfully ask, "Where did such views of religion come from?"

2. It must also be a matter of *observation*, in the sense that I have said, that the kingdom of God within a man must reveal itself in his outward life, temper, and spirit; in his business transactions; in his social and domestic relations; in his public relations; and indeed, in *every* relation of life.

If the kingdom of God is within him, he is an upright man; he is a benevolent man; he is a man devoted to the service of God and to the interests of man. In business he is equitable, in politics he is honest and honorable. In every relationship he is a Christian.

3. How very different is this account of the religion of Jesus from the experience narrated in the seventh chapter of Romans, which is plainly a *legal* experience, in which the kingdom of God is not set up, but is

striving to get possession of the heart.* The eighth chapter of Romans portrays an experience in which the kingdom of God *is* set up in the heart; in which "the righteousness of God is fulfilled in us who walk not after the flesh, but after the spirit."

The seventh chapter of Romans describes an experience the opposite of which is the eighth. Here religion is all bondage, resolution, purpose, and failing. Here, instead of righteousness, and peace, and joy in the Holy Ghost, the soul is bound fast in the cords of its own sins; floundering in a pit of mire and clay, and having neither righteousness, nor peace, nor joy in the Holy Ghost. And yet, strange to tell, this seventh chapter of Romans has been regarded as Christian experience by a great portion of the Church for centuries. There is reason to fear that millions of souls have stopped in the seventh chapter of Romans, taking it for granted that they were converted, and have gone down to hell.

4. How different is this account of the kingdom of God in consciousness from the *peaceless* religion of a great many professors. They have no peace of mind. They are restless, restive, chafing, complaining, murmuring, resisting, and are in a constant state of turmoil and agitation in regard to their relations to God. Indeed, they know that they have no peace of mind. They know that God's whole will is not cordially accepted by them. They know that they are living in the neglect of known duty. They know that they are shunning the cross daily. They know that they are not universally devoted to God. They know that they are not devoted to the interests of men. Of course peace is impossible to them, and they are aware that they have not this peace of mind and this state of cordiality between themselves and God. And yet, they think themselves Christians! But the kingdom of God is not within them, for Christ does not reign in their hearts, and they are in no sense prepared for heaven. Now, if the kingdom of God is not within them, why should they call themselves Christians?

It is very common for persons in this state to fall back and say that they have no dependence except upon Christ; that they depend upon Christ. But surely, this is a mistake. They do not truly depend upon Christ, unless Christ has really set up His throne within their hearts. If they have true faith in Christ, they have true peace, they have true righteousness, they have true joy in the Holy Ghost; but wanting these, it is a sheer delusion to say that they depend upon Christ.

But they say, "I do not depend on anything within myself. I do not depend on my prayers, on my own righteousness, on my peace of mind, on my joy, or upon any experience I have." "No," I answer, "you *should not* depend on any of these as the *ground of your acceptance with God*. But *the condition of your going to heaven*, as being that without which you cannot go to heaven, you *must* depend on this righteousness, and peace, and joy in the Holy Ghost. Without this state of mind you can never go to heaven."

---

*See especially *Principles of Victory*, "Legal Experience," pp. 87-98.

However perfect it may be, it is not that *for* which, on the ground of justice, you could be admitted to heaven, but it is that without which heaven is a natural impossibility to you.

Do not, therefore, I pray you, say, "Oh, I am to be saved by *grace*, therefore I lay no stress upon my own holiness." But I ask you, my dear sir, "What is salvation?" Is not an element of salvation personal holiness, or righteousness? True, if saved at all, you are saved by grace. But mark! To be saved by grace is to be made *holy* by grace, to be made *righteous* by grace. It is to have, by grace, the very state of mind which the text describes, righteousness, peace and joy in the Holy Ghost.

Let no one then pretend to fall back upon Christ if he does not allow Christ to reign in his heart. The religion of many is sheer Antinomianism. They really suppose that they are going to be saved by an *imputed*, without an *imparted*, righteousness.

They know that they are living in the daily indulgence of sin; that they *do* shun the cross, and always have done so; that they never have made a clean breast of confession, or washed their hands by restitution; in short, they have never become personally upright, honest, holy; and yet, they think they are going to be saved by Christ! They say, "We have believed, and therefore we are forgiven and accepted." They think that by *one act of faith* they come into a *state of perpetual justification*.

But this is naked Antinomianism. If this be true, then the law must indeed be repealed and abolished; for if the moral law remains in force, the soul must be condemned if it indulges in sin.

5. How different is the religion of this text from the *joyless* religion of multitudes of professors. Indeed, it is mournfully common to see professors of religion who seldom or never profess any religious joy. It is no wonder they do not, for they themselves will admit that they are living in the constant indulgence of known sin. In this state, true religious joy is entirely out of the question.

If in this state they have *any* joy, it will be rejoicing in *themselves*; in their own supposed safety, and not in God. A joyless religion is a very repulsive religion.

6. To have this kingdom of God in consciousness is indispensable to our rightly *teaching* religion. I say teaching *religion*. We may warn others of their danger. We may prove to them their guilt. We may hold forth the threatenings, and even the promises. We may teach them the *doctrines*, but this is not teaching them *religion*, it is not presenting to them religion. It is teaching them certain things *about* religion, or rather, saying certain things *of* religion. But religion is a *state of mind*, a *voluntary* state, a state of love, with which joy and peace are necessarily connected. Now unless we have this joy and peace, it is impossible that we should convey a correct idea of what religion is.

If we do not *ourselves* love, if we have not *personal* peace and joy, if we attempt to preach religion, then we shall continually betray ourselves, and show that we are preaching but a hearsay Gospel, and trying to teach a religion which we do not experimentally understand.

The fact is that experience always has a language of its own, and this language can never be supplied by any theory. To preach peace and good will, they must be a matter of personal experience and consciousness; to truly preach joy, the heart must be flowing with it.

7. The experience of this kingdom in consciousness is essential to *rightly living it* before the world. It cannot be really counterfeited. A man may be very sanctimonious in his outward life and looks, but after all there will be cant in it; there will be something unnatural; it will be a manifest affectation. To be lived, Christianity must be experienced. If it be in the heart, it will be looked, it will be acted, it will be spoken. It will be made manifest in the very tones of the voice, in an obliging manner, in painstaking to honor God and to do good to men. It will be unselfish, honest, generous, cheerful, and joyful. But these things cannot be so counterfeited as to set *well* upon a man.

8. Where this consciousness really exists, it will produce *conviction.* It cannot conceal itself; it will be noticeable in any relation of life.

A husband will notice it in his wife; he will be struck with it; it will produce conviction. A wife will be struck with it in her husband; parents in children, and children in parents. In every relationship of life, it will produce conviction.

Religion is a thing so diverse from the spirit of this world; the kingdom of God is so opposite to the kingdoms of this world and to the kingdom of Satan, that where it is really set up in any heart it must so express itself in the life and temper and spirit so as to force conviction wherever it has an opportunity really to manifest itself.

9. If the human soul has not this consciousness, it will of course seek worldly good. To seek for happiness, satisfaction, and enjoyment is natural to man; and he will either seek his own selfishly, or he will seek the general good unselfishly. If the kingdom of God is established in him, he is an unselfish devotee to the glory of God and the good of man. In this he will find his enjoyment, here he will find the truest enjoyment and the highest kind of enjoyment.

In this state of mind, he does not *seek* his own enjoyment as an end; but he inevitably *finds* it. In this state of mind, he does not seek his own peace, nor his own joy. These are not the objects of his search, nor the end at which he aims; yet he inevitably *finds* them while he does not seek, and all the more surely *because* he does not seek them. But if a man has not this enjoyment, if he has not happiness in God, he will seek it in the world. It is in vain to shut him up to a truly religious life, unless this kingdom be established in his heart. If converts stop *short* of this consciousness, they will surely turn back.

10. If the soul has this satisfaction in God, it will not go lusting after worldly good. It has found a joy too sublime, too high, too spiritual, too all-pervading, to leave the mind restless and craving after worldly good. It will not lust for worldly pleasure and worldly ways; it will not plead for merely worldly amusements, and pastimes, and social intercourse. No! It has found the society of God. It has entered into communion with

Him. It resides in the same palace with the King of Kings. It has an altar, a worship, and a sanctuary within itself; it is *at home* when engaged in the worship and service of God. But deprive the soul of this satisfaction in God, and you cannot keep it; it will go abroad, inquiring, "Who will show us any good?"

11. True converts will soon learn to watch unto prayer that they may pray in the Holy Ghost, and thus keep themselves in the love of God. At first, converts are not aware of how easily they can mar their own peace. How easily they can throw themselves out of sympathy with God. How easily they can bring a cloud over their souls and wound their own spirits. But if they are really converted, have the kingdom of God in consciousness, they will soon learn what wounds, what brings darkness, what mars their union with God, what disturbs their peace, what separates them from that clear and heavenly union without which they cannot live. They will soon learn the necessity of watchfulness, of much prayerfulness, of engaging as little as is consistent with duty in promiscuous conversation. They will learn to guard against idle words, vain conversation, worldly associations, a mis-spending of their time, a misuse of their money, a misuse of their tongue—in short they will learn to gird themselves up, and to walk softly with God. They will find this indispensable to their peace, indispensable to their joy, indispensable to their maintaining their righteousness. They will soon learn that they must either part with God, or part with sin; that they must gird up their loins, and live wholly a religious devoted life, or they can never have religious joy and righteousness and peace at all.

12. Spurious conversations may generally be known by their not realizing the necessity of watchfulness and prayer and constant communion with God.

It shows that they have not tasted of the grace of God; that they have not had communion with God; that they have not known what it is to be born of God, and to have the kingdom of God set up within them.

By watching the tendency of professed converts, you may generally tell whether true religion is really a matter of *experience* with them. If we find them loose in the use of their tongues, unwatchful, running hither and thither to please themselves, not caring to spend much time in prayer, not disposed to search their Bibles, not tender and easily wounded by any slip or sin into which they may fall—we may know they are not truly converted. The King has not set up His throne in their hearts. Holiness to the Lord is not written there. They know not what it is to walk and commune with God.

13. Sinners know that what I have described must be true religion, and must be what they themselves need.

While preaching at a certain place, I was discoursing upon religion as an experience; upon the love of God, the peace, and the joy of the salvation of Christ. As I came out of the pulpit, I was met at the foot of the pulpit stairs by a prominent lawyer, a stranger to me, who wished to be introduced to me. He said to me: "Mr. Finney, after tea, I wish you would make a religious call with me. I wish to introduce you to a friend of mine." I replied, "I suppose it is for a *religious* purpose." He answered, "Yes." I told him I should be happy to accompany him. He called on me after tea, and took me to the house of his friend, and introduced me to an aged lady, who immediately expressed great joy to see me, and began to tell me what the Lord had done for her soul.

She poured out a sweet religious experience in a conversation of half an hour. Her joy was overflowing. She said the very atmosphere she breathed seemed to be love.

This lawyer sat where I could look him in the face without appearing to do so. I had learned that he was not a religious man. I saw the muscles of his face quiver. It was with difficulty that he could suppress his emotions while the old lady was pouring out from her full heart this flood of religious experience.

After hearing what she had to say, we rose up and left. As we stepped out into the street, he stepped before me and said, "See here! What do you think of that! I know that that is the Christian religion. I know that that is what I need. I was never so determined not to rest short of it as I am now."

Thus I have found in common, when preaching religion as a matter of experience and consciousness, to find it carrying conviction to the mind even of the most skeptical. I have often heard of their saying: "There, I understand that now; I see that is and must be true religion; this is what we all need, or certainly we cannot go to heaven."

14. Without this experience, we cannot enjoy what we call religious duties. If we attempt to perform them without this experience, we shall do it only as a *task*, as a matter of habit, or something that must not be neglected; yet, as something in which we have not *true satisfaction*. But *with* this experience, prayer is a real luxury, and we will love to multiply occasions of prayer. So great is the enjoyment of communion with God, so sacred, so calm, so divinely serene and satisfying, that the soul is never, in this world, so deeply satisfied as when in the deepest communion with God.

Religious conversation with truly spiritual persons is a feast of the soul in which the kingdom of God is set up.

15. Painstaking labor, and even self-denial, for the salvation of souls and the glory of God, is spontaneous. It is the natural outburst of an inward flame of love; an inward spring of joy and peace where the kingdom of God is set up.

But where this kingdom is not, much prayer is a great burden. Persons are shy of religious conversation. They have no heart to it. And labor *for* souls and *with* souls is what they can hardly bring themselves to do. It is a real cross to go and labor personally with souls, a real trial, a matter of fearfulness and timidity where the kingdom of God is not truly set up in the soul. Men are ashamed and afraid to go and labor earnestly with their neighbors for the salvation of their souls, while they themselves are in bondage and have no real experience of what they teach.

Even ministers are ashamed to labor directly and personally with souls, if they have not this kingdom of God *burning* within them.

16. Without peace and joy we cannot earnestly and honestly recommend religion. If our religion is a bondage, void of peace and joy in God, we may warn others of their danger and their guilt; we can commend religion to them as a matter of personal prudence, as a thing not to be neglected lest they should lose their souls; but we cannot recommend it in such a sense as to draw people out of the world into a *present* embracing of it. The fact is that man wants enjoyment for the *present;* he wants something *now* to interest him; he wants something that he can *now* feel, *now* realize, *now* interest himself in; and *now* find some satisfaction in. But if we have not this peace and joy, all our representations will naturally repel rather than attract the mind.

They will admit: "Oh, it is something we must attend to, but not now. Your religion is a necessity, we admit, some time before we die. We *intend* to become religious; but it is religion to *die* by, and not to *live* by. It is something to be associated with deathbeds and funerals and mournful occasions; and not something in which we can find a *present* interest, enjoyment, and unction."

17. This is the true and only antidote to worldly-mindedness.

With this kingdom of God set up in his heart, a man is crucified to the world and can well afford that the world should be crucified to him. With this love, peace, and joy in experience, he will naturally turn away and hide himself in God, rather than mix up unnecessarily with the bustle, the strife, the bitterness, the slang, the egotism, and the insanity of this world.

There are many that stop short of this experience in consciousness; and of course if they are professors of religion, they make up the masses who are pleading for worldly enjoyment, for social intercourse, and for the cultivation of worldly taste. They run after amusements, they journey, they do *everything* to find enjoyment. They must see sights. They must get up worldly pastimes and parties. These things they will seek because they have nothing better in experience.

If we ask why it is that the great mass of professors of religion are so worldly-minded, the answer is at hand: "They have not the kingdom of God in consciousness."

Not being rooted and grounded in love; not having the peace of God ruling in their hearts; not having the joy of God a perennial fountain welling up within them: "How can it be expected that they will not do as they do?"

But the most surprising thing is that these worldly professors still hold on to the idea that they are truly religious. If they would be consistent, and say, "Why we have no religion. We have no consciousness of righteousness and peace and joy in the Holy Ghost. We have no joy in God. And do you expect us to deprive ourselves of all enjoyment? We have no satisfaction in our religious experience; and do you expect us to deprive ourselves of seeking satisfaction elsewhere? We know not God, and therefore we must have the world." Now if they would say this, and be consistent, they would cease to be stumbling blocks; people would understand them. The world would not hide behind them. They would not then be a standing contradiction of religion, and a shocking dishonor to Christ; for in that case they would avow their unreligious character.

But as it is, strange to tell, they will maintain their religious profession. They think themselves really religious. But they are *not* religious. They seek the world, and lust after it, simply because they have no religion in consciousness.

18. It is easy, therefore, for us to discriminate between those who love God and those who love Him not.

They, in whose heart the kingdom of God is established, follow on to know the Lord more and more perfectly. They are under the influence of a divine charm or enchantment; the love of Christ is constraining them. They have tasted and seen that the Lord is gracious; why should they turn back and lust after the fleshpots of Egypt? Why should *they* gad about to seek love? They have found the home of their hearts in Christ. They have found their resting place, their joyful habitation, their all-satisfying portion. They cannot exchange these *spiritual* joys for the *gross* pleasures of earth. They cannot exchange these sacred moments of communion with God for communion with this world. They cannot afford to abandon God's *heavenly* ways for the *insane* ways of a wicked world.

19. But lastly, do any of you ask, "How shall I come to have this experience of the kingdom of God in my soul?"

The answer is plain and scriptural: "Receive Christ, open your heart." He says, "Behold, I stand at the door and knock; if any man hear My voice, and open the door, I will come in to him, and will sup with him, and he with Me."

Give Him the key of the whole habitation, of every room and every closet, and let Him cleanse the whole—cleanse every apartment; and write "Holiness to the Lord," upon every wall, and every ceiling, and every door, and everything within. Open your heart, and commit yourself to Him for this very purpose, that He may write His law and establish His throne forever within you. Do it *now*, submit to this *now*. Invite Him in. Lay all upon His altar, and ask Him to baptize you with the Holy Ghost.